The Online Journalist
Using the Internet and Other Electronic Resources

The Online Journalist
Using the Internet and Other Electronic Resources

Randy Reddick
Texas Tech University

Elliot King
Loyola College

Harcourt Brace College Publishers

Fort Worth   Philadelphia   San Diego   New York   Orlando   Austin   San Antonio
Toronto   Montreal   London   Sydney   Tokyo

Publisher	Ted Buchholz
Senior Acquisitions Editor	Stephen T. Jordan
Senior Project Editor	Steve Welch
Production Manager	Serena Manning
Senior Art Director	David A. Day
Editorial Assistant	Margaret McAndrew Beasley

ISBN: 0-15-502018-8

Library of Congress Cataloging-in-Publication Data
Reddick, Randy.
    The online journalist : using the internet and other electronic resources /
    Randy Reddick, Elliot King.
        p. cm.
    Includes bibliographical references and index.
    ISBN 0-15-502018-8 (pbk.)
    1. Journalism—Data processing. 2. Internet (Computer network) 3.
    Information networks. I. King, Elliot, 1953- . II. Title.
PN4784.E5R43 1995   94-41564
070.4'0285--DC20   CIP

Address for Editorial Correspondence: Harcourt Brace College Publishers, 301
Commerce Street, Suite 3700, Fort Worth, TX 76102.

Address for Orders: Harcourt Brace & Company, 6277 Sea Harbor Drive, Orlando,
FL 32887-6777. 1-800-782-4479, or 1-800-433-0001 (in Florida).

Printed in the United States of America
4 5 6 7 8 9 0 1 2 3   039   9 8 7 6 5 4 3 2 1

Preface

First there was the printing press, then the telegraph, the telephone, and television. Now there are online communication networks.

As with the new technologies of the past, the Internet and other online information networks will profoundly affect the art and craft of journalism.

Journalists know their world is rapidly changing. Pat Stith of the Charlotte (N.C.) *News and Observer* has said, "Those who use these tools (computer-assisted reporting) will be ahead. Those who don't will be left behind — and may not survive."

Nora Paul of the Poynter Institute has told journalists, "By taking advantage of the access to information and people available to you by using a computer, your research and interviewing can have a range and immediacy that is simply impossible without a computer's assistance."

The Online Journalist describes and demonstrates how reporters can use the Internet and other online resources to do their jobs more efficiently and more effectively. It also discusses the impact this new technology will have on journalism, the pitfalls reporters and editors must avoid when they enter the new world of cyberspace, and the legal and ethical issues raised by online journalism.

Jargon-free and intended for both students and professional journalists, the book has value for everybody from those who wish to begin exploring online resources to experienced net surfers. It guides readers from making initial connections to online resources to advanced reporting for specific story assignments.

In addition to introducing the range of online resources and clearly explaining how to use all the major applications on the Internet, *The Online Journalist* also includes an extensive directory of where to find specific information of interest to journalists, a listing of online access providers, a survey of online media companies, and a glossary.

We feel deep gratitude to many people. First we would like to thank our families. They sacrificed in the name of "The Book" — our wives Anita and Nancy; our children Aliza and Marcie, Laura, Ben, Roxanne, Jennifer, Heather, and Jacob.

This book could not have been done without the pioneering work of others. Elliott Parker started the list CARR-L in 1992 and has maintained it since then. George Frajkor's JOURNET has encouraged discussion of journalism education in a virtual world. Tom Johnson challenged journalism educators in a 1992 *Quill* magazine article to get digital. This book is in part a byproduct of the discussion he started.

"Zen Artist" Brendan Kehoe, "NorthWest Netter" Ed Kockner, and "Internet Hitchhiker" Ed Krol generously made available online their guidelines to the network before the 1992–1994 flood of Internet books. Others who did likewise: Odd de Presno, "Big Dummy" Adam Gaffin, and the EARN Association. John Makulowich and John December have created and maintained resource lists of interest to journalists and journalism educators.

We were helped by many other generous contributors to CARR-L, JOURNET, the NIT list, and other relevant lists, including: Joe Abernathy, Jack Lail, Peter Weiss, Steve Doig, Tom Boyer, Russell Clemings, Steve Outing, Steve Yelvington, and Dan Gillmor. (Outing and Lail, at least, have gone off and created their own lists.)

People in the academic community nationwide who have encouraged this work: Sue O'Brien, Judy Solberg, Dolores Jenkins, Nancy Green, Lillian Kopenhaver, Ralph Izard, Guido Stempel, Hugh Culbertson, Pat Washburn, Tom Hodges. We benefited from critical reviews of the manuscript by David Abrahamson, Northwestern University; Steven Dick, McNeese State University; Ann Preston, North Dakota State University; Tom Shuford, University of Texas at Arlington; and Bill Smith, Northeastern University.

Loyola College in Maryland provided Internet access and other resources. Neil Alperstein in the Department of Writing and Media shares our enthusiasm for technology and this project. Bill Glover and Barry Schech of Information Services helped teach the technology.

Texas Tech University College of Arts and Sciences provided facilities and encouragement. Roger Saathoff and Jerry Hudson of the School of Mass Communications were especially supportive. Richard Fisher and David Coons of Academic Computing Services extended incredible patience through many learning experiences.

The authors,
Randy Reddick, wurlr@ttacs.ttu.edu
Elliot King, King@loyola.edu

Contents

Chapter **4 Introduction to the Internet**   55

Chapter **5 Communicating with people**   75

Chapter **6 Telnet: Remote connections**   101

Chapter **7 Gopher & World Wide Web**   117

Chapter **8 Finding & fetching files**   141

Chapter **9 News groups & relay chat**   161

Chapter **10 Putting online tools to work**   187

The Online Journalist

Using the Internet and Other Electronic Resources

Chapter

1

An introduction

Tom Regan of The (Halifax) *Daily News* was doing a story on Canada's troubling national debt. "Several politicians and right-wing business groups were running around yelling 'The sky is falling!' and demanding that the government make enormous cuts in Canada's social programs," Regan writes. "I wanted to find out if there was any substance to these dire predictions."

What Regan did was to post some notes to Usenet news groups and to Bitnet listservs related to Canadian politics. In his postings he asked "for anyone with real information to reply to my query." Then he used an Internet program called Gopher to find static documents on the Canadian economy. All this took him about a half hour, he reports.

"When I checked an hour later, responses to my queries abounded," he writes. He had notes from a professor in Montreal and the names of "three international economists from major U.S. financial firms who said Canada's debt crisis was being overblown." Another note led him to an expert on Canadian economics living in Australia.

"Without the Internet, it would have taken weeks to research the story, and I would have been limited to 'experts' in and around Nova Scotia," Regan concludes.

Regan is among a growing number of journalists who have discovered tools new to the trade. These tools enable reporters to use computers as a means of communicating with other people and of accessing information stored throughout the world.

Sergio Charlab, special projects editor at *Jornal do Brasil,* had a challenging assignment. An important book about computers and the human mind had been translated into Portuguese. Charlab said that *The Emperor's New Mind* by British mathematician Roger Penrose "is interesting, but it was not easy for a non-technical person to analyze its thesis." By posting messages to what he felt were appropriate Usenet news groups, Charlab found others who had not only read the book but had written papers critical of some shortcomings in Professor Penrose's theory.

Ultimately, Charlab obtained the e-mail address of Professor Penrose and "interviewed" him. All this without one telephone call. The review of the book and the interview piece ran in the *Jornal* on Oct. 23, 1993.

The mission of this book

This book is about empowerment.

Empowerment of individual journalists and of entire organizations.

Empowerment of other information providers.

What this book teaches can help good journalists produce even better reports.

This book describes a group of information-gathering tools that make some kinds of high-level reporting less dependent on company resources than on a journalist's initiative. In the past, elite media with enormous news budgets have sent out correspondents to centers of power and to locations of

Some Network Terms used in this Introduction

Bitnet	An international network of computers originally created for researchers and to share information. Breeding ground of the listserv and many mail lists.
File	A descrete collection of information given a unique name and stored on a computer disk. Two major file types are *ASCII* or *text* files, containing only typewriter characters, and *binary* files, which contain computer program code.
Gopher	A computer program designed to help people locate and retrieve desired information in a global networking environment.
Internet	A worldwide network of computer networks. The Internet incorporates a series of computer communication rules or protocols allowing a sort of universal exchange among computer systems of widely varying types.
Listserv	A computer running software that automatically archives and distributes messages to subscribers of electronic mailing lists.
Mail list	A register of individuals who have by subscription expressed desire to exchange information electronically on a stated topic.
Network	The interconnection of two or more computers for the purpose of exchanging files and other information.
News group	A topic area given a network name. People use news reader programs to log on to news servers and read news group messages and/or post messages to the group.
Usenet	A global network devoted to coordinated distribution of news group messages.

history-making events at home and abroad. They have had access to the inaccessible.

Today, "ordinary" reporters using global computer network resources have instant electronic access to important documents, government data, privately held information, the world's greatest libraries, and expert sources and government officials — without ever leaving their desks. Instead of going to Washington, Ottawa, London, or Cairo, New Delhi, Beijing, Taipei, Tokyo, or Cape Town, today's journalists may bring to their own desks resources from important centers of the world. And the same tools that reach around the world work down the block and around the corner.

Moreover, a reporter "fishing" for people who have firsthand knowledge of newsworthy events can reach tens of thousands of potential sources in just a couple hours. A carefully worded query posted in the proper news groups, entered into commercial forums, and sent out to the right electronic mail lists can quickly net a bountiful harvest of eyewitnesses to some event, of victims to some plot or oversight, of people with other firsthand knowledge that qualifies them as a news source.

Finally, every reporter who has held a beat has had to interview somebody on topics about which the reporter had little background or expertise. Aside from being uncomfortable, the reporter is likely to ask ill-informed questions. Such questions elicit answers which do little to inform readers or audience members. Many news sources — among them U.S. military authorities — make it policy not to waste time with poorly informed journalists. Again, through network resources the journalist can quickly locate and download "white papers" on just about any topic imaginable. Tucked away in news group cubby holes, listserv archives, and various specialized computer directories are "FAQ" (Frequently Asked Questions) files that anticipate many questions raised by people new to the interest group.

Who this book is and is not written for

You do not have to be a Macintosh Maven, an MS-DOS Master, a Windows Whiz, a Unix Virtuoso, or any other kind of computer guru to be proficient at harvesting online information. This book tells journalists what buttons to push to find the information they are seeking. It does so using plain English. *The Online Journalist* assumes that most journalists have little desire to become computer programmers or to learn computer languages.

Instead, *The Online Journalist* assumes that most reporters have in mind certain information they need and that they want the information in a hurry. If they get the information quickly, they can spend their deadline time crafting the best story rather than wrestling with inflexible machines. Not only will journalists proficient with these tools have more time to write, their reports can be more thorough and comprehensive. It is the aim of this book to enable journalists to get quickly and easily the information they need in their work. Other books on the Internet are more general and diffuse, aimed at less specific audiences. Journalists who develop keen interest in the Internet may want to read some of the other books mentioned at the end of each chapter of *The Online Journalist*, but generally all that you need to use these tools is included here.

Another assumption we make at the outset is that both journalists and the organizations who employ them are working on limited budgets. Access to a wealth of online information comes at a cost any news organization can afford. For that matter, the determined reporter, "converted" to the network, could probably pony up the $20 a month or so that seems to be the going rate for full Internet access. "Going rate" is used cautiously here, because there is no uniformity in rates. Students, staff, and faculty at Internet-connected colleges and universities generally get free access. This has led Tom Johnson, freelance journalist and professor at San Francisco State University, to suggest journalists should enroll in less demanding 1-hour courses throughout the year as a way of gaining access.

The *Virginian-Pilot* in Norfolk, Va., provides Internet access to all its reporters. In Raleigh, N.C., the *News and Observer* has become an Internet access provider for its subscribers. Many media organizations are establishing their own access. Commercial online services such as CompuServe and Delphi are offering access to the Internet. Finally, there are dozens of service providers springing forth each week promising Internet access for everything from $25 a year to $27 an hour. Chapters 4 and 5 as well as Appendix A address the access question.

A final assumption made by this book is that its readers have used computers for word processing. This book describes the process of finding information online and bringing that information to your computer. The assumption is that at least in terms of text files you find online you will be incorporating material from those files into your work — on computer.

What this book is and is not

Although this book describes how to make use of computer-based tools to do better research for stories and projects, this book is NOT a computer book. It is written in English — generally speaking the newsroom variety of English, cleaned up a little.

There is no attempt in this book to be all-inclusive or encyclopedic. Instead, we have focused on a limited selection of network tools that are

- easily accessible through the Internet or, if commercially based, are priced for the common person.
- either indispensable tools (like e-mail) or they provide a high rate of return for the time invested in learning them.

We have thus intentionally avoided some network facilities altogether. And we have intentionally refrained from providing exhaustive discussions of those tools we do describe.

Instead, *The Online Journalist* teaches how to use online tools and how to get further help for each tool. This is especially important when we are describing a moving target like the Internet, which changes shape from week to week. Each tool is described in a setting that illustrates how the tool may be (or has been) used by journalists.

As it is with other tools, the user becomes more proficient and skilled with frequent use. *The Online Journalist* describes the tools and provides electronic addresses of computer sites housing information or providing services of particular value to journalists. It is hoped that you will test the tools and hone your skills by employing them at many sites. Appendix C contains an extensive list of electronic addresses for online resources. That list is organized into traditional beat areas for news reporters.

Although *The Online Journalist* occasionally describes commands unique to VMS or Unix systems, it generally assumes most readers will be accessing online resources from a personal computer of the Macintosh or IBM compatible variety. It has been the studied intent of this book to describe the online world as it is seen by people using the lowest common denominator in terms of equipment, software, and access. That means you get connected to distant computers and talk to those computers through a program with a plain, text-based, command-line interface. However, this book also describes briefly a couple kinds of services and network tools (like the World Wide Web) that thrive on graphical user interfaces demanding more powerful personal computers, more sophisticated software, and special kinds of network connections.

What you need (& must know) to get online

Some of what you need and what you need to know to get online are described in greater detail in Chapters 3, 4, and 5. But in simple terms, you need a computer, communications software on that computer, and a connection to the online world. That connection might be a network card connected to a local area network (LAN) at your office. Or it might be a modem connected to a telephone line from your home. Chapter 3 outlines some options with modems and with communications software. Unless you plan to run some of the more sophisticated graphical network interface programs (like Mosaic and Cello) referenced above, the simplest of popular computers will do fine. A Mac Plus or a plain old IBM PC will do all the things necessary for gathering information online. A computer with a hard drive makes a lot of things more convenient, but even a hard drive is unnecessary if you are using just basic communications software. Because you work with words, it is helpful to have a word processor available at the same computer you are using to access the online world.

On the software side of things, shareware and public domain programs are fine. A *public domain* program is one to which the author has "given" to the public and relinquished all exclusive rights. A *shareware* program is one in which the author has retained rights and for which the author expects to be paid. However, shareware is made available free for a reasonable trial period. If you continue to use the software you are obligated to pay for it.

How to use this book

The best advice on how to use this book depends largely on what you know already, how comfortable you are with computers, how brave or determined you are or otherwise motivated to learn what's available online, and what kind of Internet access you have. The timid, fearful, or cautious soul may want to take a different approach from the determined, bold, and aggressive. If the only access you have to the Internet is e-mail, you may not want to spend much time reading about Gopher or the World Wide Web.

Chapters in *The Online Journalist* are arranged with three concerns in mind. The prime goal is to empower journalists with tools for harvesting information from a wealth of online resources. In concert with this goal, it has been our aim to introduce online tools sequentially, keeping in mind two modifying concerns: 1) the most common types of online access available 2) the learning investment required for the return you get in terms of a useable wealth of information obtained. We note that sometimes these two constraints work in opposite directions. For example, the network navigating tool known as Gopher (Chapter 7) provides access to a vast wealth of information for relatively little effort invested in learning. However, Gopher is not as widely available as e-mail (Chapter 5) and perhaps not as widely available as Usenet news (Chapter 9). Because Usenet news is more chaff than wheat, we placed it later in the text. Because e-mail has great flexibility for getting what the journalist wants, it has been placed earlier.

Given these concerns, Chapters 2 and 4 are survey and background chapters. Chapter 2 offers an overview of what is available online. Chapter 4 gives some history of the Internet and a brief introduction to some of the Internet tools. Between these two chapters is a discussion of the online world outside of the Internet. That world includes bulletin board systems (BBSes), commercial database services, and online services that are hybrids of each of these. Chapter 3 also describes a lot of the basics for getting connected to the online world so that journalists who need help just getting started may have it.

We selected the material in Chapter 3 — bulletin boards and dial-up online services — as the place to start in part because those services require only a telephone and a modem for connection. It is also a good strategy for getting familiar with your communications software to do so with a limited number of other variables. When you meet with the unexpected, you can sort out more easily whether it's the software you are using or your host. Additionally, it has been our experience that those requiring extra help in making online connections are more likely to find help dealing with local bulletin boards than with Internet access. In the case of the hybrid online services like America Online, CompuServe, Delphi, GEnie, and Prodigy (sometimes called the "Big Five"), providers generally have easy-to-understand books describing their services and how to use them. Finally, we selected the material in Chapter 3 as a starting point in part because all the Big Five services provide some kind of Internet access. Many of the larger BBS systems offer at least Internet e-mail and sometimes Usenet access.

After providing some background on the Internet in Chapter 4, we enter the Internet realm through a discussion of e-mail. E-mail was chosen not because it was the easiest aspect of the Internet (in practice, it can be one of the more complicated), but because it is the most widely available. Also, it can have tremendous payback for journalists. Chapter 5 describes e-mail in some detail.

As we have done at the beginning of this chapter, we start each new chapter with an example of how some online tool can be or has been a help to journalists. Chapter 6 describes Telnet, a program native to the Internet. Telnet is used to log in to remote computer sites It is extremely simple to use — it simply connects you to a remote computer. Once you are connected, you are on your own. However, Telnet can be used to gain access to many other Internet tools.

Chapter 7 describes two Internet navigating tools or "front end" programs, called Gopher and World Wide Web. These programs, unlike Telnet, are add-ons. That is, their availability and use is not native to the Internet. However, they both provide ways of finding information on a worldwide basis and of bringing that information to your computer. Gopher organizes information in hierarchical menus, while World Wide Web uses hypertext links to follow lines of thought or threads of related information.

Chapter 8 describes another tool native to the Internet: FTP (file transfer protocol) and the add-on program called Archie, which is used to search FTP sites for desired information. Chapter 8 also describes a network searching and retrieving tool called WAIS.

Chapter 9 deals with two interpersonal network communications facilities, Usenet news and Internet Relay Chat. Each of these programs attracts a lot of useless chaff, but each can be used for gain by journalists.

Chapter 10 attempts to bring together all online tools by discussing research strategies and how to incorporate network tools into them.

Chapter 11 offers a brief discussion of legal and ethical issues raised by use of network tools.

Appendices to *The Online Journalist* include a short essay on getting Internet access, a glossary of online terminology, and a long list of online resources for journalists and how to access them. The list is organized along the lines of traditional news beats.

Alternative curricula

Although *The Online Journalist* was designed for sequential use, it is possible to use chapters out of sequence. There are two major caveats in doing so, however. First, all tools chapters following Chapter 3 assume that you are relatively comfortable with your computer's communications software and that you understand the vocabulary described in Chapter 3. Second, there are terms described in Chapter 4 for which understanding is assumed in subsequent chapters. Also in Chapter 4 are accounts of Internet history and background material that will make easier the understanding of some portions of subsequent chapters.

As long as you understand these reservations, it is possible to take Chapters 5–9 in any sequence. If, for example, you have only mail and Usenet access to the Internet, you could focus on Chapters 5 and 9. If you already have Internet access, and you want to learn how Gopher or World Wide Web may help you as a journalist, you can go straight to Chapter 7.

Alternative sequence 1: You do not yet have Internet access

Journalists without Internet access can still reap benefits from online resources. You would want to read (and master) Chapters 2, 3, 5, and Appendix A. Chapter 5 is the e-mail chapter, and many BBS systems offer e-mail access to the Internet. All of the Big Five hybrid services do.

Alternative 2: You have full access but you are intimidated

Regardless of your status, you need to learn the kinds of things described in Chapter 3. You need to get connected, to log in to other computer systems whether they be the local library, a bulletin board system, or a large network. You need to get familiar with the communications software you will be using on your computer. You should get practice in creating log (or capture) files, which save to disk the text that passes your screen while you are logged on somewhere.

For the timid or cautious person, once you have mastered the Chapter 3 concepts and you have grown familiar with your communications software, you could jump to Chapter 6. You might want to scan Chapter 4 for vocabulary and background; but Telnet, the Internet protocol described in Chapter 6, is simple, straightforward, and forms a good foundation for other Internet tools. In the course of learning Telnet in Chapter 6, you would do well to try Hytelnet, also described in that chapter. Hytelnet will help you find Telnet sites of interest to you and will provide you with coaching on how to log in.

Much more powerful than Telnet, but almost as easy to master, is Gopher. Chapter 7 describes Gopher. At the present writing, no other tool offers so much to the journalist for so little investment of effort as Gopher. Much space is given in *The Online Journalist* to Gopher and to describing how to use it and its companion searching tools, Veronica and Jughead. Furthermore, sites housing Gopher servers (often called Gopher "holes") frequently offer easy access to other Internet resources discussed in other chapters of this book.

After Gopher, what?

Where you go after you learn Gopher depends on you. At some point you should read Chapter 4, which is an overview of the Internet without any specific network skills instruction. Similarly, Chapter 2 is a general survey of the online world, absent any specific instruction. On the skills side, World Wide Web (Chapter 7) browsers are easy enough to use, but are not likely to be as beneficial a work tool for journalists as Gopher is. You should plan to learn e-mail (Chapter 5). E-mail is the basic means for communicating with other people. E-mail operations are first cousin to Usenet news operations, at least in terms of how you communicate with other people. And e-mail distribution lists share common purposes with Usenet news groups. Getting connected by mail to other journalists or other people with an interest in the subjects and issues of your beat is a rapid way to strengthen your current work.

The difficulty with e-mail is that you must learn a simple mailing program and a (often primitive) mail editing program in order to use mail. There are enough of these programs available so that it is impossible in a book of this scope to discuss them individually. You will have to learn how you work your program from the people who provide you with an Internet connection.

After you have mastered mail as well as Gopher and Telnet, using WAIS and Archie to search for files and FTP to retrieve them (Chapter 8) should go relatively smoothly. Finally, you will want to round out your online repertory by at least reading about Usenet news groups and Internet Relay Chat (Chapter 9). These two utilities generally do not warrant a lot of time on a regular basis because there is at least as much chaff in them as there is wheat. But under some circumstances they can strengthen your work.

To summarize, the skills development curriculum for the cautious is:

1. Basic telecommunications and BBSes — Chapter 3
2. Internet overview and vocabulary — Chapter 4
3. Telnet (and Hytelnet) — Chapter 6
4. Gopher (World Wide Web optional) — Chapter 7
5. E-mail — Chapter 5
6. FTP, Archie, WAIS — Chapter 8
7. Usenet, IRC — Chapter 9

This book was conceived at a time when there were very few books describing the Internet and how to navigate that vast portion of the online world. Most of what was written about bulletin boards was written for hardcore computer heads. The authors, separately and independently, discovered vast treasures of resources for journalists in the online world. They met online. Both felt that a book written by journalists for journalists pointing the way to riches available online was badly needed. Here it is. We hope you will find what it teaches as rewarding as we and other journalists who have stumbled onto "the Net" have.

When something doesn't work

Neither the Internet nor other online resources described in *The Online Journalist* is yet an "information superhighway." But like other heavily travelled highways, portions of the Internet seem perpetually under construction. You will encounter delays. You will find roads closed.

When you try some of the addresses provided in this book, you will get busy signals and messages tantamount to "that number has been disconnected."

Guaranteed.

When you do, move on to other resources. You may find some delays are only temporary; try them again some other time. At other times, you may get connected, but what you will see on your screen will not match the screen image printed in the book. Frequent facelifts are common on computer networks. A little patience and understanding while the highway is a-building will reward you later. Now let's take a look at what the online world is all about.

Chapter 2

The online world

In January 1994 Vice President Al Gore subjected himself to a question and answer session in which more than 300 people participated. In the space of 90 minutes, Gore faced a battery of questions about problems ranging from educating children with special needs to ending the civil war in Bosnia.

The session was historic not for the answers the vice president provided but for the way the questions were asked. This was not a press conference nor a speaking engagement organized by a specific organization. It was the first ever live, online conference with a United States vice president. The questions were provided by people who had signed up to participate in a forum on CompuServe, a commercial information service. Gore was stationed at a personal computer in the West Wing of the White House.

The questioners and the questions were completely unscreened. The people who asked their questions first received answers. Others watched the interaction on screen. (See Figure 2-1)

This chapter covers four topics. In Chapter 2 we

- discuss the way access to information has traditionally played a pivotal role in journalism and how computer-based communications networks are broadening that access.
- show why increased access to information will lead to better journalism.
- introduce the major technological components of computer-based communications networks.
- scan the diverse kinds of information available online.

Online access to information promises to be extraordinarily important for journalists. Access will allow reporters to fulfill their roles better. The overview provided in this chapter will prepare you to work with the specific tools described fully in the chapters that follow.

Access and journalism

Interesting, timely, and accurate information is fundamental fodder for good journalism. For the last century, access to information has primarily defined the work reporters do. Beats and specialization revolve around access. Police reporters work with information from the police. Court reporters become experts in understanding legal information. Sports reporters traffic in batting averages and zone defenses.

For years, the White House beat was considered the most prestigious in journalism. At the bottom line, the role of a White House reporter has been defined by access to information from the White House. The first White House reporters hovered close outside the Executive Mansion itself, monitoring who entered and left for meetings with the Chief Executive. In the early 1900s,

```
% Moderator recognizes question #6
  glen Falkenstein (102)


(#102,glen Falkenstein) What do you think is goiong to end the problem in bosnia?
(#196,Vice President Gore) We (the US) have believed for some time
(#196,Vice President Gore)  that the Bosnian government forces should
(#196,Vice President Gore) not be subject to the internation
(#196,Vice President Gore) embargo on the arms they
(#196,Vice President Gore) need to even the odds. And we have proposed airstrikes
(#196,Vice President Gore) to prevent the agressors form taking
(#196,Vice President Gore) advantage of the situation
(#196,Vice President Gore) while the arms are delivered.
(#196,Vice President Gore) But our allies, whose votes we need in
(#196,Vice President Gore) the Security Council, don't
(#196,Vice President Gore) agree. We will continue to work for peace, though,
(#196,Vice President Gore) in other ways — including maintenance of the toughest
sanctions against
(#196,Vice President Gore) Serbia in history. And the biggest airlift of
(#196,Vice President Gore) humanitarian supplies since the Berlin
(#196,Vice President Gore) airlift. And if a real agreement
(#196,Vice President Gore) can be reached, we will help enforce it.


% Moderator recognizes question #8
  David Rogers (26)


(#26,David Rogers) Mr. Vice President...
(#26,David Rogers) Hello from a Houston, Texas student...
(#26,David Rogers) What effect will the information highway...
(#26,David Rogers) have on our health care system...
(#26,David Rogers) in our future?
(#196,Vice President Gore) It will make it possible to conduct remote
(#196,Vice President Gore) diagnostics with much higher accuracy,
(#196,Vice President Gore) and to link patients to the right specialist
(#196,Vice President Gore) regardless of geographic location...
(#196,Vice President Gore) And by making the transfer of large volumes of financial
(#196,Vice President Gore) information much cheaper, it will save money.
```

Fig. 2-1: Part of transcript from Vice President Al Gore's first online conference on CompuServe.

Theodore Roosevelt began meeting formally with reporters on a regular basis. His actions granted a certain status to those reporters. From then on, White House reporters were privy to information that reporters working in Philadelphia, Chicago, or Los Angeles just could not get on a timely basis.

That situation is rapidly changing. With the development of commercial databases, computer bulletin boards and the Internet, journalists working anywhere can have the same access to much of the information once restricted to White House reporters. Since 1993, the White House has aggressively developed its electronic communications links. The White House set up an electronic mailbox in June 1993 and received more than 100,000 e-mail messages in its first six months of operation. More than 220,000 electronic requests for information were processed by the White House staff from September 1993 through January 1994. More than 1,600 documents were published electronically including transcripts of daily press briefings by the president's press secretary and the president's press conferences. An electronic self service public documents library has been established. Reporters

THE WHITE HOUSE

Office of the Press Secretary

For Immediate Release   December 10, 1993

PRESS BRIEFING
BY DEE DEE MYERS

The Briefing Room

1:27 P.M. EST

MS. MYERS: There are no announcements, so if you all have questions —

Q Tell us, what was the Kirkland meeting?

MS. MYERS: The President met this morning with Lane Kirkland. It was the — just the two of them. They met for about 45 minutes. They discussed a wide range of issues, an agenda on which they'll work together in the coming year, including things like striker replacement, OSHA reform, health care reform and a number

of other things. It was a very fruitful meeting, and I think the President feels very good about it.

Q Can you describe the tone of it?

MS. MYERS: It was very productive. It was —

Q Friendly.

MS. MYERS: It was friendly. It was frank. They had a good discussion. They had a very good discussion. Again, it was just the two of them.

Q NAFTA?

MS. MYERS: I think they talked about a number of issues. But they looked ahead as opposed to looking back.

Q Yeah. What did he think about GATT?

MS. MYERS: I don't know if they talked about GATT.

Q You're not saying that they didn't review some of the differences, are you?

MS. MYERS: I'm saying that the bulk of the meeting was directed toward the common agenda and what they can do to work together in the future. That was the —

Q   Who initiated it?

MS. MYERS: The President called Mr. Kirkland after the NAFTA vote. They decided at that time that they would meet, and the President invited him to the White House.

Q   Did the President call for a truce? I mean, did it come down to that kind of discussion?

Fig. 2-2: Partial transcript of press briefing by presidential press secretary Dee Dee Myers following a vote on the North American Free Trade Agreement (NAFTA) downloaded from an online source.

in Seattle had almost the same access to White House information as reporters in Washington D.C. (See Figure 2-2)

White House information is only one example of increased access for journalists. Business reporters can now obtain Securities and Exchange Commission filings electronically. Science reporters can explore the databases of the National Institute of Health, the National Science Foundation and the National Library of Medicine among other resources. Court reporters can access court filings and decisions. In almost every area of interest to journalists, reporters dramatically increase their access to information through electronic communications networks.

In the same way that telephones allowed reporters to interview people around the country, electronic communications networks allow people to locate and obtain information from locations around the world. In short, online information allows reporters to do their jobs better no matter where they are physically located.

The payoff of increased access

The question is, do reporters need access to more information? After all, isn't there already a glut of information? Moreover, with so much information available, will reporters be reduced to simply sifting through information produced by others to pass on to busy readers?

The answer is complex but clear. The more access to information reporters have, the better reporters will be able to fulfill their mission to inform the public about key issues and interests of the day. More access to more information can only lead to better journalism.

The late investigative reporter I.F. Stone demonstrated in the 1960s and early 1970s the power of exploring public sources of information ignored by other people. Relying exclusively on not-so-obscure, but little publicized public documents, he revealed how the U.S. government misled the American people about its policies in Vietnam. To review most of those documents, Stone had to be in Washington. Increasingly, a reporter anywhere in the country has that ability.

Increased access to documents can also reduce reporters' reliance on specific sources, allowing them to be more independent and objective and making it more difficult for politicians and handlers to put a specific "spin" on events. For example, in the summer of 1994, the Clinton administration pushed a $30 billion crime bill. Some Republican senators charged that the bill was filled with pork barrel projects. Most of the reporting about the bill consisted of charges being hurled back and forth in Washington and the potential political repercussions for President Clinton of the bill's defeat.

But with that bill accessible online, reporters from Altoona to Anchorage could have downloaded and analyzed what kind of impact the proposals would have had in their communities. They could have then interviewed local sources to get their reactions to the spending measures. Local officials could have reflected on the impact of the bill – not on inside-the-beltway politics but in their own communities. Using online access, reporters can make national and international news more relevant to their own communities.

While not all legislative proposals may yet be easily accessible online, some are; and the access is broader each day. The House and the U.S. Senate each has its own Gopher server. Many states (Hawaii, California, Texas, Nebraska, and New Jersey are among the first) are providing some form of legislative information online. As President Clinton unveiled the federal budgets in 1993 and 1994, they were available online within hours. Should they wish, reporters anywhere can now analyze the federal budget according to their own criteria rather than the criteria of politicians in Washington.

Far from reducing reporters to sifters of information, the explosion of access to a wider range of sources of information *will make the role of reporters much more valuable*. Reporters will be able to develop more authoritative stories more quickly. More importantly, reporters will be the only ones in position to synthesize information from disparate sources into stories that are relevant to their readers.

For example, let's say a legal reporter wants to investigate the performance of the local court system. Among the key questions: how long does it take civil suits to be resolved; how many judges does the civil court have and what is the total budget; how satisfied are the litigants who use civil court to resolve their dispute?

In addition to surveying local court records and interviewing local, self-interested participants, the reporter with online access could compare the local court performance to court performance in other similar cities. The reporter could identify experts, key players and knowledgeable observers around the country to provide insight and perspective. If there were appropriate federal information, that could be identified and located as well. The reporter could network with other reporters working on like topics, drawing on their expertise and experience. And all this research could be conducted without traveling and within the normal daily work routine.

Reporters craft useful, interesting stories. Online access to wider sources of information means that more reporters can pursue more stories of greater interest to specific readers or viewers. More fact filled and broader in scope, those stories should be of greater value than ever before.

The online network infrastructure

Negotiating the online world is as important a skill for journalists as good interviewing techniques and a smooth style of writing. But the world online is complex. Not only is it relatively new, it is still under development. It changes rapidly.

To be able to understand those changes, it is important both to be familiar with key terms and to have a basic understanding of the infrastructure itself. In the same way that it is important to understand generally what happens when you dial a telephone, it is important to understand generally what is happening when you send and retrieve information via computers.

The key technology underpinning all online communication is computer networking, which refers to physical links among two or more computers. Because computers are linked, a person sitting at one computer can send or receive information stored on another computer. That access can take place in several different ways. The computers can be linked through telephone lines; they can be linked via a local area network, which generally links computers in a department of a university or company; or they can be linked through a wide area network, which links computers that may be some distance from each other.

For example, if you want to access information on another computer in your company or university, you will probably use a local area network. However, if you want to access information from a government database, you will probably use your personal computer to dial the computer on which that information is located directly, connecting via the telephone line. Or you will connect to another computer, which in turn will connect to the computer on which the information is actually located.

Dial-up access, bulletin boards, and commercial services

Most often, people who want to access information online will be working with a personal computer. The most widely available way for a personal computer to access information stored on another computer is via the telephone line. For computers to use telephone lines, they need modems and communication software. Modems, connecting your computer to a standard telephone jack, convert information from your computer into a form that can be transmitted over telephone lines and reconvert information received via telephone lines into a form that can be understood by computer. Communications software controls those activities, telling the modem to dial out or to answer an incoming call and other functions.

Using your modem, you may call another computer to access information. In many cases, at that point, the computer you have called is the one on which the primary activity takes place. If it is, that computer is usually called the *host computer*. The computer calling the host computer is known as the *remote computer*. When one computer allows another computer to call it via the telephone lines and access information from it, that computer is said to provide dial-up access. All you need for dial-up access is a computer, modem, communications software, a telephone line, and the telephone number of the computer you wish to call.

Dial-up access frequently works in the following manner. Using your communications software, you call another computer. After your computer establishes a link with the host you have called, you are asked for passwords and/or connection instructions. This procedure is called logging in (or logging on). Your computer typically acts as a "dumb" terminal for the computer you have called. In other words, the information and most of the commands that you use are actually on the host computer, and your computer "pretends" to be simply a terminal through a part of the communications software known as *terminal emulation*. The only time you use commands from your own software is when you want to transfer information from the host computer to your computer or vice versa.

After you have finished using the information on the host computer, you generally will go through a log-off (or log-out) procedure. After you log off using your own communications software, you must instruct your computer to hang up.

Three types of computer information services often rely on dial-in access — computer bulletin boards, databases, and commercial information services such as America Online and CompuServe. Specific services will be more fully described in the next chapter. The general structure of these services will be described here.

Computer bulletin boards

Long-distance bicycle racing is not as popular in the United States as it is in Europe. So when the Tour d'France was run in the past, enthusiasts in the U.S. had to settle for short, outdated articles in the back pages of the sports section of the newspaper.

No longer. During the 1994 event, people could log into the Bicycle Bulletin Board, a computer bulletin board service for cyclists in Carlsbad, Calif., and enjoy fresh coverage. Observers from the course itself as well as people watching the race on the BBC in London posted reports and impressions regularly. Journalists who wished to report on the event but could not attend in person could still communicate with many people on the scene. Furthermore, they could interview people in the U.S. and elsewhere who were interested.

Perhaps not as fanatic as many soccer fans during the World Cup, cycling aficionados take their sport very seriously. The Bicycle Bulletin Board gave reporters a mechanism for increasing the number of sources with whom they could communicate as well as opening up the possibility of new story angles.

Electronic bulletin board systems, often called BBSes or bulletin boards, are computerized information services that can be accessed using a computer, modem and telephone line. By some estimates, there are more than 40,000 bulletin boards in operation today.

With such an array, their structure and content vary greatly. In fact, many computer bulletin boards are run by entrepreneurial individuals using rudimentary technology. They may have one or two telephones attached to an old computer. There are several inexpensive software packages that allow people to set up their own bulletin board systems. Computer bulletin boards operated by an individual contain information of interest to the person who sets up and maintains the system – the system operator or "sysop."

At the other end of the spectrum, the federal government operates several bulletin boards through which people can access information the U.S. government has collected. These computer bulletin boards contain huge amounts of information and are enormously useful to reporters. (See Figure 2-3)

Generally, bulletin boards will have some or all of the following features. They may have electronic mail; that is, users can send and receive private messages to and from the system operator or other people who are registered with the system. They may have forums or conferences through which people who are connected to the bulletin board send public messages that can be read by everybody who accesses the system. Some allow for live interactive communication – the ability to chat – with other people who are logged into the system at the same time.

Many bulletin boards have searchable databases. The system operator has stored (or has allowed others to store) files that can be downloaded from the bulletin board to the user's computer. Sometimes bulletin boards can be efficient means of obtaining specific information such as bibliographic references, full text articles, and information about organizations. Text files of information can be downloaded from most BBSes, then later edited and/or printed at the user's computer. Many bulletin board operators may also store shareware and public domain software that users can download as well.

Some bulletin board operators charge people for access to the board. In those cases, users must register in advance and are billed in a variety of different ways. But many bulletin boards, perhaps the majority, are free.

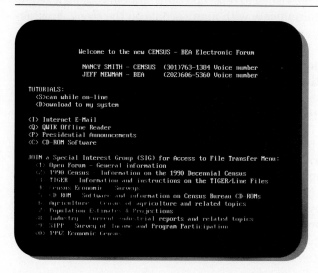

Fig. 2-3: A screen from the U.S. Census Bureau's electronic bulletin board.

They are operated as a hobby, a service by a larger company such as a magazine publisher or other type of information provider, or they are a service of a government agency trying to disseminate information to interested parties.

Commercial information services

In concept, commercial information services such as CompuServe are similar to BBS systems. Both BBSes and commercial information sources provide all the same services (including private electronic mail, live interactive communication, conferences and forums, and information and software that you can download to your computer).

Commercial services, however, provide a much broader range of information. They also provide a range of tools that help people find and use the information they need. Commercial services often charge an hourly rate for access and a premium for specialized services. (See Figure 2-4)

Perhaps most important for journalists, commercial information services develop relationships with other information companies to offer their products online. For example, many offer users access to reports from the Associated Press, UPI, Agence France Press, Reuters, and other wire services including the wire services "day book," which lists potentially newsworthy events occurring in a specific city.

Providing wire service reports is a vivid example of the way computer-based communication networks expand access to information. In the past, very small newspapers, other magazine publications, and colleges and universities could not justify or afford the expense of receiving wire service information. Although publications cannot republish the wire service reports they receive from online services, they can use those reports to stay up to date with breaking news. Also, using what is called a clipping service,

Fig. 2-4: Welcome screen to Dow Jones News Retreival Service.

reporters can save articles on topics of interest to them as background for longer reports.

The full range of information available through commercial information services as well as some of the potential pitfalls these sources of information present for journalists will be discussed more fully in the next chapter. The gamut is extremely wide and potentially very useful for journalists. The drawback is that the more you use a commercial database, the more expensive it becomes.

Indeed, there are two classes of commercial information services. The first such as the Lexis/Nexis system is directed primarily at corporate users. Lexis provides computerized access to legal information while Nexis provides access to newspaper articles. The price for these services puts them beyond the reach of many smaller companies and most individuals. And while some universities do have subscriptions, most do not.

Other services such as Prodigy, America Online and CompuServe are aimed directly at consumers. If heavily used, they become expensive. Still, they can be affordable to freelance writers and students and are certainly affordable even for small companies.

Conceptually, electronic bulletin boards and commercial databases can be considered alike because of the way they are accessed and used. Generally, using a personal computer, you directly call the bulletin board or commercial service you want, and then, using commands on the host system, you access information that is on that host system. They can be thought of as a branch of a library or a store. You are access restricted to whatever is in that location, although that store can have many different departments and products. And, you will see shortly, commercial information services will sometimes offer you passage to another store. Nevertheless, you must continue to pay for the time you are logged onto the system.

Internetworked systems

As you will see in the next chapter, accessing information through dial-up BBSes and commercial databases is a relatively straightforward operation. Once you know the telephone number of the computer you wish to access and you know the log-in procedures, you can get started immediately.

Accessing information through computers that are internetworked can be a little more complicated. Internetworking represents the ongoing evolution of computer networks in general. As companies, government agencies, and universities have expanded the number of computers they have, they have linked those computers together into networks to allow people to easily share information and applications programs. These networks are known as local area networks. In a local area network, one or more computers may function as a center for several other computers. That center is known as a server and frequently contains files that everybody on the network uses. It also contains the software that allows each of the computers on the network to share information with each other.

Over time, servers in different locations have been connected as well, often using dedicated data lines and specialized computers called routers. In addition, computers are sometimes networked using fiber optic lines and other technology that allows digital information to move at much higher speed than on telephone lines. The development and implementation of high-speed data transmission lines is what has enabled the information super-highway. Internetworking represents the connecting of smaller computer networks to form yet larger networks.

The development of large networks of networks has depended on two factors. First physical links among computers had to be installed. Second, computers had to "speak the same language" — to use similar rules or communications protocols for identifying, transmitting and handling information.

In practice, internetworking currently functions in the following way. A university or private concern will provide individuals with personal computers. Those personal computers will be networked together with other personal computers, work stations, minicomputers and mainframe computers depending on the specific location. The networks, in turn, are connected with other networks. Using their personal computer working through their server, individuals can access information residing on the computers in the more distant networks. The key is having a computer that can access a network, which can, in turn, access information on other computers on other networks. While the computers in the internetwork are sometimes linked together via the telephone line, they usually use higher speed dedicated data transmission lines.

Conceptually, accessing information in this way is different from using your computer and modem to dial the computer on which the information is located directly. Instead, it is more like entering a large building with many rooms. Each room you enter has several other doors. You keep opening doors until you find the information you want. High-speed lines allow you to move from room to room quite quickly.

The most famous collection of internetworked computers is the Internet, which will be more fully explained in Chapter 4. However, the clearest example of the way an internetworked system functions to allow users to access information in remote locations may be the library system put together by the Colorado Alliance of Research Libraries, or CARL. CARL has developed software that allows libraries scattered throughout the nation to be linked with each other. For example, users at Loyola College in Maryland can access the library system through terminals in the library itself, through Loyola's campus local area network server, or by dialing in using a personal computer.

After accessing the system, users can survey the holdings of the Loyola/Notre Dame library, which are rather limited. But, by selecting Item 3 from the main menu, users can survey the holdings of the University of Maryland, Montgomery County Public Library and Maryland Interlibrary Consortium. Users

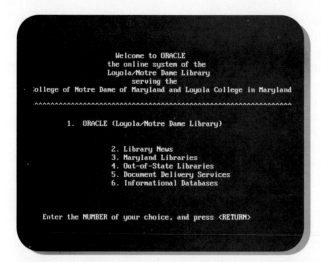

Fig. 2-5: Screen giving access to other libraries internetworked through CARL.

can also use the public access catalogs from colleges from Florida to Hawaii, including the Lane Medical Library at Stanford University, the Los Angeles Public Library and the Atlanta/Fulton County Public Library. (See Figure 2-5)

Being able to access those additional libraries is only the first step. Let's say you decide to see what is available at Morgan State University, which is just down the street from Loyola. From Morgan State University, you can also access libraries from around the country including Arizona State University. From Arizona State, you could access yet more colleges and universities that participate in the CARL network.

Each time you select the public access catalog at a different university, your personal computer or terminal functions as if it were a terminal connected directly to the computer on which that information is stored. What is most significant, however, is that the menu or user interface for each system is exactly the same. It is as easy for you to find information on a public access catalog halfway across the world if it is part of the CARL system as it is to access information in the library you use every day. More importantly, once you get access to a CARL library system, you have access to the information on the catalogs in many parts of the network, depending on the specific arrangements made by your local librarians. Journalists should be aware that many universities are now affiliated with CARL.

Internetworked libraries illustrate another distinction between these kinds of systems and bulletin boards and commercial information services. In most cases, bulletin boards and commercial computer databases were developed specifically as communication tools to allow people to share information via computers. Library catalogs were not developed specifically for access by computers. The material that can be accessed through internetworks represents the portion of information generated at a specific location which the developers or owners have decided to share with or open to the public.

Gateways and other links

Although computer bulletin boards and commercial databases can be thought of differently from networks like CARL libraries, in practice the distinctions have become increasingly blurred. Many commercial databases now serve as gateways or have links to other commercial databases. For example, users of the CompuServe Information Service now have access to certain newsletters that are part of what is called the PTS Newsletter Database. The PTS Newsletter Database is also found on the Dialog Information Service, another commercial computer database. It is available on CompuServe through a special arrangement.

Using one commercial database as a gateway to another generally involves two charges – the first for connecting to the first commercial database and then a surcharge to access the information owned by the second service.

These gateway services are different from networks like the CARL system. Not only are there charges, but in many cases the user interface and menus differ sharply from service to service. Consequently, users may confront a sharp learning curve when they try to locate and access specific information.

In addition to gateways between commercial computer databases, many computer bulletin boards also have links to each other. Information posted on one bulletin board may be automatically sent to scores of others without the original sender even knowing. Frequently, the system operators of computer bulletin boards have incomplete knowledge of information posted on their system. Once again, however, the links between computer bulletin boards are not conceptually the same as links in a system like the Internet. Although information is shared, somebody logged onto one bulletin board usually cannot then automatically connect to other bulletin boards through that first one. Also, the user interface and menus from bulletin board to bulletin board vary greatly.

What's available online

Asking what kind of information is available online is a little like asking what's in the Library of Congress and other massive library systems. One might as well ask what's available from agencies of the federal government; from leading universities, research centers and think tanks; from large companies, publishing houses and organizations in the business of collecting and disseminating information; from tens of thousands of entrepreneurs who collect and offer information in areas of their own interests. What's available also comes from hundreds of thousands of people who use computer networks to communicate with each other every day through discussion lists, news groups, postings to bulletin boards, and in a variety of different ways.

And remember, those sources are not limited to just the United States. International information links are strong in many areas.

Clearly, there is a lot of information out there – too much to catalog. In fact, nobody knows exactly what is available on line and where it is. The growth represents both an opportunity and a hazard for journalists. The opportunity is that sitting at your desk, you can access information that you may not have even known existed. The hazard is that you will waste a lot of time looking for information that is not relevant to the projects on which your are working.

With that in mind, the following is a partial list of information and services accessible online through computer bulletin boards, commercial databases, and networks such as the Internet that are relevant to journalism. All of these categories of information will be more fully explored in subsequent chapters and a catalog of these sources is in Appendix C.

Government information

The federal, state and local governments are the largest producers of public information, and reporting on the activities of government is the biggest single area of concern to journalists. At the federal level, many agencies including the White House, the Food and Drug Administration, National Institutes of Health, Department of Agriculture, National Science Foundation, Environmental Protection Agency, Social Security Administration, the National Archives, Securities and Exchange Commission, and scores of others now provide access to their information via computer bulletin boards or through the Internet. One federal BBS system (FedWorld) provides access to more than 130 other federal BBS systems. Many state court systems have begun to offer electronic access to some of their records. U.S. Supreme Court decisions are available online.

The range of information these agencies provides varies. Some, such as the National Archives, primarily offer access to their catalogs and directories, allowing users to identify information they will then have to get using more traditional methods. More importantly to journalists, many agencies now distribute their press releases and major reports online. Online access represents a vehicle to get both timely information and background material quickly.

Human sources

In general, most people look to online techniques to access documents. For journalists, however, electronic communication also offers a new way to identify and communicate with people. Talking to people who have relevant information will continue to be one of the fundamental ways journalism distinguishes itself from other types of fact-finding activities.

Online access to people is provided in several different ways. First, there is electronic mail in which individuals can send private messages back and forth to each other. Sometimes people who refuse to accept a telephone call from a journalist may be willing to respond to an electronic mail message. Electronic mail is a very convenient and efficient method to communicate.

Beyond e-mail are news groups and discussion lists. Although technologically they operate differently, in practice, both discussion lists and news groups are like conversations among hundreds or even thousands of people who are interested in a specific topic. For reporters, these online conversations can serve as windows into the concerns of the people involved in those issues as well a source of e-mail addresses to communicate directly with individuals later. There currently are thousands of discussion lists and news groups operating covering topics from United Nations activities concerning global warming to sado-masochism.

Third, public relations agencies and others now frequently use online communications specifically to reach reporters with potential sources for their stories. For example, public information officers in colleges and universities have assembled lists of university-based experts in different fields, which they forward to reporters upon request.

Finally, many computer bulletin boards, commercial computer databases and the Internet have what is called "chat." Chat is the functional equivalent of the telephone. People who are online at the same time can communicate with each other simultaneously. At times, chat conversations can appear like telephone calls on a party line. A lot of people can participate at the same time.

Libraries and special depositories

The revolution in electronic communication has transformed the image of librarians from the custodians of dusty monuments to learning to that of front-line warriors in the information age. Librarians have played a leading role in making information accessible to journalists and others. In one dramatic example, the catalogs of the Library of Congress are now accessible online. The Library of Congress is a powerful tool for journalists.

In addition to the Library of Congress, major public libraries including federal depository libraries in many cities, and college and university libraries, many specialized libraries are now online as well. For example, the catalog of the French National Institute for Research in Information and Automation (INRIA) is accessible online, as is the U.S. Environmental Protection Agencies Library, the Columbia University Law Library, and the Australian Asian Religions Bibliography. Clearly, the range of special repository and library-based information is enormous. In addition to the libraries themselves, very helpful reference material can be found as well. The CIA World Factbook, which contains dossiers on 249 nations, can be accessed online, as well as the CIA World Map and the USGS Geological Fault Maps.

Books and magazines

Increasingly, publishers are experimenting with online versions of their publications. Many magazines now offer online editions, which often consist of a scaled-down version of the entire magazine. Moreover, magazines such as the *New Republic* and others are offering electronic access. From time to time, drafts of books (particularly books about the Internet) circulate electronically before they are published.

In addition to current publications, newspaper and magazine archives are available online. Often receiving the full text of an article involves a cost, however there are several places in which you can identify useful articles online for free. For example, the Montgomery County Public Library has an index of *The New York Times, Washington Post* and *Wall Street Journal.*

Other good stuff

While government data, access to human sources of information, libraries and special collections, and other publications are probably the kinds of information available online most useful to journalists, there is a wealth of additional information as well. Public domain software and shareware is readily available online. Public domain software is software for which the copyright is no longer enforced (or doesn't exist), so anybody can legally use it. A lot of software developed at research laboratories and other government-funded sites is released directly to the public domain. Shareware is a way to distribute software in which a user pays a license fee only after he or she has tried the program and decided he or she is actually going to use it. Some of this software can help journalists become more productive.

In addition to software, there is an ever-expanding array of information available online. Most commercial computer databases offer a range of financial services including tracking and trading on the stock market as well as access to the Official Airline Guide, Zagat's Restaurant Guide and much more. Hobbyists reflecting a wide range of human interests have set up shop online. Basically, if you look long enough and hard enough, you can probably find information on just about any topic you could imagine as well as the e-mail addresses of people with expertise in those areas.

Finally, people like to play games with computers and there are many different types of games available. One of the more interesting aspects of the Internet is the ability to play elaborate fantasy role-playing games in virtual locations called Multiple User Dungeons, or MUDs.

The future of the infrastructure

Distinctions among the different components of the online infrastructure should continue to blur over time. Nevertheless, for the foreseeable future, the online world will be segmented in several different ways. The first is cost. Large amounts of information, particularly information developed by libraries and universities will continue to be free. But companies will charge for many other kinds of information.

One of the most important questions for journalists that is currently being debated is whether government information should be available electronically without cost or at low cost. In the past, from time to time, the federal government has sold its information to a third-party supplier, which then resold that information to the public at a fairly high cost. In 1994, the Securities and Exchange Commission, however, backed off a plan to sell exclusive rights to the electronic records of the information it gathers to a commercial information service, which would then resell that information. Instead, it began to test electronic access to the public at a nominal cost.

Maintaining low-cost public access to government records in an electronic form will be a key priority for reporters and editors. Ironically, media companies including newspapers can find themselves in a complex situation concerning the low-cost availability of government-generated information in electronic formats. Some see adding value to government information and then reselling it as a potential new source of revenue.

Cost of access is a significant issue as well. Currently, companies pay a monthly flat fee for a connection to the Internet, the most important internetworked system. After the fee is paid, you can use the Internet as often as you like without additional charges. You can send electronic mail to Russia or Israel at no additional charge. This makes the Internet extremely cost effective for journalists and others with limited budgets.

There are those who believe, however, that there should be a usage charge for the Internet. And as responsibility for developing and maintaining the information infrastructure shifts primarily from the government to private corporations such as telephone companies and cable operators, the cost to access specific networks could go up.

The third area in which the different components of the online infrastructure will continue to be distinguished will be in the speed at which the lines themselves can carry information. As high-speed lines are installed, new kinds of information, particularly audio, video and graphics-based information, will move freely from computer to computer. Despite all the hype in the press, installing the necessary high-speed lines is a costly, time-consuming process and will take several years, if not decades, to complete. Consequently, for the foreseeable future, certain kinds of information will be available only through specific providers and to specific recipients who are connected to the high-speed lines. The local telephone connect to the home promises to be the slowest link in the network. That means for a period of time many people including journalists may be shut out from using some advanced and complex information services as they become available.

In the early 1900s, Lincoln Steffens traveled from city to city documenting municipal corruption. His book *Shame of the Cities* is a classic of muckraking. Its power came from the information he collected. The online infrastructure will give you access to more information more efficiently than ever before in the history of journalism. The result should be better stories with more information which better serve the needs of readers and viewers.

The challenge for journalists is twofold. They need to learn how to access the necessary information. And they have to be able to fashion that information into compelling journalism.

Chapter **3**

Connections by phone

You may never have heard of Paso Robles, Calif. That doesn't matter. What matters is Vic's Cafe. Every city beat should have a place like Vic's Cafe in Paso Robles.

During World War II, many people visited Paso Robles while they were stationed at nearby Camp Roberts. The U.S.O. building on 10th Street later became home to the city's recreation department. The police department rose next door, the municipal court was up the street, and City Hall was kaddy-corner across the street. There was a park in the center of town – between 11th and 12th Streets. On 13th Street, as Paso Robles entered the last quarter of the 20th century not much different from the previous quarter century, stood Vic's Cafe. There Larry Eastwood ran a diner situated between the Continental Barber Shop and Redi's Western Wear.

The day started early at Vic's Cafe. Larry opened his doors around 6 a.m. City police, nearing the end of their early morning shift, were among the first customers. Their radio message, "10-7 Vic's" signaled the start of a new day. Jay Lyon, head of public works was there before 7. John Steaffens, a big, affable man who wore large plastic-framed glasses and had puffy cheeks, parked the pickup truck which identified him as fire chief right in front of Vic's Cafe. Proprietors of nearby businesses, sales clerks in downtown stores, and others dropped in. Politicians, police, public servants and just plain folks were there.

Before most other concerns opened, Vic's Cafe was awash with talk of the city's business. Talk ranged from whether or not the coach made the right decision at the Bearcats' last football game to what to do about water pressure at the old hospital, destined to become a Christian school.

Vic's Cafe was a reporter's heaven, a perfect place to measure the pulse of a community at the start of the day.

Late in the afternoon, about 5 p.m. or so, a slightly different crowd, generally with more commercial interests, began gathering at the Cattleman's Bar upstairs at the Paso Robles Inn. Other "watering holes," like Johnny Busi's Chianti Room (facing the park on Pine Street), attracted crowds of still another character. At midday, the post office served as gathering place for some folks. Orcutt's Market had its following as did Dauth-Leisy's. Some people preferred Bill Morgan's drug store, while others preferred the conversation at George Theraldsen's pharmacy. People involved in the community allied themselves with a couple theater groups, the chamber of commerce crowd, Bearcat Boosters, Band Boosters, and a whole gaggle of service clubs.

There are a couple messages in all this.

First, people have ways of defining communities and of defining the "subcommunities" to which they belong. Second, members of any given "community" tend to congregate in well-defined places. The reporter assigned to City Hall soon learns the haunts of all those who make the decisions and call the shots. Beat reporters worth their keep find a Vic's Cafe where community pulse may be tapped. It's true in the real world as well as the online world.

This chapter is devoted to surveying that portion of the online world occupied by bulletin boards and commercial hybrid services home to many "virtual communities." In this chapter, you will learn

- what you need to get online.
- how to find and log into local bulletin board systems (BBSes).
- a few things about "virtual communities" that exist online.
- what is offered for journalists on bulletin board systems; commercial database services; and hybrids like CompuServe, America Online, GEnie and Delphi.
- how to capture the text of online sessions to disk files you can then edit in your word processor.
- where to go for more help if you need it.

If you are already a veteran telecommunicator with hours of time logged in at commercial services and local BBS systems, you may want to merely scan this chapter. You will need to have a fair command of its concepts for all subsequent chapters beginning at Chapter 5. Chapter 3 assumes you have some familiarity with computers, computer keyboards, and that you have working knowledge of a word processor and know what a computer file is.

It is the aim of this chapter to help you get used to the process of computer telecommunications – to get accustomed to connecting to distant computers, to retrieving files from them, to telecomputing "events" – and to get comfortable with the software your computer uses for telecommunicating. If you are entirely new to the online world, the best place to start is close to home. It is often easier to get help at home, and the time you spend learning is not burdened by the cost of long-distance telephone calls.

Navigating the neighborhood bulletin board

The Vic's Cafes of the world, the neighborhood grocery stores, barber shops, post offices, community centers, and churches all have counterparts in the online world. When personal computers first began to become a part of people's lives in the late 1970s and early 1980s, it was natural that people with computers would want to connect up with each other. They created the virtual equivalent of the grocery store bulletin board. Some computer enthusiast would set up a machine in his or her bedroom or garage. The machine would run software that allowed other people with computers and modems to call in and post notices for all to see. Such a system was called a *bulletin board system*, or *BBS*. The person who owns the computer and sets up the BBS is called a *sysop*, short for system operator.

The BBS allowed callers to respond to the messages – publicly or privately – and in some cases allowed people to "chat" with each other in real time. In other words, if I called your BBS and wanted to chat with you, I could choose a menu item called "Chat" or "Page the Sysop." That might set off some kind of alarm so that the sysop – who might well be doing other things at the time – could respond. The sysop also had the ability to initiate a "chat" session anytime you called in. Often, the BBS ran on a machine the sysop used for other purposes and used the only personal telephone line coming into the home. As a result, many of those bulletin boards were "open" only a few hours a day.

More sophisticated BBS software developed, personal computers became more powerful and less expensive, and local bulletin boards became popular "gathering places" for growing numbers of people with personal computers. Because people who "come together" online do not meet in any real space in the physical sense, the term *cyberspace* is often used to refer to the online world. Established hangouts or gathering places in the online world may be seen as *virtual communities*, and members of all such communities are sometimes called *netizens*.

Today, millions of persons daily "chat" with others online; do their banking, pay bills, and conduct business electronically; get news and weather reports by computer, make their own airline and hotel reservations; and even play games together. They "visit" libraries, read online magazines and newspapers, and save articles to their computer's clipboard or disk space. From their homes and offices they access encyclopedias and other reference materials, read movie reviews, carry on courtships, talk politics and sports, conduct meetings, and in short do everything people of the past did at the village square or general store. On a global scale, they do so with little regard to traditional geographical boundaries. The revolution in cyberspace presents myriads of opportunities for journalists.

Getting what you need to make connection

For you to get connected with the online world, you need 1) a computer; 2) a telephone line and appropriate phone numbers; 3) a modem; 4) communications software; 5) healthy curiosity, a venturesome spirit, or gritty determination; 6) (optional for some, but very useful) a friend who's been through all this before. If you don't have one, buy one. That is, stop by your local computer store, introduce yourself, and offer the person dinner or something appropriate in exchange for helping you set up and get online. If you recently bought a computer, start with whoever sold it to you.

The computer: You don't need anything fancy here if you just want to get connected. Ancient Mac Plusses with 512K of memory will work. Original IBM PCs with the same amount of memory will do fine. It would be nice if the machine you plan to use has a hard drive, but even that is not necessary. In fact, these basic machines will make every connection and run almost every program this book describes except the graphical World Wide Web browsers (Cello and Mosaic) described in Chapter 8. On the IBM compatible side, you need to assure that your computer either has a built-in modem or it has an available serial port to which you may connect an external modem. Cost? We have seen Mac Classics on sale lately for less than $900. We have seen complete IBM compatible 386SX machines for $430. Neither of these machines is top of the line, but either is adequate for telecomputing and word processing.

The telephone line: Again, you don't need anything fancy. Standard residential service works fine. You should have a modular (RJ-11) phone jack to plug into, and you should have touch-tone service. But even these are not necessary, if you're willing to experiment and tinker. As for the phone numbers, you have several sources. For starters, go to the neighborhood newsstand and pick up the current issue of *Computer Shopper* magazine. Each month it carries an extensive listing of bulletin boards arranged by area code. The list describes each board's contents. Although it runs for dozens of large-format pages, the list is not comprehensive. Pick one or two near you. Log in, and you frequently find a comprehensive list of local bulletin boards. *Boardwatch Magazine* has as its reason for existence reporting on the bulletin board scene. Your local library may also have some useful books and directories (see the "Further reading" section at the end of this chapter). In fact, public libraries and their college counterparts are among the first service-oriented segments of society to go online. Many libraries provide access to their computerized card catalog and to other databases via telephone hookup. If you know a library has a computerized catalog, ask for their dial-in number. Some will even be listed in the phone book, but you may have to have a library card to get access. Don't forget your local computer store friend. Usually the folks who sell computers and modems will have handy a phone number or two for local bulletin boards. As a last resort, you might try some of the BBS numbers listed under the national BBS section in this chapter or in Appendix C under "modem" access. Most of those will be long distance, and you will have to pay the consequence. It is better to do your learning close to home.

The modem: For less than $100 you can buy a 14,400-bps (bits per second) external fax modem complete with communications and fax software. External simply means it is a separate, stand-alone unit that you can unplug from your machine and plug in somewhere else without taking anything apart. Internal modems usually are $20-$30 cheaper, but they are not easily moved.

We recommend an external modem with visible display lights on it. These lights (there are usually eight of them) "report" the progress of your computer's communication with some other computer. This can be very helpful when you have asked some other computer to give you some information and nothing seems to be happening. If you can see those little modem lights flickering, you know that data is moving between the computers, even though you don't see any changes on screen. We also recommend you buy the fastest modem you can afford. Internal 2,400-bps modems for DOS/Windows machines sell for about $40 and will work. If you buy an external modem you will also need a cable to connect the modem to your computer. The same external modem will work for either a Mac or a PC; only the cables are different.

Communications software: Generally, your modem will come with software and coupons for free time on CompuServe or a reduced rate for Prodigy membership, or similar promotions. The programs bundled with modems are usually adequate. Some are very good. If you must buy your own software you might try a shareware package such as Red Ryder (Macintosh) or ProComm (DOS). A commercial version of Red Ryder is sold under the name of White Knight. ProComm Plus is a commercial version of its shareware predecessor and comes in both DOS and Windows varieties. Crosstalk is a commercial communications programs for both Macintosh and IBM compatibles. Qmodem (PC) and Zterm (Mac) are also popular shareware programs that are widely available. MacKermit is a shareware Kermit communications program that is widely available. Frequently packaged with modems intended for use on DOS machines are Bitcom, QuickLink, and MTEZ. Bitcom is an older program which runs on machines that are only partly IBM compatible. MTEZ is a WordPerfect product that has fax capabilities and is ProComm command compatible. On the Macintosh side, Microphone joins White Knight among commercial products deserving consideration.

Whatever software you buy, be sure it will run on your computer. If you have a low-end computer, some of the newest, fanciest software may not run on it. Most communications software programs are pretty straightforward, simple, and will work on a large majority of the machines they were written for. Two warnings are in order, however. 1) Macintosh Quadras do not always run software written for older Macintosh computers. 2) Software written for Windows running on IBM compatibles will not run on DOS-only machines.

Proper attitude: We can't do anything about your attitude. However, we can offer some tips. On attitude, if you don't have healthy curiosity, you probably should not be a journalist. If you aren't tenacious and gritty, you aren't going to get what you need for a lot of stories. Getting online can only help you. Pat Stith of the Raleigh (N.C.) *News and Observer* told the Fourth Annual Conference on Computer Assisted Journalism at the National Institute for Advanced Reporting in Indianapolis in 1993: "It (computer assisted journalism) is not cheaper – it's better. Those individuals and organizations that get into it will get ahead, and the others will be left behind."

Right friends: An awful lot of success in journalism depends upon nurturing good sources. The online world opens whole new realms of sources once you get connected. As you tackle each new online area described in this book, you would do well to have a friend you can rely on to get you over the tough spots. We suggested the computer store people. Most towns of any consequence also have some kind of computer club or another. Those folks could be a great resource. Colleges tend to be computer intensive places, and they have myriads of students, graduate students, and professors with computing expertise. High schools sometimes have computer clubs, and their student leaders are often eager to share with others the joys of computing.

Making your first connections

Armed with local telephone numbers and all the hardware and software you need, you're ready to practice getting online, moving around in cyberspace, and taking the pulse of virtual communities. Your first step is to launch your communications software program and to learn your way around it. You start a call to a bulletin board from within your communications program. Usually you have two ways to do this: automated or manual. Most communications programs permit you to build a directory of places you call frequently. In Red Ryder, you compile "Phone Books," and in ProComm you keep "Dialing Directories." The directory stores such information as bulletin board names, telephone numbers, terminal emulation required (if any), and communications protocol parameters. (See Figure 3-1)

Your parameters should be set before you start the dialing process. A "safe" set of parameters for most bulletin boards includes a baud rate of 2,400 and either N-8-1 or E-7-1 for the data structure. What those labels mean is parity-data bits-stop bits. Thus N-8-1 means no parity, 8 data bits, and 1 stop bit. Many bulletin boards today can handle faster baud rates, but the faster modems can also talk to slower ones. As for the data structure parameters, the overwhelming majority of BBS systems run either N-8-1 or

Fig. 3-1: Dialing directories in ProComm communications software keep track of bulletin boards, phone numbers, communications parameters, and scripts for automating online sessions.

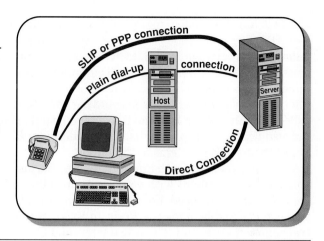

E-7-1. If you enter this information into your directory, you merely have to "point" at the bulletin board you want to call or select it with your cursor keys. You will launch a session with the selected BBS by double clicking on it or by hitting Enter when it is selected.

The second way to launch a dial-up connection is manually. (See Figure 3-2) Your communications program assumes default parameters for baud rate, parity, data bits and stop bits. You can make changes as necessary. In Red Ryder, you adjust serial port settings (Apple-command U), and in ProComm, you adjust parameters (Alt-P). If all those things are set to the proper rate, you will have some procedure in your program to "open connection" or to "launch session." From this place in the program – sometimes called terminal mode – you type modem commands. In Hayes-compatible language you would type:

ATDT 1-216-381-3320<CR>

Fig. 3-2: Dialing an online service may be done manually from most communications programs. The phone number is preceded by the Hayes command "ATDT" from touch-tone service areas and "ATDP" where pulse only is available.

The "AT" tells the modem to wake up and stand at attention; the "DT" means dial (D); using touch tone (T). A space follows, then comes the phone number followed by a carriage return (<CR> means you hit the Return or Enter key on your keyboard). Some low-end communications programs may not like having all the hyphens in the telephone number. If you are manually launching communications sessions and having trouble, drop the hyphens. If you called the number we have just given, you would connect to the PC-OHIO bulletin board in Cleveland, listed frequently by *Boardwatch Magazine* as one of the top BBS systems in the nation.

If your screen fills with unintelligible garble instead of recognizable text, you should experiment with your communication parameters and perhaps your transmission speed. For example, if your parameters were set at N-8-1 and you got garble, hang up. Reset to E-7-1. If that doesn't work, set your transmission speed to 1,200 or 2,400 bps and try each set again.

It is generally easier to launch communication sessions from a dialing directory where you have prerecorded the names and phone numbers of those bulletin boards you like to visit. It's faster, it's less mistake-prone, and the directory (phone book) method also allows you to store scripts with your phone numbers so that your communications program will automatically log in for you.

An online session

When you first connect to a local bulletin board, the computer you connect to usually gives you a short welcome screen that spells out some of the rules governing use of the BBS. Sometimes you get nothing on screen until you hit the Enter key a few times. After your host BBS welcomes you, it begins a log-in process by asking you for your name (Figure 3-3). After you type in your

Fig. 3-3: Welcome screens at most bulletin boards will seek to identify the caller. They do so by asking for a name. If the name matches an existing user list, the caller is asked for a password. If the name is unknown, the caller is asked if the user wants to become a registered member of the board.

name, the BBS computer checks its database for registered users. If the computer recognizes your name, it asks for a password. If your name is not on the list of registered users, a public BBS will give you a brief welcome message and invite you to register. A private BBS may give you a second and even third chance to log in before disconnecting you. Figure 3-3 shows the greeting screen for visitors to MicroTechNet (aka MTN) in Lubbock, Texas. It specifies use of real names only and announces that the board carries no games. If you go through the process of registering, you are asked to answer several questions about your computer, your home address and phone, sometimes your age and employment. Generally, only fully registered people have full access to the BBS.

When you get past the name identification/registration stage, you are taken to a menu of choices, generally a message or bulletin menu or a main menu for the BBS. New users and visitors to bulletin boards often receive a series of bulletins aimed at helping explain the board and how it works. Figure 3-4 shows the MicroTechNet Bulletins menu. Bulletins are numbered 1-25, and you bring a bulletin to your computer by typing the number of the bulletin followed by a carriage return (hitting the "Enter" or "Return" key). The bottom line asks you to enter the number of the bulletin you'd like to read. If you type "R" the menu will be redisplayed. The BBS computer keeps a log of your visits; and if you type "N" at the Bulletin screen, you will get a display of all new bulletins. Hitting the Enter key without giving any other direction tells the BBS to clear the screen and take you to the Main menu (Figure 3-5). The Main menu of most BBS systems offers options of reading and posting messages, joining conferences, and going to the file area where you can download (retrieve to your computer) or upload (send from your computer) files.

At the message menu, your choices typically include reading and posting messages, returning to the Main menu (or other menus), killing

---

Fig. 3-4: The bulletin menu of this Wildcat bulletin board offers several "explanatory" options aimed at new users. Calendar items for the board's community – in this case the Texas Tech University "community" – are also offered.

```
                          MicroTechNet BULLETINS

         1 - About MicroTechNet           9 - What's new in Wildcat! 3.90 (long)
         2 - Tips for using MicroTechNet  10 - To those with ACS VAX accounts
         3 -                              11 - How to use QWK mail packets
         4 - How do I download files?     12 - About the Discussion Conference
         5 - "What is a .ZIP/.SEA/... file?"  13 - What is "ShareWare"?
         6 - Not enough time to download? 14 -
         7 - "An Introduction to BBSs"    15 -
         8 - Repeat of "New User" Message 16 - Results of user poll (if any)

         17 - ATLC hours and phone numbers; TTU computer phone numbers
         18 - BBSs in the Lubbock area (from "Kaptain's Korner BBS", 762-5536)
         19 - TTU Campus Events Calendar (Thanks, D.S.!)

         TEXAS TECH UNIVERSITY ATHLETIC SCHEDULES
         20 - Football         22 - Men's Basketball      24 - Baseball
         21 - Volleyball       23 - Women's Basketball     25 - Others

         Bulletins updated: 1, 2, 3, 4, 5, 6, 7, 8, 9, 10, 11, 12, 13, 15, 16, 17, 18
         19, 20, 23
         Enter bulletin # [1..25], [R]elist menu, [N]ew, [ENTER] to quit? [  ]
```

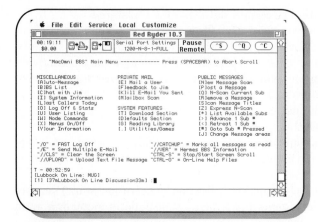

Fig. 3-5: Main menu of the MacOmni BBS is typical of most solo bulletin boards. You are given choices that take you to other parts of the bulletin board such as the file download, message, and other sections. You choose the function you want by typing a letter.

messages addressed to you, and scanning all messages not posted privately to others. A scan produces a list of messages posted, each with a one-line description of the message, who sent it, to whom it was addressed, the topic of the message, and the message's number on the bulletin board. Figure 3-6 shows a typical scan from MicroTechNet. By reading the subject entries (right column), the dates, and the names of the parties in the messages, you can decide whether you want to read any messages posted to the list. When you post a message to a list, you specify whether it is private or available to the public.

File actions: Capturing, downloading, and uploading

The Files section of a bulletin board has as its primary purpose to make available space for the sharing of software: graphics, program files, spread-

Fig.3-6: Scanning messages from the Message Menu produces a sort of directory of messages on the bulletin board. By reading the subject entries, the dates, and the parties of the message, you can choose which messages you want to read.

Fig.3-7: Messages posted to an electronic bulletin board typically look like this. The name has been changed on this message, but all else is exactly as it appeared on the board.

```
From      : A.L. SMITH                        Number    : 1768 of 2069
To        : ALL                               Date      : 09/22/93 2:47pm
Subject   : bbs phone numbers                 Reference : NONE
Read      : [N/A] (REPLIES)                   Private   : NO
Conf      : 000 - General

My wife and I are looking for bbs numbers (locally, state, or
nationally) that carry job listings, particularly in the area of public
relations,advertising, broadcast reporting, or other communications
fields.  We would really appreciate any help that anyone can give us.
We'll check back later this evening, and from time to time on this
network for numbers.  Thanks!
s
S

Read mode : (ALL) (1768 +)
Msg Read [1754-2069], [F]orward, [H]elp, [N]onstop, [Q]uit, [R]eply,
[T]hread, [ENTER = next]?
```

sheet templates, and text documents. A BBS File menu has as its choices uploading (sending files from your computer to the bulletin board), downloading (receiving files from the BBS to your computer), or listing of available files. If you choose either to download or to upload, the BBS software prompts you to select a communications protocol and to provide the name(s) of the file(s) you want to transfer.

Popular file transfer protocols include ASCII, Kermit, X-modem, Y-modem, and Z-modem. ASCII is used for files that contain only text characters – the kind you find on a manual typewriter keyboard. All other protocols may also be used to transfer text files but are designed for moving files containing program code. Program code may include formatting instructions in

Fig.3-8: A listing of files from the File menu generally produces a list of files organized by subject.

```
**** PC: Database and spreadsheet

ASE255-1.ZIP  279,561   02/22/93 | As-Easy-As spreadsheet (1-2-3 clone)
DwnLds: 20    Last DL:  02/11/94 |

**** PC: Directory utilities

ACD200.LZH    34,935   04/30/92 | Don't type CD \APP\WKS\LOTUS123 - TYPE ACD
DwnLds: 18    Last DL:  05/04/94 | LOT instead

**** PC: Disk Utilities

DCF46.ZIP    102,519   05/11/94 | a very fast one pass diskcopier
DwnLds: 0     Last DL:  05/11/94 |

DTR40.ZIP     15,215   05/04/94 | Sector-copies a disk to a file and vice
DwnLds: 0     Last DL:  05/04/94 | versa; FreeWare

RDISK20.ZIP    2,595   08/10/91 | Ramdisk you can install/remove/adjust
DwnLds: 37    Last DL:  05/18/94 | without reboot

**** PC: Education

DDLI330.ZIP   94,727   04/25/94 | Duniho and Duniho Life Pattern Indicator
```

```
File # 4? usbbs120.zip

Denied USBBS120.ZIP. Not enough time left for this file.

File # 4?

Automatically logoff after last download is completed? [Y]
Please select a protocol:

[A] Ascii        [X] Xmodem      [C] Xmodem/CRC   [O] Xmodem1K
[Y] Ymodem       [Z] Zmodem      [K] Kermit

Select [A X C O Y Z K] ? [Y]

Ready to send 3 file(s), starting with LBBS0594.ZIP.

Please begin your Ymodem download now, <CTRL> X to abort...

LBBS0594.ZIP - SUCCESSFUL!   CPS = 234
BILLMTED.ZIP - SUCCESSFUL!   CPS = 234
MTMFILES.ZIP - SUCCESSFUL!   CPS = 234
Disconnecting in 10 seconds, press [H]ang-up or [ENTER] to remain online...

Seconds until disconnect:  2
```

Fig.3-9: The download dialog walks you through the steps necessary to get a file copied from the BBS to your computer. You can move files one at a time or in "batches."

a word processor document, digitized graphics, or programming instructions for the computer. Kermit is one of the oldest protocols allowing personal computers to talk to larger mainframes. It is not the easiest to use. X-modem is an old standby. It moves data in small chunks and checks for errors along the way as the sending computer and receiving computer "compare notes" on the data moved.

While X-modem may move only one file at a time, both Y-modem and Z-modem have batch capabilities. That is, you give the computer a list of files to send or receive at the outset, and the process continues unattended until the entire list is transferred. Y-modem moves files in bigger chunks than X-modem and is somewhat more efficient. Z-modem has the added feature of automated file transfer. If you have told the sending computer that you want to use Z-modem, the process starts automatically when you are done naming the files you want. With other file transfer protocols you have to go through a number of steps to actually start the transfer.

If the files you ask for would take longer than the time you are allotted on the bulletin board, you get a message similar to the one near the top of Figure 3-9. In this session, we asked for four files to be downloaded in a Y-modem batch routine. We were told that the fourth file would force us beyond the time limit we had allotted to us. Therefore, we downloaded only three files in the batch.

Many files are stored in a compressed format on bulletin board computers. The files are "packed" or "archived" using compression software. The files take less space on the BBS computer and also take less time to download or upload. In exchange for this convenience you must "unzip," or "unarchive," the file on your computer. You can tell whether a file is archived by the extension on the file name. Files are listed typically in the filename.ext format where the extension (ext) is generally three or

Fig.3-10: Progress of downloads and uploads is shown graphically in many programs by a bar chart that grows toward 100 percent.

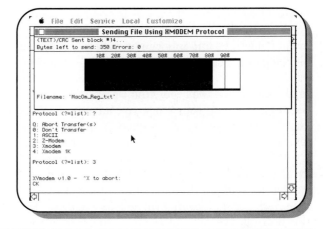

fewer characters following the dot (period) after the main file name. If, for example, you download a file named "bbslist.zip," you know that it is archived and needs to be unzipped on a PC using the program PKUNZIP. Figure 3-11 lists common file extensions and the environments with which they are associated.

Logging sessions and dumping screens

One software trick to master before you get online long distance is that of "capturing" or "logging" or "saving" an online session. Most communications software packages allow you to save to a file all the text that passes your screen. In Red Ryder, "Capture Incoming Data To TEXT File" is the first item on the File menu (keyboard shortcut Apple-R). If you are using ProComm software or one of its clones, you open a log file by pressing Alt-F1. (If you use the pull-down menus, it is "Toggle" a log file under the File

File Extension	Archive?	PC?	Mac?	Program to use to extract from archive
ARC	yes	x		PKUNPAK
COM	maybe	x		if archive, is self-extracting
CPT	yes	x		Compactor
EXE	maybe	x		if archive, is self-extracting
LZH	yes	x		LHARC
MAC	no	x		Is a runnable application
SEA	yes	x		Self-extracting
SIT	yes	x		Stuff-It
PIT	yes	x		PackIt
TXT	no	x	x	Text (ASCII) file (readable on any computer)
ZIP	yes	x		PKUNZIP

Fig.3-11: You can tell (usually) if a file is archived by the file name extension, which also tells you what program is necessary to unarchive the file for your use.

menu.) Capturing text files or logging a session has many uses. It can be used much as a tape recorder is used to capture the precise wording of quotes during meetings and interviews. When you get onto the Internet (Chapters 5–8), logging a session is sometimes the easiest way to latch onto the information that passes your screen. A great advantage of session logging over tape recorders is that you wind up with the text already in a computer file. As you are typing your story, you have no need to rekeyboard those choice quotes. You simply mark the quotes in your session file and then copy the text to the file containing the story you are writing.

Related to session capturing is doing screen dumps. Assume for a moment you are just browsing through files and messages posted somewhere on the net and you happen onto some very useful information. You didn't have your session logging turned on when the "great stuff" hit your screen. But there it sits, staring at you. You could quickly take some notes or you could dump the screen to a capture file. On a Macintosh, you do this by holding down the "Shift" and "Apple" keys and hitting the "3" key. If you are using Windows, you accomplish the same end by holding down the "Alt" key and hitting the "Print Screen" key.

In the Mac environment, the result is that a picture of your Mac screen is dumped to a MacPaint file. The first file is placed on your desktop as "Screen 0," the second as "Screen 1," and so forth. (Some operating systems may save the files as "Picture 1".) These are graphics images and cannot be imported as text to the file you may be working on at the moment. If you want text, you can mark text on your screen (by dragging your mouse over the text, for example), and then through the Edit menu function of copying (or cutting and pasting) you can move text into the document you are presently composing.

In the Windows environment, you have the same options and problems. However, all screen dumps in Windows go to the clipboard. Every time you dump a screen to the clipboard, the screen image replaces whatever was on the clipboard. Therefore, to save what is on the clipboard, you need to go into another program (word processor, graphics program) and paste the clipboard image to a file. If it's text you want to save, it is better to highlight the text in question and copy it to your word processor, which you can have running in a window separate from the communications program. Stand-alone utilities as well as utilities that are part of other programs will capture Windows screens and write them to files. The Hijaak graphics conversion program has such a utility. Corel Draw is a suite of graphics programs that includes Corel Capture.

In the DOS environment, there are dozens of screen dump utilities like "SnapShot" that will capture text images, one right after another, and store them to files with a name you have designated. Subsequent dumps in SnapShot are numbered sequentially: 01, 02, and so forth. ProComm and other DOS-based communications programs have built-in text dump utilities. Other DOS-based utilities such as Inset, DOS Cap, and Frieze will capture graphics images of the DOS screen.

Bulletin board pricing

Many BBS systems operate free of charge. Others charge fees by the month, the year, the hour, or some combination of pricing schemes. Some ask for voluntary contributions. The Windmill Company in Lubbock, Texas, for example, charges $35 per year. Your membership on the Windmill BBS includes with it some limited Internet access. Membership on the Agape BBS is free. If you want Internet mail access from Agape, you pay by the message. Some local bulletin boards are linked to others in separate networks of bulletin boards. The oldest of these is FidoNet. Others include ILink, VBBSnet, WWIV, and RAnet. These "extended" bulletin boards allow people logged in to exchange messages with other people in distant communities who are logged into *their* local board which is part of the net. Some allow local BBS members to join conferences that include people from other geographical locations. Some provide at least e-mail access to the Internet. In Lubbock (a town of 187,000 people), there are 61 BBS systems enumerated on a frequently posted list of BBSes. Five of those list subscription fees, and three are private. More than a dozen indicate some kind of affiliation with larger networks.

Each board develops its own personality, dictated largely by the sysop and in part by the members who sign on. Sometimes a board's name gives clues to the board's contents. Some boast of the thousands of software files they have available for download. Others tend to gather people interested in a particular issue or hobby. Some specialize in role-playing games. One gathers people of a particular religious persuasion. Another serves as a place where writers "convene" online. Still another bills itself as the center for people involved or interested in health concerns. The variety is as boundless as the human spirit.

The uses for journalists

Most local BBS systems will provide for journalists little more than another place to meet people and to "talk" with them. National boards, reached through long distance calls, contain files with more hard news value. However, following messages on carefully selected local boards can be a way of measuring community pulse on issues. Just be sure you understand what section of the community you are measuring.

The main thrust at this stage of online learning is that you connect to several different BBS systems and explore what they have to offer. Read some of the messages to get the flavor of what each board sees as its mission. Log or capture some sessions; download a file or two. In short, get used to

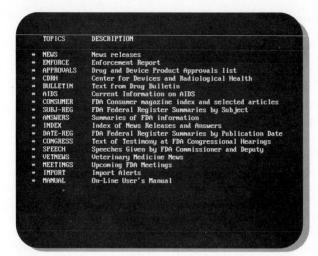

```
TOPICS      DESCRIPTION

*  NEWS       News releases
*  ENFORCE    Enforcement Report
*  APPROVALS  Drug and Device Product Approvals list
*  CDRH       Center for Devices and Radiological Health
*  BULLETIN   Text from Drug Bulletin
*  AIDS       Current Information on AIDS
*  CONSUMER   FDA Consumer magazine index and selected articles
*  SUBJ-REG   FDA Federal Register Summaries by Subject
*  ANSWERS    Summaries of FDA information
*  INDEX      Index of News Releases and Answers
*  DATE-REG   FDA Federal Register Summaries by Publication Date
*  CONGRESS   Text of Testimony at FDA Congressional Hearings
*  SPEECH     Speeches Given by FDA Commissioner and Deputy
*  VETNEWS    Veterinary Medicine News
*  MEETINGS   Upcoming FDA Meetings
*  IMPORT     Import Alerts
*  MANUAL     On-Line User's Manual
```

Fig.3-12: The Food and Drug Administration BBS is topic-oriented. Choose the topic you want to get information on, and the BBS takes you to that part of the computer.

your communications software using local telephone calls. Then when you must go long distance for a national BBS or when you start navigating the Internet you will have more certain footing from which to explore vast new territory.

The treasures of (inter)national BBSes

When you move out beyond the neighborhood bulletin board to boards of regional and national scope, you attain new levels of information. Major government agencies run bulletin boards. Large non-profit organizations and special interest groups put up boards as a way to disburse their message and to communicate with their various publics. Few of them, however, have 1-800 phone numbers.

One that does is the Food and Drug Administration. You reach it by dialing 800-222-0185. Your parameters should be 7-E-1. When you first get connected, you might have to hit the Enter key a few times to get the board to respond. This is not unusual. You will get a menu of available choices from which you select the FDA BBS (choice 1 at this writing). Then press Enter. When you are asked to log in, you type "bbs" (lower case) and hit Enter. You then will be asked for your name in a typical BBS fashion. If your name is not in the FDA BBS database, then you are asked if you would like to register. If your name *is* found, you are asked for a password. Once past all this, you are prompted to enter the Topic area for your inquiry. If you don't know the topic area, you just type the command "topics," and get a list of acceptable topics (Figure 3-12). You can get help online by asking for it ("help" command), and one of the topics – Manual – retrieves an online user's manual for the FDA BBS. The board is a little difficult to get used to, but if your beat

Fig.3-13: The Top Menu at the FedWorld BBS includes a gateway (choice D) to scores of government agency BBSes. The system welcome screen bears the name of the U.S. Commerce Department and gives warning against abusing the system.

```
Min online today: 0 minutes                Time per day: 180 minutes

                        F e d W o r l d (TM)
                National Technical Information Service
--------------------------------------------------------------------------
              [M]  FedWorld Marketplace (Doc Ordering Sys)

     [B]  Information Center              [E]  Public Mail/Forums
     [D]  GateWay system                  [P]  Private Mail
          (connection to Govt systems)    [U]  Utilities
     [F]  Library of Files                [W]  Who's on
     [O]  Subsystems/Databases            [G]  Goodbye (Logoff)
     [Q]  Quick Bulletins

          [N]   NEWSROOM (updates & new information)
          [J]   Federal Job announcements


              There are 12 other user(s) on-line now.

MENU=> TOP
Please select (M,B,D,F,O,Q,E,P,R,U,W,G,N,J or ? for help):
```

includes things the FDA is involved in, your time in learning the system could be worthwhile.

The grand master of all government bulletin boards is FedWorld, accessed by phoning 703-321-8020. FedWorld is an umbrella BBS operated by the National Technical Information Service (NTIS) under the U.S. Commerce Department. Through the FedWorld BBS (see Figure 3-13) journalists have access not only to NTIS documents and databases but also to more than 130 bulletin boards run by dozens of other government agencies through the FedWorld GateWay system. When you choose the GateWay from FedWorld's Top Menu, you are taken to a menu with screens full of BBS listings (Figure 3-13 shows the first screen). The BBSes listed cover subjects ranging from agricultural topic libraries to space exploration and from federal job opportunities to government computer systems security.

Because the FedWorld board is available both by phone and by Internet Telnet protocol, and because FedWorld represents a one-stop connection to myriads of government sources, FedWorld had become extremely crowded by the end of 1993. The result was that there were times it was nearly impossible to make connections with FedWorld. When you did make connection, FedWorld could be extremely slow to respond to your commands. When it did respond, it was slow in executing. For example, during one connection in the fall of 1993, it took FedWorld nearly two minutes to send one of its opening screens. Sluggish performance in the network world is a fact of life where people have scrambled to get to places on the Information Highway in numbers exceeding the capacity of existing facilities. As data and information providers make adjustments to increased traffic, performance should improve. FedWorld again upgraded its access in the summer of 1994.

```
###:Name                        :Comment
 ─────────────────────────────────────────────────────────────
  6:CIC-BBS (GSA)               :Consumer Information Center
  7:CLU-IN (EPA)                :Superfund Data and Information
  8:CPO-BBS (Census)            :Lists open jobs at the Census Dept
  9:CRS-BBS (DOJ)               :Amer. With Disabilities Act Info
 10:Computer Security (NIST)    :Computer Sys Lab Computer Security BBS
 11:DCBBS (DC Govt)             :DC Government Information
 12:DMIE (NIST/CSL)             :NIST/CSL Data Management Information
 13:EBB (DOC)                   :Economic data and information
 14:ELISA System (DOD)          :DoD Export License Tracking System
 15:GSA/IRM BBS (GSA)           :Information Resources Management,Issues
 16:EPUB (DOE)                  :Energy information and data
 17:FDA's BBS (FDA)             :FDA info and policies
 18:FDA/DMMS (FDA)              :PMA, IDE, 510k & guidance documents
 19:FERC-CIPS (DOE)             :Fed Energy Regulatory Commission
 20:FEBBS (FHWA)                :FHWA information and data
 21:VA Vendor BBS (VA)          :Learn about business opps at the VA
 22:FEDERAL BBS (GPO)           :GPO and Govt Data (Fee Based)
 23:OSS-BBS (GSA)               :GSA On-line Schedules System
 24:Eximbank BBS (EXIMBANK)     :Export/Import Bank data and info.
 25:JAG-NET (USN)               :Navy Judge Advocate General
 26:Labor News (DOL)            :Dept of Labor information and files
 27:Megawatt 1 (DOE)            :Information on energy and DoE
```

Fig.3-14: The FedWorld GateWay system offers connections to scores of other government bulletin boards.

Alternative connections, other numbers

In some cases, agencies accessed through the FedWorld GateWay are also available directly. ALF, the National Agricultural Library's Forum is available at 301-504-5496. The Census Bureau BBS is available at 301-763-7554, the Commerce Department at 202-482-3870, the Justice Department at 301-738-8895, and the Small Business Administration at 800-859-4636. Just as FedWorld is available by Internet Telnet connection, many of the same facilities accessed through FedWorld's GateWay are also available by Internet.

Other dial-up numbers of interest to journalists include

- Cal Tech's Jet Propulsion Laboratory (818-354-1333), where there are GIF images and text files on NASA space missions.
- Normandeau Newswire (212-274-8110), which is full of the news you don't/can't get anywhere else, especially on alternative life-styles.
- Environmental Protection Agency Clean Up Board (301-589-8366), dedicated to reporting EPA cleanup activity.
- Internal Revenue Service's 1040 BBS (202-927-4180), has lots of information about forms, rules, filing regulations.
- Strictly Business! BBS (614-538-9250) in Columbus, Ohio, which specializes in information for small business people.
- American Justice Federation (317-780-5211), a board dedicated to preserving civil liberties.
- The WELL (415-332-6106) in San Francisco, which is a legendary big board with full Internet access.
- The World (617-739-9753) in Boston, which is another legendary big board with Internet access.

Fig.3-15: The Strictly Business! BBS in Columbus, Ohio, offers to its members information and services aimed at small businesses.

On your local boards watch for conferences and forums aimed at writers. They often have matters of interest to journalists. There are forums and conference groups specifically dedicated to journalists on the Internet as well as in the dial-up world. For the dial-up connection for journalists, we need to visit one of the commercial online services.

Free-Nets

Many communities have in them a local "Free-Net." Cleveland, Ohio, was the first. Typically, Free-Nets are locally based networks generally initiated by volunteers with computing interests. Their purpose is manifold, but includes making online information more widely available to residents of their host communities. Local government information, community calendars, and places to chat about what's going on at home are among the fare on Free-Nets. But Free-Nets offer much more.

Foremost, Free-Nets provide for their users at least some access to the larger world of networked computing. Behind the Free-Net concept is the mission of making telecommunications resources available to everyone. They are the products of National Public Telecommunication Network. Dialing into a Free-Net is much like dialing into any other BBS. You have a local number, and you gain access to the resources of the host system according to its rules. Free-Nets also have access to and are accessible from the Internet. Many Gopher (Chapter 7) and some Telnet (Chapter 6) sites offer access to Free-Nets. During 1994, the idea of Free-Nets seemed to enjoy new popularity as new community Free-Nets were announced about every other week. Free-Nets access is described in Appendix A.

GUIs, commercial databases and hybrid services

If you want to get online with other journalists, one sure way to do it is in the JForum on CompuServe. CompuServe and its cousins America Online, Delphi, Prodigy and GEnie are hybrid services. They offer some of the features and services of larger bulletin boards as well as some of the features of commercial database services. In some cases, they provide gateway access to those services as well as to the Internet.

Local bulletin boards cater mostly to small, localized groups of people who "convene" online to exchange information, observations, and opinions. Most are computer savvy, and so it is that a regular feature of local boards includes the sharing of computer and "how to" files. Because BBSes of national scope draw from a larger user pool, they can afford to be more focused. They also tend to assess membership and/or usage fees. Even the government boards charge for some online services. At some point, providing online services becomes a commercial venture. Provide a service people are willing to pay for, and you are in business.

CompuServe

"If you can only get one service," Nora Paul of the Poynter Institute writes, "this is the one to get." We agree. CompuServe is the granddaddy of the hybrid services. It entered the public online information business primarily as a service for home computer users. In June of 1994 CompuServe boasted more than two million users, adding 80,000 new subscribers per month. For a basic monthly fee of $8.95 the user has unlimited access to a number of services including AP news wire, weather reports, sports scores, reference services including *Grolier's Online Encyclopedia*, *Consumer Reports* magazine, help with travel plans and arrangements, stock quotes, and electronic shopping. CompuServe users also have mail credit equal to the subscription price. You have to be pretty active with mail to use up your $8.95 a month credit. But once you get active, that's easy to do.

Beyond the basic services, CompuServe conducts several online forums where people of common interests gather, and discuss the things of importance to them. The Journalism Forum is one of these places, where thousands of journalists gather and discuss topics of interest to them. They share notes on dealing with reluctant sources, on ethical issues, on jobs, and on finding information online. Conversations in 1993 and 1994 on Journalism Forum and on Internet discussion lists that cater to journalists made it clear that something like this book was in growing demand. Within the Journalism Forum, specialized groups such as science writers and press photographers gather in their own subgroups.

Participation in special interest forums is assessed per hour. With millions of people to draw from, there are forums on just about any topic you can

Fig.3-16: The Journalism Forum on CompuServe organizes member discussions into topics and tells you how many messages treat that topic. Here the topics window has been reduced to reveal the underlying JForum logo.

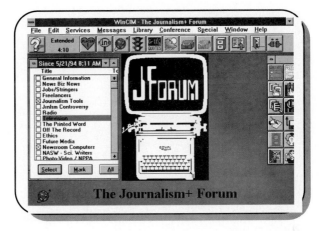

imagine. This can be very useful if you are trawling for information. Let's say for a minute you have a tip that a certain model new car has serious brake problems. You case local garages and get mixed responses. The manufacturer's public relations department and the local dealers deny any knowledge of the problem. Several forums on CompuServe and on other services deal with cars in general and by model. News groups on the Internet do the same. You post a notice in a few selected forums. The notice is read by thousands of car enthusiasts, owners, and other interested folks. You begin to get replies to your message, which you can then follow up on for verification.

So far, what we have described might qualify CompuServe as an overgrown BBS. In some ways it is. What separates it from BBSes, however, is not only its reach, but its scope. CompuServe and the other hybrid services offer fairly seamless mail interchange with the Internet. They also offer some pretty sophisticated links to other commercial services, and this is where they really become hybrids.

For example, one of the premium services on CompuServe is IQuest, a gateway to more than 800 database services. You can ask IQuest to do a search for you and retrieve documents relating to your topic. Also available are TRW credit reports, Peterson's College Database, and PhoneFile, a nationwide cross directory. CompuServe is also a gateway to Dialog, DataTimes, and DowJones Information Services. So extensive are the offerings on CompuServe that members get with their membership a monthly magazine that reports on additions and changes to the service and carries articles reporting ways to solve information problems using the service. The magazine periodically carries updates to CompuServe's printed Directory of Services.

In the days when CompuServe first came online, the service was all text and accessed by a command line. It is still available that way (Figure 3-17), and the advantage is that anyone with a computer, communications software, and a modem can access CompuServe. No special software or hardware is required. Those who prefer graphical interfaces and the convenience

Fig.3-17: The "TOP" menu on CompuServe as it is seen in a text-only interface. Contrast this with the Windows WinCim interface in Figure 3-18.

of point-and-click navigation can acquire versions of the CompuServe Information Manager (CIM) that provide such convenience. Macintosh and Windows (Figure 3-18) versions are available. So popular is CompuServe that a small cottage industry exists providing "front ends" for the service, session automators, books, and scripts helping people get into CompuServe, get what they want, and get out. While such programs and Graphical User Interface (GUIs) programs for the hybrid services put a prettier face on doing things online, they are service specific. Thus you cannot use your WinCIM program to navigate Prodigy or GEnie. But with a general communications program, you can have access to any service not limited to a proprietary interface.

America Online, Prodigy, GEnie and Delphi

Not far behind CompuServe in the race to provide commercial online access during the days of text-only interfaces were GEnie and Delphi. GEnie is a

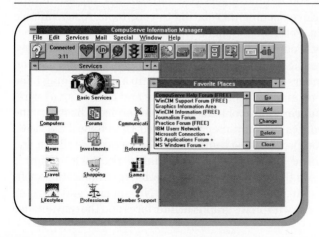

Fig.3-18: The "TOP" menu on CompuServe as it is seen in the Windows-based WinCIM program. Contrast this with the text-based interface in Figure 3-17.

Fig.3-19: America
Online uses graphical
windowing software to
present its informa-
tion online.

child of the General Electric Corporation. Delphi is independent, and until
the recent blossoming of interest in the Internet, Delphi was known only to
the hard-core online community. At this writing, Delphi bills itself as the
only online service providing full access (e-mail, Telnet, FTP, Gopher, etc.) to
the Internet. Its appeal still seems to be aimed at people who are serious
about getting things online. Like CompuServe, GEnie and Delphi offer mail,
forums, news wire, and some database access. GEnie has been the least expensive for basic services, coming in at $4.95 per month for after-hours access.

Prodigy joined the online market in the late 1980s with a unique series
of marketing ploys. First, they devised a simple graphical interface. Second,
they structured and promoted their service to have a whole family appeal
with a flat rate of $14.95 per month for their core services. Finally, they
worked a packaging arrangement with IBM on whose computers their proprietary graphical interface software ran. An added plus to the software is
that when you installed the program on your computer, the program walked
you through a process that left your computer with all the proper settings
and numbers needed to access Prodigy. It was relatively painless. They probably were successful in
bringing a number of people
– families – into the online
world.

As bold and exciting as
Prodigy's move into the market with a graphic interface
was, the graphics were still
pretty primitive, and many
of the screens appeared
childish with large lettering
and the simple graphics.

Hybrids and Press Services

America Online	800-827-6364
Burrell's Broadcast DB	800-631-1160
CompuServe	800-848-8199
Delphi	800-695-4005
GEnie	800-638-9636
PressLink	703-758-1740
Prodigy	800-776-3449

From its first entry into a broad general market, America Online (AOL) was designed with a high-quality GUI borrowed from GeoWorks. AOL provides the software free. In fact, they send it out direct mail and include it in magazine advertisements. For $9.95 per month, you get five hours of access. AOL sports online versions of *Time* magazine, the *San Jose Mercury News*, *Compton's Encyclopedia*, *Macworld*, and *Consumer Reports*. More news oriented perhaps than other systems, they also feature the CNN Newsroom (Figure 3-19). Their software includes both Mac and IBM versions. In the spring of 1994 they began shipping Windows versions.

The hybrid services, like the commercial database services, have various pricing schemes. We have mentioned some along the way. Generally, they offer basic services for a flat fee ranging from about $5 to about $15 per month. You can add on permanent options very much as cable TV subscribers elect to take optional services like HBO or the Disney Channel. Other service options are added on a per-use or per-hour basis. For example, the basic fee for CompuServe is $8.95 per month. This permits you unlimited access to several areas including AP wire, *Consumer Reports*, *Grolier's Online Encyclopedia*, weather reports, online shopping malls, and $8.95 worth of electronic mail delivery.

For $2 a month a journalist might add on the Executive News Service option. This permits you, among other things, to open news clipping folders with CompuServe. You tell the CompuServe computer you want it to save all articles mentioning Bill Clinton *and* health care (or any other terms or combination of terms). You also tell the Executive News Service which periodicals you want it to clip from and how long you want this process to continue. You can have several folders going at once. You then check your news folders as often as you like – every few hours or every few days.

Database pricing

The hybrid services offer gateways to more sophisticated operations that make a living solely on providing online information. More than 8,500 commercial database vendors are listed in Gale Research's Directory of Online Databases. These include the likes of Dialog, Datatimes, Dow Jones, Lexis/Nexis, PressLink, Burrelle's Broadcast Database, and others already well known to newsroom librarians at larger news operations. They provide news clipping services, broadcast transcripts, newspaper, magazine, and book texts, topical information retrieval, credit reports, reference services, government documents, telephone directories, and more. They do this with some pretty stiff pricing, and that has led to new job descriptions for newsroom librarians for the operations who can afford such folks.

This book, we stated in Chapter 1, is about empowering workaday journalists and news operations on tight budgets with the ability to access information store houses worldwide. This is a book about leveling the paying field among news operations. Consequently, we do little more than mention the high-price services. You can pay one of them $124 per hour to search the Securities and Exchange Commission's EDGAR filings for financial information about corporations, or you can do the search yourself – *free* – using Gopher (Chapter 7) at town.hall.org. You can pay Lexis by the hour to track Supreme Court decisions, or you can access them free at the Legal Information Institute Gopher (gopher.law.cornell.edu) at Cornell University. We are not saying that everything the commercial services provide is available free on the Internet, but some of their valuable information is.

Further reading

If you want to know more about the commercial online database services, we recommend two books: Nahum Goldmann's *Online Information Hunting*, Blue Ridge Summit, PA: McGraw-Hill, 1992, 236 pages; and Nora Paul's *Computer Assisted Research: A Guide to Tapping Online Information*, 2nd ed., St. Petersburg, FL: Poynter Institute, 1994, 44 pages. Goldmann's book goes into to great detail on developing search strategies and using the commercial services wisely so you get what you want for the least amount of money. Nora Paul's *Guide* is aimed more at just pointing news folks in the right direction. The *Guide* names a few of the more news-oriented services available, gives a thumbnail sketch of what they have to offer, describes their pricing structures, and tells how to get in touch with them. Not available in bookstores, it may be ordered ($3) directly from Poynter at 801 Third Street South, St. Petersburg, Florida 33701. This booklet is under annual revision to keep pace with a rapidly changing online environment.

Two other books are helpful in understanding the dial-up online world:

1. Howard Rheingold, *The Virtual Community: Homesteading on the Electronic Frontier*, Reading, Massachusetts; Addison-Wesley, 1993.
2. Peter Rutten, Albert F. Bayers III, and Kelly Maloni, *Net Guide*, New York: Random House, 1994.

Magazines that monitor the dial-up online world, include:

1. *Boardwatch Magazine,* devoted exclusively to BBS type systems.
2. *Wired.*
3. *Computer Shopper,* which has other purposes, but prints a fair listing of BBS numbers by area code each month.
4. *Online Access.*

Chapter

4

Introduction to the Internet

On March 19, 1992, *USA Today* published an article about residential over-crowding. The story reported that the poorer the family, the greater the number of people per room in houses and apartments. No surprise there. But the state with the most crowded households was seemingly affluent Hawaii.

That story was the latest in a series of interesting insights in "The Nation's Newspaper," as it likes to call itself. In September 1991 it had reported that non-white populations represented a majority of the people in 51 cities. In July of that year, the newspaper had identified Crawford County, Mo., as the population center of the country and in April it had revealed that New Mexico had the country's most diverse population while Vermont had the most homogeneous. Also, Los Angeles had passed Miami as the most diverse large city.

These stories were not the result of in-depth investigations. In each case, reporters relied heavily on information from the U.S. Census. Cleverly used, Census statistics can be a virtually endless source of interesting national and local stories. Since 1990, the information has been widely available on CD-ROM.

But to fully explore the possible stories contained in Census material, reporters need to be versed in the data itself. As Shawn Macintosh, special projects editor for *USA Today* cautioned a group of investigative reporters and editors, reporters need to have a story idea before they begin chasing data. That is why it is significant that journalists can now access data and communicate with Census Bureau personnel online. Indeed, you can access Census information through commercial services like CompuServe, by calling the Census Bureau's electronic bulletin board service in the Washington D.C. area, or through the Internet.

Commercial information services and bulletin boards such as those described in Chapter 3 clearly demonstrate the potential value to journalists of using online information. The problem is that commercial information services can be costly. By definition, they are operated by for-profit companies and are geared primarily to corporate clients with budgets to support the costs of searching for specialized information. In 1992, according to its newspaper librarian, the *Washington Post* spent more than $1 million a year using commercial information services. Smaller newspapers, magazines, broadcasting outlets, and particularly freelance writers may not be able to support the costs of extensive online searching on commercial services.

Bulletin board services also have drawbacks for journalists. While very useful, bulletin boards frequently specialize in very narrow kinds of information. Consequently, it may be difficult to identify a bulletin board service with exactly the kind of information you need. Moreover, you may need to devote a considerable amount of time looking through a bulletin board service to find what you need.

But reporters who wish to access Census data have an alternative. The information is also available through the Internet. The Internet can be conceptualized as the equivalent of a network of computers. Through the Internet, thousands of computers throughout the world can send information back and forth. Millions of people with Internet access can locate and retrieve information stored on those computers. People can also use this extensive network to send messages to each other. Unlike commercial information services, users are not charged for access time. Unlike bulletin board services, you do not have to make long distance calls and you can easily move among different sources of information.

Properly used, the Internet provides journalists with immense information stores to flesh out stories on which they are working. Journalists are no longer limited to the information in their newspapers' libraries (if their newspapers have libraries) or nearby university and public libraries. They can now access libraries, universities, and other computers around the world searching for the information they may need.

Almost as significantly for journalists, the Internet supports electronic mail. That means, the Internet provides a method for journalists to locate and communicate with their human sources beyond face-to-face and telephone interviews. One of the most popular features of the Internet and related networks is the capacity for people with similar interests to engage in online, public discussions about topics of mutual interest. These newsgroups and discussion lists represent a way for journalists to identify new sources of information.

This chapter will cover five topics

- a description of the Internet.
- a short history of the Internet.

- a survey of many of the tools journalists can use on the Internet.
- issues involved in gaining Internet access.
- issues associated with the Internet that will be important to journalists over the next several years.

The information in this chapter is important for journalists to know for several reasons. The Internet was not developed with journalism in mind. By understanding the rationale behind the development of the Internet, you will be better able to understand its structure and operation and develop strategies to solve problems that may occur as you move through the net.

Moreover, the Internet is undergoing a period of change and redefinition. If journalists do not understand that process, they will not be able to participate in a way that will ensure that the online infrastructure will evolve in a way that is consistent with the aims and needs of journalism. Finally, in addition to using the Internet, many journalists will have to describe the Internet to others.

What is the Internet?

Some veteran users of the Internet like to argue that it defies definition. In a well known story, one old timer once defined the Internet by describing what it wasn't. Quickly others shortened his definition to "The Internet – not."

While complex, the structure of the Internet is understandable. The Internet is a term used to describe the interconnection of many computer networks in a way that allows them to communicate with each other. Although the popular term "Information Superhighway" is misleading, the Internet is like the road and highway system and conceptually functions in much the same way.

Consider this extended metaphor. In the United States, you can drive a car from Los Angeles to New York. You can do this for two reasons. First, there are physical links called roads. These roads take many different forms. In front of your house, the road may be a single lane. You then may turn onto a slightly larger road and two lanes with a line down the middle. The next street may have traffic lights to control the flow of traffic. Eventually you will reach an interstate highway that has several lanes of traffic moving at high speeds in the same direction. To arrive at your final destination, you must go through the same process but in reverse. You exit from the interstate highway and then travel on a series of successively smaller streets until you arrive at a specific location.

In addition to the physical links, however, to make the trip from Los Angeles to New York safely, you need to have a set of rules that govern the way all the travelers use the roads. You must know that you cannot cross a double line in the middle of a road; that you must stop at red lights; that you must travel within certain speed limits depending on the type of road and weather conditions.

The Internet is the same kind of network as the road and highway system, but instead of moving vehicles occupied by people, it moves packets filled with information. The Internet is made up of physical links, but in the same sense that no one road connects a home in Los Angeles directly to a home in New York, no one single link connects all the computers on the Internet. Like streets, computers are linked in successive levels. At your university or company you have a local area network to provide a direct link for computers in a single department of a university or company. Frequently networks in different departments will in turn be connected with each other. Departmental and even company-wide networks are like neighborhood streets. They are under the control of the system administrators of the facilities.

In the automotive world, different neighborhoods are linked by larger streets. In the Internet world, these larger streets make up what are called regional networks. Regional networks, often called midlevel networks, connect the computers at different universities, companies and other institutions. Like larger streets, these midlevel networks enable data to travel faster than on local area networks. These midlevel or regional networks have names like SURAnet, NYSERnet and NorthWestNet.

National backbones

The specialized computers that control the flow of information on the midlevel networks are also physically linked to what are called national backbones. The national backbones use lines that transmit data at yet higher speeds and higher capacity computers to handle information traffic. In the United States there are several national backbones for the Internet, including networks run by the Department of Defense, the Department of Energy and NASA. The largest and most influential backbone, and the one which has enabled the Internet to be used by a wider community of people, has been the high speed network initiated by the National Science Foundation, called NSFNet.

In addition to being linked to regional networks, the national backbones are connected to each other. The Internet itself then is the word used to describe the interconnection of these successive levels of networks. As such, the Internet is the series of physical links that serves as the road system for computer-based information. It encompasses the local networks within organizations through which information moves slowly but only for short distances; the midlevel networks linking universities, companies and other organizations; and the national backbones, which allow a lot of information to travel long distances at very high speeds.

As you will see, it is important to understand that the Internet is not any single network. It is not even any single national backbone network like NSFnet. Instead, it is the interconnection of thousands of networks around the world. But the physical links are only one part of the Internet. The sets of rules or protocols that allow the information to travel from computer to computer on the Internet are equally as important. If a computer or computer network does not support that set of rules, it is not part of the Internet. In other words, to send and receive information via the Internet, computers must package information in the same way. If a computer cannot do that, even if it has a physical link to a network, it is not part of the Internet.

Think of it this way. Motor vehicles and airplanes are both forms of transportation but airplanes cannot use the road system. There are many types of networks and ways to send information between computers. But only computers that follow the specific rules associated with the Internet can use the Internet.

The dominant protocol or set of rules used on the Internet is called the Transmission Control Protocol/Internet Protocol (TCP/IP). The IP part of the protocol is the address for every computer that is physically linked to the Internet. Each computer has a unique address. The IP part of the protocol identifies the sender and destination of information.

The TCP part of the protocol controls the way information is sent through the Internet network. It is according to the TCP protocol requirements that the ability to log onto remote computers, transfer files and perform other applications on the Internet have been developed. At one level, TCP serves as a quasi operating system for Internet applications, allowing Internet applications to interact on computers that, themselves, have different operating systems such as Unix, VMS, DOS or Macintosh OS.

In summary, the growth of the Internet has stemmed from two factors. Physical links consisting of high-speed data lines have been established connecting the computer networks — or internetworking, as the jargon sometimes has it — of universities, governments, businesses, and other organizations. These links have created a de facto national network. Second, the widespread acceptance of TCP/IP protocols allows information to travel transparently through the linked networks, which make up the Internet even though different computers have different hardware architectures and operating systems.

Network control

Understanding of the structure of the Internet sheds light on several important questions. First, who controls the Internet? The answer is that no one entity controls the Internet. Instead, there is a layer of control at every network level.

For example, the people responsible for the administration of your local network may choose not to develop a complete link to the Internet but only to support electronic mail. They can decide how much information on the central computers at your site will be available to other people on the Internet. Most importantly, they decide who gets an Internet account and the rules governing that account.

In turn, the midlevel networks have network operation centers and network information centers that provide database, registration and directory services. Individual universities and companies negotiate their connection with the Internet through these regional bodies.

Finally, the national backbone networks have their own governing organizations. Because the National Science Foundation's NSFnet is the most significant backbone network for non-military users, its acceptable use policy has long defined how the Internet may or may not be used. For example, extensive use of NSFnet for private or personal business and many types of for-profit activities are unacceptable under these guidelines.

As the Internet has grown, however, the rules governing its use have come under scrutiny and there are many proposals to change the usage policy. As the Internet has grown to include companies, it is increasingly being used for commercial as well as educational and research activities.

The growth of the Internet, however, does not rely just on the growth of physical links among computer networks and on the development of higher speed data transmission lines. The protocols that manage the flow of information are continually being developed as are new ways to navigate through the net to access information. Because the functioning of the Internet itself relies on those protocols being accepted by different groups, and there is no one central governing body, since 1992 those kinds of developments have been supervised by a non-profit organization called the Internet Society, which has absorbed the Internet Architecture Board.

Cost structure

The lack of a centralized management organization has also had an impact on the cost of using the Internet. Building, maintaining and developing the Internet is an ambitious and costly undertaking. To date, the national backbones have largely been subsidized by the federal government and some of the regional networks have received state funding. Currently, universities, business enterprises and organizations generally pay a flat monthly or annual fee to connect to either a regional network or a national backbone. Once connected, however, organizations are usually not charged on a usage basis. Consequently, most universities do not charge individual users for using the Internet.

Looked at another way, the cost of the Internet is like the cost of cable television. With cable, you pay a monthly fee and then you can watch as many programs on as many different channels as you like. With the Internet, once the monthly charge is paid, users can generally use as many services as often as they like without additional charges.

This current pricing structure is significant for journalists. It means that you can search through the Internet as diligently as you want for relevant information and can communicate with as many people as you can identify via e-mail without worrying about receiving a huge bill at the end of the month. Moreover, it means the Internet can open sources of information — both archival and human — that would be too expensive or difficult to access in any other way.

For example, an editor of a specialized science magazine was looking for someone to write articles about new developments in laboratory automation. Working through the Internet, he came in contact with scientists in St. Petersburg, Russia, who were active in that area. Over the course of several months, the editor and the scientists collaborated to develop two articles. At one point in the editing process, the editor was exchanging information with the scientists on an almost daily basis. He did not have to worry about accruing huge costs. Also, the time differential between the U.S. and Russia was not a problem.

Some people would like to change the pricing mechanism for the Internet. They would like to see users charged for the time they are actually online or for the specific services they use. If the pricing mechanism is changed, it could have a dramatic impact on the functionality of the Internet for journalists, particularly those working for smaller organizations.

While the Internet is clearly the largest computer network of its kind, it is not the only one. There are other similar networks such as Bitnet, which links universities, and FidoNet, which links thousands of bulletin boards, and Usenet, which was created to facilitate online discussions. Nevertheless, the Internet is by far the dominant network of its type. Moreover, many of the alternative networks are beginning to create links to the Internet at least via electronic mail.

A history of the Internet

The growth of the Internet can be measured in three ways: the number of host computers connected to the Internet, the number of users connected to those host computers, and the amount of information or traffic carried on the Internet. Because of its decentralized structure, precise usage figures are hard to determine. But by all measures, the Internet is rapidly growing.

By some estimates the number of users is growing by 50 percent per year and the amount of traffic is growing at a rate of 20 percent per month. At least one analyst anticipates the number of host computers connected to the Internet may jump tenfold from nearly one million in 1993 to 10 million by the turn of the century. And that analyst may be right. From January 1993 to January 1994, the number of host computers climbed 69 percent from 1.3 million to 2.2 million.

The number of users may climb even faster. Currently, many observers believe that each host computer represents three to 10 users. But the number of users per host may climb as more people learn how to take advantage of opportunities provided by the Internet. Some people project that by the late 1990s, more than 100 million people will have access to the Internet. If those projections prove accurate, and it is impossible to say with certainty that they will, the Internet will eventually represent a communications network that will rival the telephone system in its importance and usefulness to journalists.

Military origins

Ironically, the Internet was not originally conceived of as a global communications system. Like some other useful technologies, the Internet has its roots in the need for military preparedness. In the late 1960s, the Advanced Research Projects Agency of the Department of Defense began funding projects to develop an experimental computer network to support military research by allowing people spread across the country to more easily share their computer files and send messages to each other.

The interest in developing networks of this kind represented a logical step stimulated by the explosion in the use of time sharing minicomputers at the time. In time sharing, dedicated or dial-up lines connect dumb terminals to a host, which, at the time, was either a mainframe or minicomputer. All the terminals do is send instructions to the host. The host computer divided its time among several different jobs although it could only respond to one instruction at a time.

Timesharing allowed many users to access a single computer at the same time. Clearly, the next step was to be able to link the hosts into wider networks to electronically exchange information.

The Department of Defense had specific requirements for the way it wanted to link host computers. It wanted the network to be able to function even if parts of it had been disrupted, presumably in a war. The researchers decided that by using an addressing system, which they called the Internet Protocol (IP), the communicating computers themselves could ensure that the information was successfully transmitted or received and every computer on the network would be able to communicate with every other computer on the network. This kind of arrangement, in which every computer on the network can fulfill all the communication tasks among computers on the network is called peer-to-peer networking.

In 1969, an experimental network called ARPAnet was launched with four nodes. The participants were UCLA, the Stanford Research Institute, UC Santa Barbara and the University of Utah. By 1971, there were 19 nodes shared by 30 universities with funding from the Department of Defense.

Developing ARPAnet was complicated because different sites used different types of computers, and the protocols that were developed had to work on many different computer architectures and operating systems. The challenge was to develop rules of communication that would allow information to be sent over many different kinds of networks without regard to the underlying network technology. These protocols began to appear in the mid-1970s and were known as the Transmission Control Protocol, or TCP. By the early 1980s all the systems associated with ARPAnet standardized on TCP/IP.

Supercomputing centers established

The next impetus for the Internet came in 1987, when the National Science Foundation decided to establish five supercomputing centers around the country and link them through its own high-speed network known as NSFnet. Since the cost to connect researchers directly to the supercomputing centers with dedicated high-speed data lines would have been prohibitive, NSF encouraged research institutions to form regional networks, which, in turn, were linked to the supercomputing centers. That strategy has led to the basic structure of the Internet, with its multiple layers of networks.

The exponential growth in the use of the Internet began with the launch of NSFnet in the late 1980s as researchers in academic and governmental settings took advantage of the new opportunity to collaborate. In 1990, an effort was undertaken to include commercial and non-profit organizations as well. By the middle of 1993, by some estimates there were more than three million commercial Internet users and that number was growing at a rate of 10 to 20 percent a month. Commercial organizations have the fastest rate of connection to the Internet of any single type of user community.

Host, server, and client

Describing the programs associated with the Internet and applying them to the tasks of journalism will be explored in depth in the next several chapters. This section will provide a brief overview of the different types of software tools available and briefly describe their differences. In a sense, it will survey what's available in your Internet tool box before you go out to work and use each one.

Internet applications are not the same as application programs for personal computers. Unlike personal computer software, in which everything happens locally on your personal computer, with Internet applications, some parts of a specific task are handled at your local computer and some parts of the task are handled by a remote computer.

As mentioned earlier, when the process that has evolved into the Internet first began, timesharing was the emerging model for computing. Dumb terminals sent instructions to a "smart" computer called the host. The host actually performed all the tasks. As personal computers became commonplace in the 1980s, this structure began to shift. In a network, some tasks were performed by the computer on the person's desk while other were performed by a centralized remote computer. This approach to networks is called the client-server model. For any specific application, part is done by the

Fig. 4-1: From your desk you connect to the Internet either directly or through a host computer. Client software provides you with an interface to servers. That software may reside at your desktop, your host, or elsewhere on the Internet.

client software running on one computer and another part is done by the server, which is on another computer.

Internet software applications combine the client-server and host-terminal models of computing for nearly all the applications described in the pages that follow. A server or "daemon" program runs all the time on one computer. A server accepts from client programs requests for information and requests to perform other tasks. Client programs run on the computers that people actually use to connect to the Internet and to communicate with the servers.

The terms *host*, *client* and *server* are used extensively in the literature about the Internet and computer networking in general and it is important to keep them straight. The *host* computer accepts you as a guest for its connections to the Internet. *Client* software organizes information into menus, hypertext documents, or some other format designed to be helpful to you and sends out requests to get things done. *Servers*, which may be located on the specific host computer you are using or on other computers on the Internet, answer requests from client software by sending to the client data and information in a format the client can use in helping you.

When you use an Internet software application, the *client* software will be either on your personal computer, the computer you log onto for access to the Internet (your *host*), or on yet another computer to which you connect in order to use client software you may not have yourself. The *server* often is located on yet another computer. The terms are confusing because the Internet is a peer-to-peer network. Each computer on the network potentially can be a *host*, run *client* software, and provide *server* functions, although not all do. Moreover, during the course of a search for information, you may find yourself logging on to several different computers.

For example, let's say you are working on a story about teaching about sexually transmitted diseases in the school system. You heard that there is some interesting information about health education projects stored on a computer at the University of California, Davis. You decide to log onto the computer at UC Davis to explore those files. First, you log onto the computer that provides you with Internet access. At that point, that computer is the *host*. Then you activate the *client* software that allows you to connect to the computers at UC Davis. A *server* program directs you to the UC Davis computer.

As you navigate through the Internet, you will find yourself logged onto different host computers, sometimes gaining access to different client programs and also accessing different servers. It can be complicated. Fortunately, the purpose of advanced Internet software is to hide this complexity from you; and to a large degree it succeeds.

Internet software applications

Internet software can be divided into four categories. Basic Internet tools allow you to log onto and transfer information to and from other computers on the Internet and to send electronic mail to people with access to the Internet and other computer networks. These basic applications reflect the original twofold intention of the Internet – to facilitate collaboration and communication among researchers and to place the responsibility for communicating within each computer connected to the network rather than on the network itself.

The second set of Internet applications allows you to locate information stored on computers connected to the network. To be able to effectively use the information available through the Internet, you have to be able to identify where the information you want is. These tools help you find specific types of information.

Once you have located files, you want to be able to retrieve them. Because of the client-server-host structure of the Internet, this means you often have to log onto a different computer to transfer the files. The third set of Internet application tools automate the process of moving around the network and transferring the specific information for that you are looking.

The last category of Internet applications represents an interactive aspect of the Internet. People who are logged into the network at the same time can interactively communicate in real time. Messaging programs permit personal exchanges delayed over time.

There is an old saying that if all you have is a hammer, everything looks like a nail. With the Internet, you have much more than a hammer. On the other hand, even if you do not have access to the full set of Internet tools available, you will find even the basic tools extremely useful in locating and collecting information and communicating with people. In fact, even if you only have electronic mail access to the Internet, you can still locate and retrieve files, although it is a slower, more tedious, less efficient process.

Basic Internet programs

Electronic Mail: Electronic mail is one of the most useful features of the Internet and is often the application that gets people started. Electronic mail is a method to send messages back and forth among people with Internet addresses as well as people on other networks with mail connections to the Internet. The Internet supports several different useful forms of electronic mail including person-to-person communication that is delivered to the electronic address of the intended recipient; one-to-many transmissions and ways to allow your message to be seen by many people even if they don't receive it in their electronic mail box. In addition to interpersonal communication, electronic mail will let you enjoy the benefits of some Internet services even if you don't have the appropriate client software. Electronic mail will be discussed in Chapter 5.

Telnet: Telnet allows you to log onto another computer on the Internet. That computer is known as the remote computer. Once you are logged onto a remote computer, it is as if your keyboard were attached to that computer. You can do what the people who regularly use that computer can do. Frequently, if the computer you use to access the Internet does not have specific client software with which you want to work, you can use Telnet to connect to another computer that does have the right tools. For example, the law library at Washington and Lee University provides access to a wide range of other databases and client programs. Telnet will be explored in Chapter 6.

FTP: FTP stands for "File Transfer Protocol." As the name implies, it facilitates moving files from one computer to another. It has become the common language for sharing data. Unlike Telnet, in which you often must know a specific password to actually successfully log onto the remote computer, anonymous FTP has become commonplace. With anonymous FTP, anyone on the Internet may transfer files from (and sometimes to) a remote system using the word anonymous as the user identification. FTP will be discussed in Chapter 8.

Locating files and people

Hytelnet: Hytelnet incorporates extensive guides to Telnet sites around the world. Once you locate a site, Hytelnet hands you off – with instructions – to Telnet to log onto and to explore other sites. Hytelnet will be discussed in Chapter 6.

Archie: Archie is a program that locates files that can be transferred via FTP. The Archie program reads an index of more than 1,000 FTP sites. It is updated constantly and its "what is" command describes the files you have found. Once you have located files via Archie, you can transfer them via FTP. Archie will be described in Chapter 8.

Veronica and Jughead: Veronica and Jughead are programs that locate files that can be accessed through the Gopher software described below. These programs survey the directories of thousands of Gopher sites around the world. They are discussed in Chapter 7.

WAIS: WAIS, or Wide Area Information Servers, is another vehicle for locating and retrieving information. There are several hundred databases indexed and linked through WAIS. Like Gopher, WAIS helps you find and access resources on the Internet even if you don't know exactly where they are located. But instead of paging through menus, with WAIS, you search for phrases in the documents stored on the WAIS-linked databases. In other words, when you ask your WAIS client program to find something, it asks each server to check its index for the words you specified. It then returns a list of documents that could be appropriate along with an evaluation of how well the information in each document matches your search criteria. You then have the option of retrieving the document. WAIS will be discussed in Chapter 8.

Finger, Whois Knowbot, and Fred: Finger, Whois, Knowbot and Fred are services that can be used to help locate the e-mail addresses and other information about people who have Internet addresses. These services and other options for locating people on the Internet will be discussed in Chapter 5.

Navigating tools

Gopher: Gopher was the first program to integrate the information search and retrieval process on the Internet. Like other Internet applications, Gopher consists of servers and client software. More than 2,000 Gopher servers have been linked. When you find something you want, the gopher client software retrieves it for you through menu-based commands. With Gopher it does not matter exactly where the information you want is located. It does not matter what kind of information you want to retrieve. Nor does it matter what tool you need to use to retrieve that information. You use tools from a menu to perform each operation. Gopher will be fully discussed in Chapter 7.

World Wide Web: World Wide Web is perhaps the most exciting new tool for the Internet. It is based on a technology called hypertext. With hypertext, words in one document can be linked to other, related documents. For example, let's say you have found a bill in the U.S. Senate in which you are interested. The names of each of the authors of the bill can be linked to brief biographical sketches that are actually stored on a completely different computer. Let's says the biographical sketches include the amount of money senators raised for their reelection campaigns. That information could be linked to a document that lists all their campaign contributors. Lynx is a World Wide Web hypertext client. Web clients are called browsers.

Graphical World Wide Web browsers like Cello and Mosaic respond to hypermedia links beyond just text. Along with text, they fetch graphics, video, and sound if links to those kinds of information have been built into the document. The World Wide Web is an ambitious attempt to link connected information wherever it may be located on the Internet, allowing the user to easily access and retrieve related files. Several easy-to-use client programs such as Cello, Mosaic and Lynx have been developed for the World Wide Web, which will be discussed in Chapter 7.

Interactive applications

Internet Relay Chat: Internet Rely Chat (IRC) turns the Internet into the equivalent of an international CB radio network. IRC is organized into different channels with different themes. When you log onto an IRC server, you see a list of channels and then can join the conversation. You can also establish private channels of communication with IRC, allowing you to interview somebody privately online. IRC will be discussed in Chapter 9.

News groups and discussion lists: News groups and discussion lists allow for delayed (not real time) conversations. Using either news reader software or e-mail, people post messages, which can be read by many people. Discussion lists and news groups will be discussed in Chapters 5 and 9.

The software tools for the Internet are constantly under development. Because most are being developed by Internet users themselves, clients for most of the advanced applications are still in the public domain and can be accessed using the basic Internet functions. Some companies, however, have begun to sell client programs on a commercial basis as well.

As sophisticated as the application tools get, the basic operation and purpose of the Internet remains the same. At its core, the Internet is a communications network among computers. It allows you to locate and retrieve information on other computers linked to the Internet as well as send and receive messages to and from other people on the Internet and elsewhere electronically.

Accessing the Internet

Gaining access to the Internet involves two separate factors. The first issue is establishing an account on a computer that is connected to the Internet. It is less common that your own personal computer will be directly connected to the Internet. Instead, you will establish a connection with a host computer, which, in turn, is connected to the Net.

The second factor relates to the manner in which your computer is connected to the computer through which you access the Internet. To return to the street analogy used earlier in this chapter, the first step is to make sure that you live in a neighborhood that is connected to larger streets, which connect to other neighborhoods. The second step is to make sure that traffic rules in your local neighborhood work.

For many, getting an account on a computer that is connected to the Internet is very easy. If you are at a university, almost certainly your school is connected to the Internet already. If you are working at a larger company, your employer's computers may be connected.

In both those cases, your first stop should be the computer system administrator or computer support personnel. They will tell you what you have to do to establish an account on a computer that will give you Internet access, as well as some of the relevant aspects of the computer setup in your organization.

But if you are working at a smaller media company or are a freelance writer, getting access to the Internet can be a more complicated issue. The first alternative is to affiliate with a university or other organization that has Internet access. At some schools, even if you take only one course, you can establish an account on a central computer with access to the Internet. Also, some user groups and community free-nets like those described in Chapter 3 are now establishing Internet access for their members.

A second alternative is to establish an account with what is called a public dial up service. As more people have found out about the Internet, several companies have begun to sell access to the Internet on a monthly basis. You dial into their computer as though it were a bulletin board. From there, you are connected to the Internet. A partial listing of some dial-up Internet providers is in Appendix A, as well as a method, once you have Internet access, to get a complete listing.

A third way to access the Internet is through commercial information services, which were described in Chapter 3. America Online, Delphi, CompuServe, the World, Holonet and the WELL, among others, provide access to Internet functions in addition to the specialized information services they offer. Commercial information services, however, charge by the hour and sometimes have limits on the amount of electronic mail you can send and receive. They may have other restrictions on Internet access too.

To complicate matters, once you have access you still may not be able to use every feature available on the Internet. There are several different levels of access to the Internet. Some networks offer what is called electronic mail access to the Internet. Although computers on these networks cannot use applications like Telnet and FTP, they can send and receive electronic mail. Fortunately, you can get some of the benefits of the advanced applications of the Internet using electronic mail. Those methods will be described in Chapter 5. Moreover, just being able to send and receive electronic mail can be very useful to journalists.

Type of connection

Once you are sure that you have an account on a computer that has access to the Internet, you have to be aware of the way you are connected to that computer. The most efficient way to connect is to be on a network that is running TCP/IP. Your computer has its own IP number and is connected to the network through a network card. That means that you can run client software on your personal computer and control the number of different Internet software applications you use. Almost as desirable is a telephone dial-up connection in which the host supports one of two protocols: SLIP (Serial Line Internet Protocol) or PPP (Point-to-Point Protocol). You will want a high-speed modem (at least 9,600 baud) for this arrangement. If you have either a direct TCP/IP connection or a SLIP or PPP connection, you can use client software available for the Macintosh or IBM-compatible computers.

If you cannot get direct connection or SLIP or PPP connection, try to select a host that makes available to you a full range of Internet protocols (FTP, Telnet, mail) as well as providing you with at least Gopher, and preferably WWW, clients. Without a local client, you will not be able to take advantage of the bookmark features of Gopher and the World Wide Web. Figure 4-2 describes levels of Internet access and connections in a table format.

If you are not on a network running TCP/IP and do not have your own IP number, somebody else – usually the system administrator – controls the number of Internet application programs running on your host. For example, at some universities, to access the Internet you will connect to a

Fig. 4-2: Hierarchy of preferred connections and services offered by providers. If you have Direct or SLIP (or PPP) access, you may have your own clients on your personal computer. If you have only dial-up access, you will have to rely on your host for all client services. Without some local client, you cannot take advantage of Gopher and WWW bookmarks.

Hierarchy of Connections

Direct	Your computer has network card hard-wired to the Internet (generally large institutions). Most desirable.
SLIP, PPP	Computer has dial-up (modem) access and host supports SLIP or PPP protocols.
Dial-up	Host accessed through telephone dial-up with no special communications protocols. Least flexible.

Hierarchy of Services

Full/plus	Host provides Telnet, FTP, and mail access. Also has other clients such as Gopher, WAIS, Lynx, a news reader.
Full	Host provides Telnet, FTP, and mail access but without other extended clients.
Partial	Host has e-mail access, typically provides a news reader, perhaps Telnet.
Mail only	Host merely has an e-mail gateway to the Internet.

central computer that is connected to the Internet. Once connected, your personal computer operates like a dumb terminal. The only Internet client software you can run from your home computer are the clients your system administrator has agreed to carry on the central computer.

Unfortunately, many system administrators will not run software to access newsgroups or other services, claiming their centralized computers are too busy with other chores. Your alternative in that situation is to use basic Internet functions like Telnet to log onto remote computers with the client software you need.

Impact of online journalism

Although it is rarely studied, when the use of the telephone exploded around the turn of the century, it had a profound impact on journalism. Suddenly, journalists could collect much more information much more quickly. Reporters at the news scene would call in their reports, shortening the time between the event and the printed article. An entire new job classification, the rewrite person, emerged.

And as telephone technology improved, its impact on journalism continued. Instead of reporters calling in information to newspapers, they could call out to sources as well. For Washington-based stories, for example, reporters could tap sources across the country or even the world. Telephone interviews became a standard reporting procedure.

The Internet will have a similar impact on journalism. Currently, the Internet is about at the same level of development as the telephone system in the 1890s. There is no universal access. It is not easy to operate. And only a select number of reporters currently use it.

Nevertheless, even in its current form, the Internet is very useful because it allows reporters to perform their fundamental tasks of collecting and communicating information in a much more comprehensive and efficient fashion. It gives reporters access to sources of information, both documentary and human, that they would have never known existed before. And it gives that access in a very timely fashion.

Capacity improvements certain

Just as the telephone network has improved in the last 100 years, the Internet will dramatically improve too. The advances will come in three areas. First, the speed at which information can travel on the network will increase. Second, the variety and amount of information available through the Internet will increase. Finally, methods to identify and access information will improve.

The effort to increase network capacity has been dubbed the development of the Information Superhighway. The term is misleading because it implies that at some point everybody will be connected to one network.

They won't. The term Information Superhighway is also often misused by cable television companies eager to increase their channel capacities and regional telephone companies who wish to deliver video over their lines to the home.

When government officials talk about the Information Superhighway, however, they frequently are referring to improving the data transmission capacities of the national backbone networks like NSFnet, which the federal government has largely funded.

Improving the data transmission capacity of the national backbones could potentially increase the efficiency of the Internet. But when the Information Superhighway is discussed, how the relationship of the regional, midlevel networks to the national backbones, and, in turn, relationship of the local networks to the regional networks, will be managed is not generally mentioned. That relationship will be key in determining how useful the Internet will be to the public and not just to specialists.

Improving data transmission speeds throughout the network will be significant because it will allow for more and different kinds of information to be sent via the Internet. Currently, the Internet is useful primarily for text information. Though it can be done, graphics, audio and video information cannot always be efficiently transmitted except by those parts of the Internet connected by higher speed lines. That will change as transmission speeds improve and data compression schemes advance.

More information, easier to find

In the future, more information will be accessible through the Internet. The federal government is the largest collector of information in the world. It is just starting to make much of that information available through the Internet. State and local governments, court systems, and other public agencies also are just beginning to come online.

Moreover, only about one-third of the hosts currently connected to the Internet allow other Internet users to access information stored on them. That should change over time as well, as security issues are resolved and people's comfort level with the Internet increases. At some point, it is conceivable that anybody who produces information for public circulation will also provide that information via the Internet or a successor network.

Finally, ways to locate and access information on the Internet will improve over the next several years. The leaders of the computing industry have long held a vision in which information stored on computers anywhere in the world would be accessible to people sitting at their personal computers. Tens of millions of dollars are being invested to help realize that vision. Part of the payoff will be in improved software to find information through the Internet.

Future policy

The potential development and direction of the Internet raises public policy issues of which journalists concerned about freedom of information must be aware. First, as network technology improves, the telephone companies and cable companies are anxious to take control and responsibility for it. If private companies take control of the basic technology, journalists will be one community that will need to make sure that the private economic gains of those companies does not supersede the public interest in providing access.

Along the same lines, the cost to access information gathered by the government has already become an issue. On one hand, private information providers have lobbied to receive exclusive rights to specialized information that they believe has commercial value in return for paying a royalty to the government. Others argue that information gathered by the government has been paid for by taxpayers already and should be available to the public in a computerized form at a nominal cost.

This issue is called the privatization of public information. Although it would seem that journalists clearly would like to keep low the cost of accessing government information in computerized form, some large publishing companies with well known newspapers are actively reselling government information at stiff prices. These companies see the privatization of public information as a potential new profit center. The controversy could pit working journalists against their potential employers.

Finally, as the software to access the Internet improves, more people will be able to easily access more information. Not only will that make the Internet more useful to journalists, it could change the nature of publishing. Newspapers, for example, are currently investing millions of dollars to develop a newspaperlike interface to computerized information. As that interface develops, the duties and responsibilities of reporters to their companies and to the public will change. By the middle of 1994, more than 70 newspapers already had online publishing projects underway. Scores of newsletters and journals are also being published via the Internet.

The policy issues regarding the Internet will be resolved over time. But the Internet is extremely useful today. In the next five chapters, you will learn how to apply the Internet to your current reporting assignments.

Further Reading

For short books approaching the Internet from an introductory level, three "old classics" recommend themselves.

1. Brendan Kehoe. *Zen and the Art of the Internet: A Beginner's Guide*, 2nd ed. Engelwood Cliffs, N.J.: PTR Prentice Hall, 1994.
2. Tracy LaQuey with Jeanne C. Ryer. *The Internet Companion: A Beginner's Guide to Global Networking*, Reading, Mass.: Addison-Wesley, 1992.
3. April Marine, ed. *Internet: Getting Started*, updated 1993 ed. Englewood Cliffs, N.J.: PTR Prentice Hall, 1994.

Chapter **5**

Communicating with people

The case riveted the attention of America. When Polly Klass was abducted from her home in Petaluma, Calif., during a pajama party with her friends, millions of Americans were horrified. And many Californians were motivated to join in the search for the young girl. Lawrence J. Magid, a syndicated columnist whose articles appear in the *Los Angeles Times* and elsewhere was among them. He felt compelled to drive to Petaluma to volunteer for a search team.

But then he reconsidered. "I live and work in cyberspace," he said. So he turned to his personal computer to disseminate information about Klass via electronic mail across the country. When Klass's alleged abductor and murderer was apprehended, Magid continued to establish online forums about missing children. Through his efforts, by the fall of 1994 the National Center for Missing and Exploited Children was receiving 600 e-mail messages and contacts daily.

For journalists and others, e-mail and other online communications have become significant channels of communications. Since the beginning of the 1990s, the use of electronic mail has exploded. In 1992, a survey of corporate management information service and telecommunication managers in 160 of the Fortune 1000 companies indicated electronic mail was the most important technology in meeting their companies' messaging needs. Since then, the ability of people to send and receive electronic messages not only within a company but to people with access to the Internet, other networks, and commercial information services has grown dramatically.

For many people, electronic mail has already surpassed the telephone as their primary form of non-face-to-face interpersonal communication. For years Bill Gates, chairman of the board of Microsoft Corp., routinely received and responded to hundreds of e-mail messages a day. That number climbed into the thousands after his e-mail address was published in the pages of a major business magazine.

Electronic mail is the most used feature of the Internet. Using electronic mail, reporters can identify potential sources for stories, gather information from those sources, and check and recheck the accuracy of information they have collected. Like the telephone, electronic mail expands the reach of reporters, enabling you to obtain quotable information from around the world efficiently and at low cost. Moreover, e-mail makes collaborative work much easier. Reporters working in different cities or even different countries can work as closely together as if they were in the same newsroom. The potential of collaborative reporting made possible by e-mail has not yet started to be explored.

But because it is such a useful tool, using e-mail raises many difficult questions that reporters must resolve. Like the telegraph, the telephone, high-speed printing presses, broadcasting and satellites, e-mail will change the routines of journalists. Using e-mail in journalism is basically uncharted territory and by definition, uncharted territory has unknown hazards.

This chapter will:

- explore the basics of e-mail including how to get started with e-mail, interpreting e-mail addresses, and understanding the e-mail network.
- suggest several ways to locate e-mail addresses for people.
- describe how e-mail can be used to create an online electronic discussion group.
- look at the rules of etiquette associated with e-mail.
- reflect on the tactical and ethical issues the use of e-mail raises for journalists.

E-mail basics

Conceptually, sending e-mail is not very different from sending regular mail, affectionately called "snail mail" by e-mail users. You create a message. Then you address the message to a specific recipient and deposit it into a transmission system that carries the message to its destination. Once it arrives, presumably the message is read and discarded or filed. The primary difference is that with e-mail, the message is sent from a computer and received by a computer.

Of course, e-mail has many advantages over snail mail. The first is speed. A correspondent in St. Petersburg, Russia, reported receiving replies to e-mail sent to the Washington D.C. area in less than four hours. Moreover, you don't have to wait for the mail to be picked up or delivered. You can send e-mail at any time of day.

The second advantage is convenience. Most of the software programs for e-mail allow users to reply automatically to messages with just a few key strokes. Moreover, you don't need to find an envelope or stamps. Furthermore, many programs allow you to copy the section of the e-mail correspondence to which you wish to respond. Thus, when you respond, you can easily include the exact text to which you are responding. The information you receive via e-mail can easily be forwarded to a third party, with a note or response from you. This feature can be particularly useful when you want sources to react to each others' comments. Finally, e-mail messages can easily be stored in appropriate files on your computer to be retrieved at convenient times.

The third advantage of e-mail is informality. Unlike formal business letters, e-mail often is closer in tone to conversation. Messages can be very short and to the point. People do not yet expect a great deal of superfluous salutations and other extraneous materials in e-mail messages. Formality often takes time. With e-mail, in many cases the information counts the most. Misspelled words, grammatical errors, the use of incomplete sentences and other grave transgressions of written correspondence are often excused by e-mail users who understand that people may be working with unfamiliar word processors.

The fourth advantage of e-mail is novelty. Because it is new, for some, e-mail still has a degree of urgency about it. Once people begin to use e-mail, they often check it frequently and, because it is easy, they often respond to messages immediately. Moreover, people who travel a lot often access their e-mail messages while they are on the road. And many people do not yet have subordinates screening their e-mail messages for them, although some have computer programs to perform that task, so your message has a good chance to get to the recipient no matter how busy that person may be.

Complexities of e-mail

But e-mail can be complicated. Perhaps most problematic, e-mail requires you to use several different pieces of software. If, like many people, you access the Internet and electronic mail by first logging onto a host such as a VAX or a Unix workstation, to write short messages you may find yourself working with a text editor with which you are unfamiliar. Longer messages created with a word processor may have to be converted to a suitable format such as ASCII and then transferred from your personal computer to the computer through which you have e-mail access.

After you have composed your message, different software may be used to send it or to read and manage your incoming messages. In some cases, you may use the communication software on your personal computer. But in other cases you may find yourself using network software or mail utility software that operates on a completely different computer. In many situations, you will not enjoy the easy user interface you find on personal computers running Windows or on Macintosh computers.

The second complexity with electronic mail is addressing. Although the Internet has a standard format for addresses, you can frequently send e-mail to people who are not on the Internet and different mail programs have different ways to signal where the mail should be sent. For example, in the VAX/VMS mail utility, mail sent to people on the Internet must be prefaced with IN% and the address must be enclosed in quotation marks. The entire address for mail sent using the VAX/VMS mailer to somebody on the Internet might look like IN%"king@loyola.edu".

On CompuServe, however, to send mail to somebody on the Internet, the address has to be prefaced with >internet:. And CompuServe does not require the use of double quotation marks. Thus, the entire address sent via CompuServe to somebody on the Internet might look like >internet:king@loyola.edu.

The third complication associated with e-mail is privacy and security. Although e-mail has the illusion of being at least as private as a telephone call, it is not. E-mail messages can be reviewed by the administrators of the computer systems through which the messages are sent. For example, the commercial information service Prodigy has rules about the content allowed for certain e-mail messages and claims the right to enforce those standards. The FBI has been known to monitor e-mail in its efforts to track criminals. Perhaps most worrisome, many companies monitor their employees' e-mail. The legality and ethics of monitoring e-mail has not been settled, and there are strong cases to be made on both sides of the issue.

Furthermore, if messages are stored on disk, e-mail can be retrieved by system administrators as well. The most dramatic recent example came when investigators probed the activities of Oliver North in connection with the Iran-Contra arms-for-hostages arrangements in defiance of Congress in the mid-1980s. Investigators were able to retrieve e-mail messages North thought he had deleted from the hard disk of his office computer.

Privacy and security at the destination of a message are also an issue. As with faxes, when you send e-mail, you do not know exactly who receives the message and when. In most cases, incoming messages will be stored on a centralized computer. Frequently, system administrators or other managers can access and review files in individual accounts on those computers. More-over, it is not uncommon for executives to have subordinates review their e-mail. For example, a reporter once e-mailed his picture along with a confir-mation of a time to interview a person. When he walked into the office, ev-erybody knew who he was. A secretary had read the message and seen the picture first. Finally, from time to time, people will share computer accounts so more than one person could have access to any message you send elec-tronically.

The final complexity associated with e-mail is the network itself. E-mail is not restricted to the Internet. In fact, the e-mail network currently represents the coming together of both top-down and bottom-up development. In the late 1980s, large telecommunications companies like AT&T, MCI and Western Union established their own electronic mail networks. To use them, people had to subscribe and then pay fees according to the number of messages they sent or according to some other criteria. Along the same lines, companies like CompuServe, America Online and GEnie provided electronic mail services to their subscribers. And, of course, e-mail was a feature of the Internet. Prior to the late 1980s, different systems could not pass messages back and forth.

At the same time, companies were developing internal electronic message systems. For example, IBM has had some form of electronic mail internally for more than 30 years. As local area networks became more common in companies, the use of internal e-mail grew as well.

Over the past several of years, different e-mail networks have been patched together. But those patches are not seamless and that can present difficulties for people who wish to use e-mail.

Creating and sending an e-mail message

Creating and sending short electronic e-mail messages is very easy regardless of the computer system you are using. The steps generally will be the same regardless of the system you use, however, the specific commands needed to complete each step will vary from system to system. Currently, even VMS and Unix have very friendly mail programs and there are several programs for the Macintosh and Windows. You will have to consult with whomever you depend on for e-mail access to learn the exact set of commands to complete the following steps.

To create and send a short mail message, first you access the mail program you are using. For example, when you log onto a VMS system, the first thing you see is a "$" which is called the system prompt. At the system prompt, you type in the command "mail." This changes the system prompt to what is called the mail prompt, which looks like Mail>.

Once you are into your mail program, you will tell the system that you want to send a message. In VMS Mail, which is an older program, you type in the command "send." In other mail programs you can use your mouse to click on the send command.

The computer responds with "To:" and you enter the address of the person to whom you wish to send mail. After you enter the address, which will be discussed later in this chapter, the computer responds with "Subject:" After you enter the subject, you begin composing your message. When you compose a message, you will be using a text editor. The text editor probably will not work exactly like your word processor so, depending on how user-friendly it is, you may want to obtain a list of commands from your computer resource person. Often, text editing in the mail program is awkward. It may be hard to move between lines to correct mistakes. In those cases, you may want to compose longer messages using your regular word processor and then upload that message to send it.

When you finish composing your note, you will exit. Exiting sends the message to its intended destination.

Sending relatively short e-mail messages is easy, even if you must use unfriendly software such as the basic Unix and the VMS mail utilities. New programs such as Pine for Unix and VMS and Eudora for Macintosh and Windows computers make it even more efficient. The mail utilities on commercial services such as CompuServe are also straightforward.

In addition to sending messages, in many cases you will want to keep a record of the message you sent. One of the advantages e-mail has over the telephone interview is that you have a written record of what the source said. In some situations it is nice to have a copy of what you said as well.

Most mail programs allow you to send copies of a message to other destinations. If you are working with a Unix mailer, for example, you will see a Cc: after you have finished writing your message. Simply type in your own address to keep a copy of the message. The "Cc" or carbon copy function also allows you to send the same set of questions to many different people.

When it arrives at its destination, a message will have a header in the following format: TO: Recipient's e-mail address FROM: Sender's e-mail address SUBJECT: Subject of the message. There are ways to include your personal name in the FROM line, if you choose. Nevertheless, you should always include your e-mail address as well, either in the FROM line or in the body of the message to ensure that the recipient knows how to respond to you via e-mail as well.

Many people like to create what is called a signature file. A signature file, which usually will include your name; contact information such as address, telephone and fax numbers, and e-mail address, as well as personalizing information like a saying or a graphic; is automatically appended to the end of every message you send. In programs such as Pine, signature files are extremely easy to create. In programs such as VMS mail, they may require three or four lines of programming. A signature file still can be created but you may have to consult with a veteran user.

Receiving and responding to e-mail

When you begin to send e-mail messages, you should anticipate receiving responses as well. Unlike a blinking answering machine, you generally will not know if you have mail unless you access the computer through which your e-mail is routed and check for mail. For example, if you use CompuServe for e-mail, you have to log onto CompuServe to check your electronic mail box. If you have an account on a central computer, you will have to check there.

Once you start using e-mail, you must make a commitment to check your mail box regularly. If not, not only are you sure to miss messages, but you give up two of the main advantages of e-mail, the timeliness of the delivery of information and the ability to immediately respond.

A sound strategy is to incorporate checking your electronic mail box into your daily routine. For example, you may want to check your e-mail first thing in the morning, at some point in midday, and perhaps in the evening. Another strategy is to check your mail box whenever you check your telephone messages.

A third approach is to make sure you begin doing other tasks on the same computer that handles your e-mail. For example, some people prefer a commercial information service for e-mail because they access other information such as the AP news wire from the service as well. Others subscribe to an online discussion group, which will be described later in this chapter, to give themselves the incentive to log onto the computer every day. If you belong to an online discussion group, the chances are you will receive mail every day. The point is to check your e-mail regularly. If you check your mail box regularly, reading, responding to and managing your e-mail files is easy.

Once you log onto the computer that handles your e-mail, you will receive a notice if you have any mail. If you do have messages, enter your mail utility program and you will receive a list of messages. In some systems you may have to use a directory command to view the list. You will see who sent you the message and the subject of the message. (See Figure 5-1)

You can then read the full text of a specific message by entering its number. Once you have read the message, you can delete it, file it electronically, respond to it, or forward it to another person at another address. The commands to perform each of those tasks vary from mail utility to mail utility, but virtually all mail utility programs include each of those functions.

Fig. 5-1: A mail directory in VMS Mail, retrieved by giving the "dir" command after entering the VMS Mail utility.

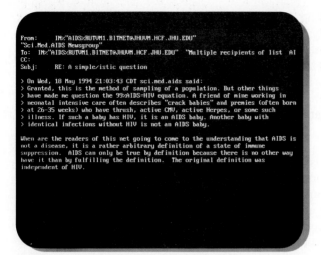

Fig. 5-2: An e-mail message showing a response to quoted text. The quoted material is set off by > signs at the beginning of each quoted line in a process some mail programs call annotating.

Managing your mail files

Responding to mail, forwarding it, or deleting messages are generally simple, one-command operations. Each is an important function for journalists. Ease of response means that journalists can more efficiently check their facts. Furthermore, many programs allow you to quote a message you received when you respond to it, allowing you to ask for further clarification if needed. See Figure 5-2 for an example. Forwarding messages helps facilitate collaborative work. You must regularly delete messages so you don't clutter your hard disk. You can delete messages one at a time or in batches.

The key feature for journalists working with electronic mail, however, is to be able to save the information they receive in a format that will be convenient to use when they are ready to write a story. This can be a complicated process for two reasons. First, if you access electronic mail by first connecting to a central server, transferring mail to your personal computer may take several steps.

Second, and perhaps more significant, information stored electronically may not be the most convenient when you are ready to write your story. In many cases, the information you receive via e-mail will mainly supplement information you have gathered through face-to-face or telephone interviews, and you will want to keep that information together. For longer documents, you may want to review the documents in their entirety first and highlight the spots that are relevant to your story.

Some people feel comfortable opening multiple documents in their word processors and then switching back and forth as they write stories. Others, however, do not. In either case, you will want to put the information you receive via e-mail – and through other online tools – into the format that is most useful to you and store it in a way that is most accessible when you begin to write an article.

Using mail folders

After you have initially read an e-mail message, you can file it in a specific folder within the mail utility. Folders are very useful if you are working on a number of different projects with different deadlines simultaneously and you have sent many messages to different people. Let's say, for example, you are an education reporter and you are collaborating with a colleague on an investigative series about the effectiveness of preschool programs around the state while you continue to file daily stories. You may send your colleague e-mail asking for specific documents she has. At the same time, you are covering a court case about sex discrimination in higher education and you send an e-mail message to a local professor asking for a reaction.

The first story will take several weeks to complete and you plan to review the document from your colleague in a few days. You are on deadline with the second. When you access your mail, you can file the document from your colleague in the folder "Preschool" and deal with the second one immediately.

The folders exist as subdirectories of the mail directory. You have several different options for transferring the files to the personal computer on which you are actually working. The way to transfer files from a central computer to your personal computer varies greatly from location to location. One method is to rename the mail message to move it to another directory on the central computer and then use specific transfer routines such as a program called Kermit. Although it can be complicated, if you have received some lengthy messages, dozens of pages long, this may be the best method to transfer files. To learn the exact sequence of steps for your computer setup, however, you will have to work with your local computer support personnel.

Other options

For shorter messages, you have three very effective alternatives. The first is to use "print screen" on your personal computer to make a hard copy of the text on your screen. Let's say you have interviewed a management consultant about his advice to companies trying to maintain the morale of their workers while they are reducing their work force. At one point your notes are unclear so you send an e-mail message to the consultant asking for clarification. He sends you a message back which is only five lines long.

While the message is on screen, you hit the "print screen" key on your personal computer and make a hard copy, which you can then attach directly to your other notes from the interview. Depending on exactly what is on the screen when you print it, you may wish to date and notate the hard copy as well, in case any question arises concerning when you received the additional information.

Another alternative is to automatically print what appears on the screen. Many communications software programs have a feature that turns on a local printer. In ProComm Plus, for example, the command is Alt-L. You can also print messages directly from VMS mail or Unix. In VMS, you enter the command "print/queue name". The queue name is the location of the printer on the network you wish to use.

Both of the alternatives above print the message on paper. If you wish to save the message in an electronic format on a floppy disk or the hard disk of your personal computer, one effective method is to use the "log" or "capture" feature of your telecommunications program. Session log and screen capture utilities were described in Chapter 3. The log feature allows you to capture an electronic record of everything that appears on your screen directly to a file on your personal computer. Consequently, as you read a message, you can save it directly on your personal computer, bypassing the potentially complicated procedures of transferring files from a central computer to your personal computer.

Using the "log" feature has its disadvantages, however. First, to capture a file, you must scroll through it entirely. If the message is long or you are under pressure, that could be too time consuming. Moreover, the file may be littered with extraneous information. Generally, as you read your mail, for example, a message at the bottom of the screen will tell you to hit the Return key for more information. That message will be included with every screen full of information captured by using the "log" feature.

Nonetheless, the "log" feature is very simple to use. In the telecommunications program ProComm Plus, for example, you hit Alt-F1 to open a log file. In MacKermit for the Macintosh, "log on" is under the File commands. In most cases, you can turn the log feature on and off and you can effectively "pause" the log feature, allowing you to pick and choose the information you wish to save. In Chapter 3 you were asked to practice using these utilities. They will continue to be useful as you venture onto the Internet.

Electronic mail has become so popular because it is relatively easy and clearly very useful. Often it is more useful than the telephone. Although different mail programs and mail utilities have different features, if you can send, receive, save and retrieve messages, you will find that e-mail can help you enormously in gathering and checking information.

The e-mail network and addresses

Once you have created a message, you will want to send it to the correct destination. Understanding the components of an e-mail address can also tell a journalist something about the person to whom they are sending mail as well as provide strategies if mail is returned.

It is important to keep in mind that the electronic mail network reaches far beyond the Internet. As mentioned early, throughout the 1980s, commercial providers such as MCI and CompuServe, and companies such as General Electric and Apple Computer Corp., built their own electronic mail networks. At the same time, networks such as ARPAnet, which has now evolved into the Internet, Fidonet, Bitnet and UUCP also developed electronic mail capabilities. As could be expected, every network had its own peculiar way to handle mail.

As in the early days of the telephone network, having several different, non-compatible systems was not efficient. People had to subscribe to several different commercial services and maintain accounts on many different networks. Even then, they could not be assured that the person to whom they wished to send electronic mail would have an appropriate address. Moreover, people found they tediously had to check several different mail boxes each day.

In the early 1990s, the different electronic mail networks began to be linked through what are called applications gateways. That meant that if you had an account on CompuServe, for example, you could send mail to somebody who had an account on let's say MCI Mail. Gateways are points of connection between electronic mail networks. At those gateways, mail from one network is reformatted so it can be understood by another network. Consequently, when mail is going to be sent through a gateway, the gateway has to have enough information to know how to reformat the message. That information is contained in the address. That is one reason why a correct address is so important.

As the Internet emerged as the broadest electronic mail network, its addressing scheme, which is called "domain name addressing," or DNA for short, emerged as the predominant addressing scheme. The domain name addressing scheme has two parts, which are divided by the @ sign. The information that follows the @ sign is the domain, and ultimately designates the computer on which the recipient's e-mail account is located. The information before the @ sign is the name of the recipient's account. A standard form of an address is "president@whitehouse.gov". Whitehouse.gov is the name of the computer on which the recipient's account is located. President is the name of the recipient's account.

The domain, or the information following the @ sign, follows a standard format developed in conjunction with the Internet and can have several different elements. Each element is divided by a period. Working from the end of the address backwards toward the @ sign, the last piece of information is the country in which the computer is located. For example, "ca" signifies Canada and "fr" is France. The United States uses "us" but this information is often omitted for computers located in the United States.

The next element of the domain is what is called the top level domain. For the sake of Internet addressing, computers have been categorized

Top Level U.S. Internet Domains

.edu = Educational
.gov = Government
.com = Commercial
.org = Nonprofit organizations
.mil = U.S. Military
.net = Network providers
.int   = International organizations.

Fig. 5-3: Internet addressing scheme tells what kind of organization is associated with an Internet address. In nations outside the United States, a two character suffix is added. For example .uk = United Kingdom; .au = Australia; .be = belgium; .ca = Canada; .de = Germany.

according to the kind of organization in which they are located. For example, "edu" is used for educational and some research institutions. Computers in commercial companies are designated by "com." By looking at the top level domain designation, a reporter can know if a source is associated, at least for the purpose of e-mail, with an educational or research institution, the government, the military, a commercial enterprise, etc. See Figure 5-3 for a list of top level domains.

Each domain, in turn, is subdivided by institution. Computers at Microsoft, for example, include the name "microsoft" before the "com." Computers at Stanford include "stanford" before the "edu." Many companies and institutions, in turn, have specific names for their different computers. New York University, for example, has a computer called "acfcluster." Consequently, the domain name for some people at New York University is "@acfcluster.nyu.edu." To facilitate the transfer of electronic mail, other electronic mail systems and networks have been designated as domains themselves. For example, the domain format for CompuServe is CompuServe.com. The domain format for America Online is aol.com. (See Figure 5-4)

Once you send electronic mail, it is the job of the network to get it to the computer designated in the domain information. Once it arrives at that computer, however, that computer itself must route the message to the proper recipient. That information is contained before the @ and is determined by the institution that is responsible for the domain computer. Some institutions use the first name and last name of the user joined by a "_". Others use the first initial of the first name immediately followed by the last name. Many of the commercial services use a person's ID number.

Even though the commercial services listed above use the standard domain name addressing structure to receive mail, to send mail from the service to other Internet addresses, these services may require you to add information. Moreover, sometimes if you want to send mail between commercial services – from CompuServe to MCI Mail, for example – the domain name

Fig. 5-4: E-mail is sent to commercial services subscribers by appending the following "@host. domain" designations to the subscriber's user name.

Commercial Server Domain Names	
@aol.com	America Online
@applelink.apple.com	AppleLink
@attmail.com	AT&T Mail
@compuserve.com	CompuServe
@genie.geis.com	GEnie
@mcimail.com	MCIMail
@geis.plink.com	PressLink
@prodigy.com	Prodigy
@well.sf.ca.us	WELL
@world.std.com	World

addressing format will not work. Some services have their own specialized gateways.

Although widely used, the domain name addressing system and the gateways between electronic mail systems is not yet completely consistent. Consequently, when you send electronic mail, you can never be sure exactly how long it will take to arrive. While many messages will be delivered to their destinations within a matter of seconds, others can take a day or more. Furthermore, if the network has problems delivering the message, it may try for some time before returning the message to the sender.

From time to time you will have messages returned to you. Either you will have incorrectly addressed the message or a gateway will not have functioned as you anticipated. When mail is returned, you will also receive a message from what is called the postmaster, which is the software handling your message at different points in the network. If you closely read the message, you should be able to determine the source of your problem — usually a mistake you made in the address. If you have made a mistake in the domain, the section of the address which follows the @ sign, the message from the postmaster will read "host unknown." If you made a mistake in the part of the address preceding the @ sign, the message will read "user unknown." In that case, you know that you have a valid domain name.

Locating people

To communicate electronically with people, of course, you will need to know their electronic mail address. When the Internet first started to be developed, nobody anticipated that it would spread as broadly as it has. Consequently, no allowances were made to develop directories that could list millions of users with Internet access, much less the additional millions of users of commercial services and other networks who can now send electronic mail back and forth through gateways.

For several reasons, the best way to determine somebody's e-mail address is to ask that person directly. First, although some directories of e-mail addresses have been compiled, they are far from comprehensive and in many cases it will be unlikely that you will find the address for which you are looking. Second, just because people have e-mail addresses does not mean they actually use e-mail regularly. If you access an address from a directory and send an e-mail message, you have no idea whether the intended recipient actually checks the mail box. Third, some people maintain more than one e-mail address for different purposes. Those people generally check one address more than another. Fourth, addresses change. Organizations can rework their computer infrastructures, taking machines off line, or a person may have changed jobs and is no longer at that location. Finally, it can take a long time to query different directories to find the name. Telephoning the person, or the person's secretary, subordinate, or co-worker is often the most efficient way to learn an e-mail address.

Along the same lines, you will want to save people's e-mail addresses once you begin to communicate with them electronically. The easiest method is to add e-mail addresses to your standard address/telephone directory entries. Many mail programs support their own electronic directories as well. Often, those directories allow you to associate the e-mail address with the person's name. Once you have made the appropriate entry into the directory, to send mail, you use the person's name at the TO: prompt.

Nevertheless, from time to time, you may want to try to locate a person's e-mail address through a directory. In this section, five different vehicles for locating addresses online will be discussed.

One of the most interesting methods is a searching system called Knowbot Information Service or KIS. By submitting a single query to KIS, a user can search a set of remote electronic mail "white pages" directory services and see the results of the search in a uniform format. You can access KIS in several different ways including Telnet (Chapter 6) and electronic mail.

Using electronic mail, you send Knowbot an e-mail message asking for the name of a particular person, and Knowbot will search several different directories and then send the results back to you via e-mail. You can send e-mail either to kis@cnri.reston.va.us or netaddress@sol.bucknell.edu. You begin your message with the word "query" followed by the name of the person for whom you are looking.

For example, if you were looking for the e-mail address of Randy Reddick, the body of the message you send to KIS@cnri.reston.va.us would read: query Randy Reddick. The KIS server is sophisticated and the name can be entered in several different ways as shown: Reddick – a single last name; Randy Reddick – first name, last name; Reddick, Randy – last name, first name; Reddick, R. – last name, first initial. KIS will then look through several databases and mail you the results of the search.

Figure 5-5 illustrates both the strengths and weakness of Knowbot. Within minutes it searched through six white pages directories. Unfortunately, Randy

Fig 5-5: Results of a Knowbot search are returned to the sender as a mail message.

Reddick was not listed in any of the directories searched, even though he has used e-mail for several years. If the person is found using KIS, in addition to the e-mail address, you may receive the person's regular address and telephone number as well as the last time the record was updated. KIS has several advanced features to aid the search process. You can receive a set of instructions by sending e-mail to the KIS address with the word "man" as the body of the message. For shorter versions of the instructions, send e-mail with either "help" or "?" as the body of the message.

Another relatively new directory system is called Netfind. Like Knowbot, Netfind will automatically search several different white pages directories looking for a specific name. To use Netfind you Telnet to bruno.cs.colorado.edu. Telnet is described in Chapter 6.

After you connect to a Netfind server using Telnet, you log in as "netfind." The first item you will see is a list of additional Netfind servers. The Netfind server bruno.cs.colorado.edu also has a comprehensive list of instructions and additional information about the service. To initiate a search, you enter a person's name and their domain. Netfind will then provide possibilities and ask for additional information until the e-mail address for whom you are looking has been identified.

For example, let's say you are looking for the e-mail address of Elliot King at Loyola College. You would enter "King Loyola". Netfind would then lead through a series of steps to narrow the results of your search until you could identify the most likely e-mail address for the person.

There are many limitations to this approach. First, you still must have an idea of the person's domain and the format of the personal information that comes before the @ sign in the e-mail address for a search to have a chance of being successful. Also, many institutions that have extensive computer networks have subdivided their domains to include designations for several different host computers. Consequently, you may have to know the name of the exact computer on which the person you wish to locate has their account to find their address. Nevertheless, Netfind is a useful approach to trying to locate people on the Internet and represents an important step in the development of white pages directories.

Other locating tools

Another tool for finding people on the Internet is Gopher phone books. Gopher is described in detail in Chapter 7. "Phone books" are provided as options on the menus of many general interest Gophers. Their listings, however, are generally confined to faculty and staff at colleges and universities where Gopher servers exist. Their use presumes you know which institution the person you seek calls "home." You work your way down through a series of menus starting with the continent, and on down to the institution. About 300 colleges and universities are listed for North America. When you get to the university in question, you are prompted for your search terms.

Among the directory tools that Knowbot and Netfind use to try to locate appropriate names are Whois and Finger. With the appropriate client software, you can run those tools yourself. Whois servers can also be accessed via e-mail. Whois was first developed to list people who are responsible for running the Internet and who were conducting network research. There are now dozens of Whois servers on the Internet. Unfortunately, these servers are not yet linked, so you must identify the server you want to search. If your computer is running Whois client software and you know the address of a Whois server, you enter whois -h (name of server) (name for which you are looking) You can get a list of Whois servers via FTP (Chapter 8) from sipb.mit.edu. from /pub/whois/whois-servers.list.

You can also access Whois servers via e-mail. One address is service@nic.ddn.mil, which has the names of thousands of people who are responsible for the working of the Internet or who are active in network research. The body of the message should read "whois (name)"

Another, more useful Whois server, which can be accessed via e-mail, lists the participants in different listserv discussion groups. Listserv discussion groups will be explained in the next section of this chapter. To identify the address of somebody who is participating in a listserv discussion group, you can send a message to whois@ukcc.uky.edu. In the body of the message you enter "find (name)." For more information about using Whois for people participating in listserv discussion groups, send an e-mail message to the same address listed above with the word "help" in the body of the message.

Similarly, you can identify the e-mail addresses of people who participate in Usenet news group discussions, which will be described in Chapter 9, by sending e-mail to mail-server@pitmanager.mit.edu. The body of the message should read "send usenet-addresses/(name)".

Finger is a program that allows you to learn more information about people if you know the domain name of the computer on which they have their account. For Finger to work, however, you must have a Finger client on your computer, and the target computer must have a Finger server running. For example, let's say you are doing a story on the media tactics President Clinton used in connection with his health care program. You may wish to contact Samuel Kernell, a professor of political science at the University of California, San Diego, who is an expert in the media tactics used by politicians. Using Finger, you can determine his e-mail address. At the system prompt, you would enter "Finger kernell@ucsd.edu". In response, you would get a listing of his exact e-mail address, his telephone number and the department with which he is associated.

Finger's usefulness, however, is limited. It can only be used for people for whom you know the name of the computer on which their address is located. And you need those computers to be running a Finger server program. To make matters more difficult, for security reasons, many sites have stopped operating Finger server programs.

In the final analysis, the Internet tools available for locating people's e-mail addresses are still rudimentary. The most direct method is to contact the person with whom you want to communicate and ask for the appropriate address.

Using e-mail for reporting

Not only is the direct method of obtaining an e-mail address usually going to be more efficient than rummaging through different directory services, in most cases it will lead to better journalism. Effective interviewing — and sending individuals e-mail can be considered a form of interviewing — relies to a large degree on the building of rapport between the reporter and the source of information. If you blindly send e-mail to people you don't know well enough to contact through another method first, you will have no way to evaluate the information they send you, if they respond at all. Indeed, you cannot be sure if the person to whom you thought you were sending the message actually responded rather than a subordinate or assistant.

Consequently, sending e-mail to somebody you don't know is a tactic you should use sparingly. It can, however, be one method you can use to open doors for you. For example, you can send an e-mail message to a potential source describing your project and asking if the person would be willing to talk to you or otherwise share information. In that message, ask how you should get in touch with the source in the future – via e-mail, voice, face to face or regular mail.

Once you have established a relationship with a source, however, you will find that person-to-person e-mail can be an invaluable tool. After a long telephone interview or face-to-face session, you may find that your notes are unclear in certain crucial places. E-mail is an effective tool to ask your source to clarify information.

In fact, many journalists covering specialized and technical beats now rely on e-mail to make sure their stories are accurate. For example, a science writer with a Ph.D. in physics found himself covering environmental issues. Although he was an expert in physics, he wasn't familiar with the technology and science involved in cleanup activities. As he prepared articles, if he had any doubts at all about the way he presented the information, he would use e-mail to check back with his sources, ensuring that he quoted them accurately and that the way he told the story was not misleading.

E-mail makes it very easy for reporters to check quotes with their sources as well. Allowing sources to check quotes is controversial among professional reporters. Some are loathe to give their sources the chance to review and perhaps enhance or otherwise alter their quotes. Whether you should allow a source to see what you are going to include from an interview in an article depends on the situation. In political or enterprise reporting, sources will often want to change their remarks to make themselves look better or for some other self-serving reason. In those cases, you should resist their attempts to review the information they gave you.

On the other hand, you want your story to be as accurate as possible. If you have any questions about the accuracy of your information, you will want to have the source take another look. The key question, then, is not whether or not the source reviews the information, but what steps does the reporter take to craft an accurate and honest story with the least amount of "spin."

Frankly, in many situations, particularly in business and entertainment reporting, people will not agree to be interviewed unless the reporter submits a list of questions in advance. Once again, e-mail is a very effective method to do that.

Finally, in some cases, e-mail can serve as a substitute for either a telephone or a face-to-face interview. You send the questions and the source responds. Because messages often arrive at their destinations so quickly, an e-mail correspondence can come to resemble any other type of conversation.

If you include information you received via e-mail sent directly to you in your article, do you have to indicate how you received the information? Do you have to include a phrase such as "In an e-mail message. . ." Probably not. After all, people are quoted from press releases every day and reporters seldom add "In a press release. . ."

You do have to be sure, however, that sources with whom you are in contact via e-mail know that you are writing an article and what they say is on the record. The same complexities that exist in the reporter-source relationship in other kinds of interviewing are operative in e-mail as well.

Discussion lists and listservs

In addition to person-to-person e-mail – that is e-mail which is sent to the e-mail address of one individual from the e-mail address of another individual – bulletin boards, commercial information services and the Internet have tools that allow e-mail from individuals to be read by many people. Different forms of one-to-many communication will be discussed in more depth in Chapter 9. However, discussion groups and mailing lists have emerged as potentially significant tools for journalists. Discussion groups and mailing lists use e-mail to generate one-to-many communications. If you have e-mail access to the Internet, you can participate in these groups.

Consider this. A reporter for a magazine covering journalism wanted to do a story about stress among copy editors. He reasoned that as newspapers worked to cut costs, the workload of copy editors would increase. And, of course, even in the best of times copy editors work under extreme deadline pressure.

The challenge was finding sources. The reporter did not want to rely just on the copy editors he knew. Furthermore, many newspapers do not allow their employees to talk to reporters from other publications. And many copy editors were probably under too much pressure to talk anyway. How could he locate sources for his story?

Part of the answer was two discussion groups for journalists. The reporter posted a message to the groups describing his project. He also asked copy editors and others who wished to talk to him to send him e-mail with the best way to get in touch with them. Within a couple of days, the reporter's electronic mail box was stuffed with leads to people who were eager to share their experiences.

Discussion groups can be thought of as electronic salons in which people with similar interests gather to talk about issues of concern. It works like this. Individuals send e-mail to a specific address for the particular discussion list. That mail is then automatically forwarded to everybody who subscribes to that list. Everybody who subscribes to the list gets to read every message.

There are two parts to discussion groups. The first is the list service software, which is a specialized mailing program to manage these kinds of lists administratively. The second is the discussion list itself.

Originally, the list service software resided on computers that were actually part of the Bitnet network. Today, list service software comes in several forms and is not limited to Bitnet sites. Bitnet addresses can be easily converted into the standard Internet domain name addressing format. The list service software at a particular location often manages many different discussion lists.

The most important primary function of the list service software is to allow a person to subscribe or terminate a subscription to a particular list. To subscribe, you would send a message to "listserv@(the location of the list)." In the body of the message, you would enter "subscribe (list name) (your name)." To terminate a subscription, you would send a message to "listserv@(location of the list)" and in the body of the message type "unsubscribe (name of the list)." Instead of the command "unsubscribe" you can also use the command "signoff."

Some mailing list software use variations on this theme. Instead of sending the subscribe message to "listserv@(Location)" you send it to "(name of list)-request@(location). The list of the Society of Professional Journalists, which will be described below, works in that fashion. There also is a growing number of sites where you address your correspondence to "majordomo@(Location)" rather than a listserv.

Once you have subscribed to a listserv discussion list, you will begin to receive the e-mail messages that are being sent to the list. With some active lists, you may receive 10 to 50 messages a day. Consequently, you should check your mail box regularly. If you subscribe to four or five lists, you receive more than 100 e-mail messages a day.

To post a message to a discussion group, you send e-mail to (name of the list)@(location of the list) and then follow the normal procedures for sending e-mail. To respond to a posted message, with most lists you can simply use the reply function of your mail program while you are reading the message. Hundreds of different listserv-based discussion lists operate with people communicating about topics ranging from the use of computers in Eastern Europe to bird watching to jazz.

Lists for journalists

There are several lists of specific to journalists. Three of the most important are CARR-L, Journet and SPJ-Online. SPJ-Online is a list organized by the Society of Professional Journalists. In all three, journalists, journalism educators and students discuss issues of common interest and share leads where to locate online information.

To subscribe to CARR-L, you would send an e-mail message to listserv@ulkyvm.louisville.edu. In the body of the message type "subscribe CARR-L (your name)." To subscribe to JOURNET, send e-mail to "listserv@qucdn.queensu.ca" with the message "subscribe Journet (your name)." For SPJ-Online, send the subscribe message to "SPJ-request@netcom.com". After you send the message to the listserv, you will receive in return a message welcoming you to the list, describing the list's purpose, and giving basic commands for controlling your receipt of mail from the list. Save these messages in a place where you can easily find them. Mail lists have frequent postings from people who are asking for help getting off a list or giving other commands described in the welcome message.

To post a message to CARR-L, the address you would use is CARR-L@ulkyvm.louisville.edu. The address for posting a message on Journet is Journet@qucdn.queensu.ca. To post a message to SPJ-Online, you send mail to SPJ-online@netcom.com.

Reading and participating in discussion lists can be extremely useful. It puts reporters in contact with people who generally know a lot about a specific topic. The reporter can then follow up with those people, or ask where more information can be found or who else would be good sources to interview. Messages on these lists routinely provide tips on how and where to find valuable information on the network. CARR-L is very strong here. If for no other reason, we recommend you subscribe to CARR-L as soon as you can.

In other words, discussion lists can provide reporters with a wealth of leads to more information. You can receive a listing of listserv lists via anonymous FTP at lilac.berkeley.edu in the netinfo directory (ftp lilac.berkeley.edu login: anonymous cd netinfo). You will learn how to use FTP in Chapter 8. WAIS (Chapter 8), Gopher, and World Wide Web (Chapter 7) also provide access to listserv databases. Or you can send e-mail to listserv@mizzou1.missouri.edu. In the body of the message put "list global."

Keep in mind that these are long files listing hundreds of different discussion groups. Many, of course, will be of no interest. And if you subscribe to too many discussion lists, your e-mail box will be continually jammed. It will be hard for you to find information you need.

In addition, many of the addresses you receive in these databases will be in a bitnet format. You will have to convert them to an Internet format or access them via Bitnet. For a guide to frequently asked questions about listserv send e-mail to listserv@mizzou1.missouri.edu and in the body of the message put "get listfaq memo."

As you monitor discussion lists, from time to time participants will engage in an exchange that may relate directly to a story on which you are working. Should reporters directly quote from messages that have been posted on discussion lists?

This controversial question has been hotly debated and no clear rules have emerged. At one level, when people send messages to discussion lists, they know the message will be read by hundreds and perhaps thousands of people. Those people clearly have chosen to communicate publicly. On the other hand, they may not have realized that they are talking on the record to reporters, with the added factors that entails.

The copyrights associated with messages posted to discussion lists is another issue that has not been resolved. Should e-mail messages posted to discussion lists be considered like talk in a public forum or like published, written works in which authors have greater control over the dissemination of their words? If discussion list postings are copyrighted written works, what constitutes "fair use?" Legal issues will be further discussed in Chapter 11.

Ideally, you should use discussion groups as a place to obtain leads to information. You should then follow up with those leads through more interpersonal methods. The best journalism is frequently the result of one-to-one interaction between a source and a reporter. Learn from the material that is distributed; but if you want to use that material in a story, try to establish one-on-one contact to clarify and develop the information.

Discussion group archives

In general, when you subscribe to a discussion list, you will monitor or participate in an ongoing discussion. Often it is like walking into the middle of a conversation.

Not infrequently, the interaction taking place at any particular moment will not be of immediate interest or use. Months later, however, you may receive an assignment on a topic that was discussed earlier by a discussion group. Alternatively, after you receive a specific assignment, you may identify what you think is an appropriate discussion list and wish to know if the topic has, in fact, been discussed.

Fortunately, many discussion lists now keep archives of their past postings. To receive an index of archived files you send a message to the management address for the list (i.e. listserv@(location)). The body of the message should read index (list name). You can retrieve messages that look like they may be of interest by sending the message get (list name) (name or number of file).

You do not have to subscribe to a specific discussion group to review the archives of its messages. You can see which groups have archives at a specific location by sending the message "database list" to listserv@location. In other words, to see what archives are available at the location at which the CARR-L discussion list is manager, you would send the message "database list" to listserv@ulkyvm.louisville.edu.

Once you have the list of archives, they can be searched using key words by sending the message "search (keyword) in (listname)." You can then retrieve the message using the procedure outlined above.

Listserv software supports several other database features as well. For instructions about how to access advanced commands, send the message "info" to listserv@(location).

Netiquette and tips

The Internet and other electronic mail networks represent a new way in which people can interact. As with all human interaction, certain rules have been developed. Some are legal restrictions that are slowly being implemented and changed. Some commercial services, for example, have restrictions on content. The use of the Internet for commercial activities is also under review.

While it is important to know legal restrictions applicable to the networks you use, the rules that define what is considered polite behavior are also important. The rules of etiquette are generally flexible, but you will want to consider the following suggestions. First, check your e-mail regularly. Once you start communicating with people, they will want to communicate with you. Furthermore, if you use a central computer, you will want to delete old messages and download messages you wish to save to your personal computer in a timely fashion so you do not exceed your disk quota.

Never assume that e-mail is private. Messages you send may be forwarded to others, and security in some systems is not what it should be. Consequently, you would not want to say anything via e-mail that you would not face to face or that would make you feel uncomfortable if others heard secondhand. Moreover, your files may be accessible to somebody who has system privileges, so you will not want to store private information.

You want to make your e-mail messages as easy as possible for others to read and for them to respond to. Consequently, try to keep e-mail relatively short and to the point. Not only is it difficult to read long messages, the people to whom you send e-mail may not always be experts in operating their own mail utility programs. They may have problems negotiating back and forth through a long message.

You want to be as professional as possible. Don't forget to include your name, affiliation, e-mail address and other ways to get in touch with you at the bottom of the message. Forwarding a private message to a discussion group without that person's permission is considered very rude.

Discussion groups generally have their own set of rules. First, if you participate in the ongoing discussion, try to keep your responses to the point and relevant. Also, try to be constructive. Too often, discussion groups seem to bring out the Dr. Jekyll in many people's personalities. Being online is no excuse for being rude or crude.

If you request information from people in a discussion group, have them send their answers to your e-mail address rather than the list itself.

When you are going away for a period of time, you might unsubscribe from the listservs and mail lists. When you subscribe to a discussion group, you should save the confirmation message you will receive for future reference. If you subscribed by sending your subscribe message to a listserv (rather than majordomo or request), you have the option of using "set" commands to control your mail. For example, if you want to stop your mail while you are on vacation, you would send the command: set (list name) no mail. When you return, you would send the same message without the word "no."

In general, use common sense. Although you can mask yourself behind a cloak of anonymity, you should act as though you are face to face with others.

Other e-mail tasks

E-mail is the primary tool for interpersonal communication via the Internet and other electronic networks. That communication can either be person-to-person or one-to-many. It is as a very convenient and efficient form of interpersonal communication that e-mail is most useful to journalists.

In addition to interpersonal communication, however, e-mail can also be used to perform other tasks as well. These tasks may be less important to journalists, but useful if you get more involved in computing in general. For example, e-mail can be used to send binary, non-text, files. Sending binary files via e-mail, however, will require extra steps and knowledge of your mail utility and perhaps your operating system. Consequently, you will have to consult with your computer support personnel.

You can also sometimes use e-mail to request files from remote computers instead of using FTP. You can do this by sending mail to an FTP mail server. You can receive instructions by sending a message to ftpmail@decwrl.dec.com with the word "help" in the body of the message. You are going to have to tell the FTP mail utility if the file is binary or not and other information.

E-mail and journalism

It is no surprise that e-mail is the most widely used feature of the Internet. It is easy to use, efficient and convenient. Indeed, many journalists may find it worthwhile to subscribe to a commercial information service just to establish e-mail access. On the other hand, e-mail must be used judiciously by journalists. While some people complain that you cannot be sure of the identity of your source if you only communicate to them via e-mail, that is not really an issue. Many journalists find themselves calling people they have never met before on the telephone and interviewing them without wondering if the person has identified themselves correctly.

Although using e-mail widens the number of sources you can reach, reporters must still work to obtain information from the best sources for their stories. Just because it is easy to get information from somebody does not improve the quality of the information.

The question of the quality of the source is particularly true with discussion lists. Reporters cannot know the level of expertise of people making comments on the discussion list. Once, for example, a person posted a message on CARR-L looking for leads to archives of newspapers from West Virginia in the 1800s. One person opined that the researcher would have problems finding material because newspapers did not become widespread until the 1920s – or so the person thought he had recently learned in a journalism history class he had, self-admittedly, slept through. It is impossible to know how many other ill-informed opinions that person had offered in the past without revealing his true lack of expertise.

E-mail can also allow for much more interaction between reporters and their sources. But the increased interaction can be a liability as well as an asset. On the one hand, using e-mail, reporters can be sure their quotes are accurate and can have difficult material thoroughly checked by experts. On the other hand, the increased interaction can allow sources to doctor their quotes, increasing the amount of spin put on events. While taking advantage of the first, reporters have to guard against the second.

In the final analysis, however, e-mail is having and will have a tremendous impact on reporting. Few people can imagine reporting today without access to a telephone. E-mail is destined to play a similarly integral role in journalism.

Further reading

Two resources of particular interest for e-mail resources are:

Seth Godin. *E-mail Addresses of the Rich & Famous*, Reading, Mass.: Addison-Wesley, 1994.
Peter Rutten, Albert F. Bayers III, and Kelly Maloni. *Netguide*, Random House: New York, 1994.

Chapter **6**

Telnet: Remote connections

At 4:31 a.m. Monday, Jan. 17, 1994, ground in California's San Fernando Valley shook with a violence that produced the most costly natural disaster in U.S. history. A magnitude 6.8 earthquake jolted densely populated suburbs northwest of Los Angeles. Apartment buildings collapsed. Water mains and gas lines broke. Fires erupted throughout the valley, and sections of freeway buckled. Electrical power and telephone communications were interrupted. In all, 57 people died and 20,000 lost their homes in the Northridge earthquake.

The Northridge quake of '94 was a news story of major significance. But in the predawn hours that Monday, there was no way of knowing how serious the quake was. News people at the scene had difficulty sizing up the damage. Normal lines of communication were erratic. Public safety officials who weren't at the strike points of the quake were hard to find for quotes and information at 5 a.m. It was a holiday (Martin Luther King Day) for many, the climax of a three-day weekend. For the thousands of reporters nationwide who were not in Southern California and the millions of Americans in their audiences it was even more difficult to get information. The broadcast networks and wire services were painfully slow in sending out news.

There was no way of knowing how serious the quake was as the nation awakened that day – unless you had access to one of the Internet tools called Telnet. "Tel-net" allows us to log into (become a part of) computer networks at remote distances just as "tele-vision" allows us to "see" things happening a long way away.

In this chapter, you will learn how to:

- log into remote computer systems.
- read files on a remote computer system.

- navigate menus during a Telnet session.
- capture remote text files on your personal computer.
- use Hytelnet to find computer sites of interest.

Assumptions that this chapter makes are that the reader is reasonably comfortable with using a computer communications program, has logged on to dial-up bulletin board systems (BBSes, Chapter 3), and understands the concept of passwords to control access to computer systems. Additionally, this chapter assumes the reader has an Internet connection that allows at least Telnet access and that the reader has some understanding of Internet addresses (e-mail, Chapter 5).

Foundation for Internet search tools

Telnet is the foundation upon which all Internet finding tools rely. With Telnet, you have at least some access to all other Internet information-finding tools discussed in this book.

The good news and beauty of Telnet is that it is the simplest of all Internet tools. You need only to type the word "telnet" (or some local equivalent) followed by the Internet address (numerical or verbal) of the site you want to log into. For example, by typing

telnet fedworld.gov

you can connect to the National Technical Information Service bulletin board system which is a gateway to on-line services of many federal agencies. The process is much like connecting to your local BBS (Chapter 3).

Telnet has three drawbacks: 1) You have to know ahead of time the address and log-in procedure for the site you are visiting. 2) Most sites only allow you to browse text files. Some will allow you to mail or download files. But downloading binary files is really a job for FTP (Chapter 8), not Telnet. 3) There are only limited indices of Telnet sites on the network, and usual search routines don't regularly turn up Telnet sites. To "find" a site with material you want, you have to rely on other tools such as Gopher or World Wide Web (Chapter 7), Mailing Lists (Chapter 5), News Groups (Chapter 9), or Hytelnet (described later in this chapter).

On the day of the Northridge temblor, networked journalists who issued the Telnet command

telnet oes1.oes.ca.gov 5501

about 5:30 a.m. were greeted by the menu in Figure 6-1.

The Emergency Digital Information Service (EDIS) operated by the California governor's Office of Emergency Services (OES) is a simple Telnet site. It offers a menu of 14 "Latest Messages" from the EDIS. Each message is numbered, and one line of information about the message gives a headline, select code, the date and time the message was posted to the system,

Fig. 6-1: The Emergency Digital Information Service (EDIS) is a Telnet offering of California's Office of Emergency Services. On the morning of the Northridge earthquake, first OES release on the quake appeared as item 0393 (bottom of the menu) at 5:25 a.m.

```
             State of California - Governor's Office of Emergency Services
                    EMERGENCY DIGITAL INFORMATION SERVICE (EDIS)
                                 Latest Messages

           Number  Headline                    Select   Date/Time   Source

           0380    NEWS RELEASE.............    c2bp-    Jan 13 16:29  bfd
           0381    TEST MESSAGE.............    d0-p-    Jan 14 05:47  fema
           0382    TEST MESSAGE.............    d6cp-    Jan 14 09:24  sdsd
           0383    TEST MESSAGE.............    d6cp-    Jan 14 09:31  sdsd
           0384    TEST MESSAGE.............    d6cp-    Jan 14 09:43  sdsd
           0385    EDIS SYSTEM TEST.........    d0-o-    Jan 14 10:00  OES
           0386    TEST MESSAGE.............    d2bp-    Jan 14 13:59  sfoes
           0387    EDIS SYSTEM TEST.........    d0-o-    Jan 15 10:00  OES
           0388    EDIS SYSTEM TEST.........    d0-o-    Jan 15 16:16  OES
           0389    TEST MESSAGE.............    d0-p-    Jan 15 16:19  edis
           0390    EARTHQUAKE INFORMATION...    c0-q-    Jan 15 19:13  NWS
           0391    TEST MESSAGE.............    d2bp-    Jan 15 21:46  sonsar
           0392    EDIS SYSTEM TEST.........    d0-o-    Jan 16 10:00  OES
           0393    URGENT NEWS RELEASE......    b0-p-    Jan 17 05:25  edis

         Enter Message Number (blank to exit): 0393
```

and the source. A line across the bottom of the screen instructs the visitor to "Enter Message Number (blank to exit):" At 5:30 a.m. Jan. 17, half the "Latest Messages" were three days old, and more than half the messages indicated system tests rather than newsworthy information.

The screen image in Figure 6-1 shows we have entered "0393," the number of the latest message on the screen. It is headlined "Urgent News Release" and is timed at 5:25 a.m. Jan. 17, some 54 minutes after the quake hit. After typing in the number of the desired message, the journalist online hits the Enter key. The message displayed appears in Figure 6-2.

The first message posted to the EDIS site on Jan. 17 gave quake statistics in tentative terms and ended with a plea and a promise from the OES: "MEDIA: Please do not telephone OES at this time. Additional information

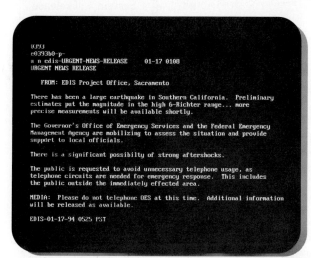

```
0393
e0393b0-p-
u n edis-URGENT-NEWS-RELEASE    01-17 0108
URGENT NEWS RELEASE

    FROM: EDIS Project Office, Sacramento

There has been a large earthquake in Southern California.  Preliminary
estimates put the magnitude in the high 6-Richter range... more
precise measurements will be available shortly.

The Governor's Office of Emergency Services and the Federal Emergency
Management Agency are mobilizing to assess the situation and provide
support to local officials.

There is a significant possibilty of strong aftershocks.

The public is requested to avoid unnecessary telephone usage, as
telephone circuits are needed for emergency response.  This includes
the public outside the immediately effected area.

MEDIA:  Please do not telephone OES at this time.  Additional information
will be released as available.

EDIS-01-17-94 0525 PST
```

Fig. 6-2: First "official" word of the Northridge earthquake appeared on the OES/EDIS Telnet site in Sacramento 54 minutes after the quake. The first message was tentative and ended with a plea for media representatives NOT to telephone the OES.

will be released as available." The plea to media folks not to telephone OES was understandable. OES kept the promise in such a way that made telephoning them unnecessary. Throughout the day, this on-line Telnet information was constantly updated. Morning postings included Caltrans (the state's highway maintenance agency) listings of highway closures and damages. Also enumerated were utilities interruptions, aftershock times and magnitudes, Red Cross relief efforts, disaster declarations, press briefings, media advisories, FEMA (Federal Emergency Management Agency) involvement, structural damages, deaths, evacuations, shelter locations. There were reports of oil spills, an hydrochloric acid spill in Saugus, a derailed train spilling 5,000 gallons of sulfuric acid in Northridge, school closures. Postings to the list included law enforcement tactical alert notices, accounts of the U.S. Air Force flying U-2 surveillance missions, the California Conservation Corps assembling resources lists, neighboring counties sending in public safety officials, National Guard deployments, and more.

During the first days following the Northridge quake, the Office of Emergency Services EDIS Telnet site was a one-stop shop for all the hard statistics of a major breaking news story, and it provided many insights and leads

```
e0422c0-p-
   r n edis-NEWS-RELEASE    01-17 0947
   NEWS RELEASE

FROM: Governor's Office of Emergency Services, Sacramento

STATE OFFICE OF EMERGENCY SERVICES
STATUS REPORT
AS OF JANUARY 17, 1994, 1130 HOURS
SAN FERNANDO VALLEY EARTHQUAKE

1.Proclamations/Declarations

1. Local Declarations - County & City of Los Angeles, City of Hawthorne,
County of Ventura
2. Governor's Proclamation of a State of Emergency - County of Los Angeles

5.Damages/Incidents

OES Fire reports 70+ structures involved or down from fire.  All fires under
control.

LA City  - 100 incidents reported.  Numerous building collapses; mainly in
north area.  Ranging from single family homes to larger structures including an
apartment building and Northridge shopping mall.
People trapped.  Partial collapse to pancaking.

LA County - City of El Monte—unreinforced masonry moderate damage.
Cities of Sierra Madre and Alhambra—broken glass in business districts.

Ventura County - Fillmore hardest hit; partial collapse of Fillmore Hotel.
Petro chemical plant at SR 126 and Santa Clarita; potential chlorine release.
Fire at El Dorado Mobile Home Park, Fillmore.

Saugus - 1,000 hydrocloric acid and 500 gallon of sodium
hyperchloride spill.

Lake Castaic - Ruptured tank - crude oil spill with one-mile plume
(unconfirmed).

Valencia - pipeline rupture, crude oil.

Oil flowing into Santa Clara River.  Three more pipeline leaks in
```

Fig. 6-3: News releases posted to the EDIS/OES Telnet site on the day of the Northridge quake, such as this status report, often contained several computer screens full of information. This figure shows Section 1 and portions of Section 5 of release 0422. The release had 13 sections and referred news people to a separate release for reports on road conditions and closures. Following the first notice at 5:25 a.m., new postings hit the Telnet site every 10-12 minutes well into the afternoon.

for sidebars and color pieces. During the first two days after the quake, new intelligence was posted every few minutes. For weeks following the quake, OES continued to provide new information. As the relief efforts shifted to relocating the homeless and providing federal disaster relief assistance to victims, pertinent information continued to be posted several times a day.

This Telnet operation serves as an example of how on-line information services can aid journalists in the news business as well as the agency sources on whom news people rely. The OES/EDIS Telnet operation did most of the work of a news conference, only better. News people had no need to physically arrive at a site. Those "arriving" online late could still pick up the "fact sheets" and news releases. Pertinent quotes did not have to be rekeyboarded, but could be moved directly into the journalist's copy. Using on-line technology, journalists in places as remote from Los Angeles as Sioux City, Iowa, or Boston, Mass., or Temple, Texas, or Paderborn, Germany, could "attend" the conference and get all the pertinent data in their freshest form. The system worked well for OES, too. Uninterrupted by calls and visits from media folks or by the need to orchestrate formal conferences, state information officers could gather necessary data from all their people at the scene, package the information once, and post the material to the Telnet bulletin board. The only thing missing from this virtual "conference" was that the press could ask no questions. No interview questions were raised at the OES/EDIS Telnet bulletin board. The on-line journalist has other tools for interviewing sources when personal visits are impossible and telephone communications are not reliable. Those tools will be discussed in Chapter 9. In Chapter 7 we will describe Gopher, the tool that pointed us in the direction of the OES site.

Other Telnet sites – log-in, terminal emulation

The OES/EDIS Telnet bulletin board is about as simple as Telnet sites come. The journalist online types "telnet" followed by an address. (In this case the address was followed by a port number, 5501. Port numbers often specify particular client software or public access.) At the OES EDIS site, the reporter gets connected to a remote computer, which immediately offers a menu of "articles" to read. Other Telnet sites are more sophisticated; they offer more choices and require more complex logging in and sometimes more complex procedures for getting at the desired information.

If you issue the command

telnet happenings.ncsu.edu <CR>

for example, once you are connected, you are greeted by a screen that affirms that you are connected, tells how to enter the escape character, and identifies the terminal emulation required by the site. The connect message also informs visitors that they may have access to "HAPPENINGS" by simply typing "INFO" at the "USERNAME" prompt (Figure 6-4).

```
Connected to HAPPENINGS.NCSU.EDU.
Escape character is '^]'.


        North Carolina State University Computing Center's VAXcluster

**********************************************************************
  *                                                                 *
  *          Happenings!, your campuswide information system        *
  *                                                                 *
  *      Access to Happenings! is available by typing INFO at the   *
  *      USERNAME: prompt following this message.                   *
  *                                                                 *
  *      Please make sure you are emulating a DEC VT100, 200 or 300 *
  *      style terminal; VT100 is the default.                      *
**********************************************************************

Username: INFO
```

Fig. 6-4: Some Telnet facilities give welcome screens containing instructions for gaining public access. At North Carolina State University's "Happenings," this connect screen tells the networker to type "Info" to log in.

Before you connected to "Happenings" you may have observed a screen message that said "Trying ... 152.1.13.23." The number sequence is the Internet address truly recognized by machines connected to the network. Had you typed

telnet 152.1.13.23 <CR>

you would have achieved the same result as you did by naming "happenings.ncsu.edu".

Other public Telnet sites may offer similar advice for logging in to access special services. If you Telnet to archie.sura.net, for example, a screen message tells you on connection that if you type "qarchie" at the log-in prompt, you will have access to the Archie client (see Chapter 7).

FedWorld, for example, is a BBS-type system available both through telephone/modem dial-up (703-321-8020) and through Telnet. To get to FedWorld by Telnet, type

Telnet fedworld.gov

When you connect to FedWorld you are prompted for your name. The first time you log in, you enter "new," and FedWorld asks you to fill out a form giving your company affiliation, phone number, and address. You then choose a password, and you are encouraged to write it down so that future log-ins will be more smooth. FedWorld offerings are described under Bulletin Board Systems in Chapter 3, but among the offerings of interest to journalists are the gateways FedWorld offers to more than 120 BBS systems run by various federal government agencies. Logging into FedWorld through Telnet saves the costs of making telephone call(s).

A typical Telnet session begins when the host launches the log-in dialog, asking for your username (or user ID) followed by a password. Sometimes the process begins when the host displays a prompt that says simply "login." Other variations exist. But in each case, you are asked first to give your name and then a password — the same process as signing onto a bulletin board. If you don't know the log-in words, sometimes typing in such words as "public" or "guest" or "visitor" gets you to the public section.

At other sites, such as the North Carolina State "Happenings," you are greeted with a message that tells you how to log in. Still other sites, such as the OES/EDIS site in California, no log-in is required. The Telnet process is the ground upon which much network activity is built. Even when you use an Internet "front end" like Gopher (Chapter 7), you are sometimes dumped into or handed off to a Telnet session.

You might want to practice telnetting to following sites:

Address	Log-in procedure	Resource
vienna.hh.lib.umich.edu	"mlink"	business/economics
cap.gwu.edu	Login "guest", pwd "visitor"	state & local govt.
neis.cr.usgs.gov	Username: "QED"	earthquake info.
fdabbs.fda.gov	"bbs", then register	US FDA
info.umd.edu	"info"	federal govt. info.
debra.dgbt.doc.ca	"chat"	AIDS, epilepsy files
stis.nsf.gov 23	"public"	Nat'l Science Fnd.

During log-in, you will not type the quotation marks. Note that the last entry concludes with a space and a port number after the Internet domain. In all instances you will want to be alert to upper and lower case designations – sometimes case makes a difference.

In Appendix C, log-in procedures are provided where they are needed. Again, the Internet changes almost daily, and we expect that some of the sites identified in this book will no longer be accessible in the manner described. Especially with Telnet, we encourage you to keep a log book of the Telnet places you "visit" and what you find there. We cannot overemphasize the importance of learning Telnet. From Telnet, nearly all the Internet tools are at least partially available.

Many Telnet sites require you to specify a terminal type during the login process. This is done so the host computer knows how to read your keyboard and in turn how to speak back to your computer. Most communications software programs allow your computer to "emulate" or to appear to be one of several different "dumb" terminals often connected to larger computers. Probably the most commonly accepted terminal on the Internet is the DEC VT100. Most communications software programs will allow your computer to emulate the VT100. If the site you are telnetting to asks for VT100 or some other emulation, be sure you configure your software to that specification. A few sites require an IBM® 3270 terminal emulation. If you do not know what is required or accepted, try VT100 or TTY first.

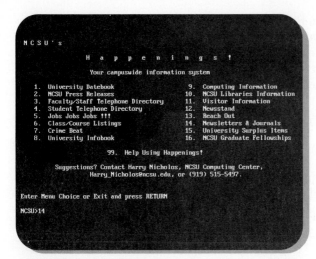

Fig. 6-5: North Carolina State University's top menu at "Happenings" gives the appearance of offering nothing but college pomp. However, menus beneath the top one offer some matters of interest to journalists on environmental or technology beats.

Menu hierarchies

The OES/EDIS Telnet service presented a flat menu with 14 choices; enter an item number and the designated file appears on your screen. More commonly, however, you are greeted by a top menu. Selecting items from the top menu takes you to lower level menus, frequently organized by topic just as local bulletin board systems are organized. There is hidden opportunity here for the journalist on the prowl.

The "Happenings" top menu shown in Figure 6-5 looks like just a bunch of college cheerleaders: university calendar, press releases, course listings, telephone directory, job listings, fellowships, campus information, and so on. This is a typical campus information system. But beneath the campus rah-

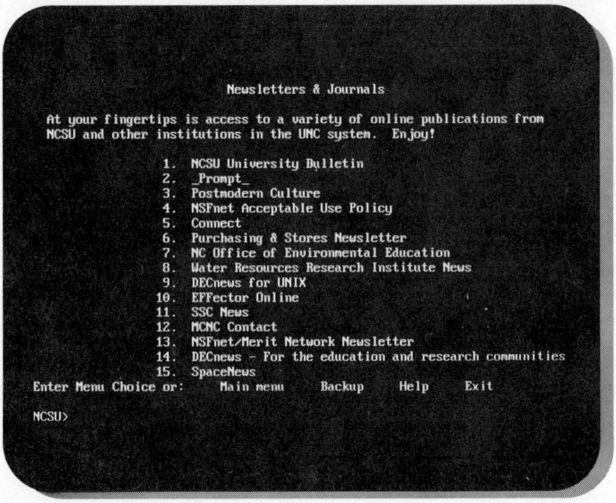

Fig. 6-6: A second-level menu at North Carolina State's "Happenings" suggests matters more useful to a journalist than all the campus information offered at the top-level menu.

Fig. 6-7: A third-level menu at North Carolina State's "Happenings" offers files of information from the Water Resources Research Institute News.

rah lurks information useful to some news people. If you had selected choice 14, "Newsletters & Journals," you would have called up the menu in Figure 6-6. Menu choices 7 and 8 in particular offer further choices in documents of interest to environmental reporters.

North Carolina State is typical of many universities. Most colleges and universities have some areas of distinction for which they are noted. An excellent engineering program may be one school's claim to fame. A well financed meteorological research center may be another's, or wildlife and range management, or early childhood education. Most great medical research facilities are connected with some university. College professors are frequently quoted as "expert" sources in news stories.

Colleges and universities have been quick to embrace the Information Age – they provide key computing power to keep much of the Internet up and running. As part of the academic movement into the Information Age, colleges and universities have dedicated computer resources to some area of specialty or another. In the list of Telnet sites given for "practice" earlier in this chapter, three sites were at educational institutions. George Washington University (cap.gwu.edu) provides the access point for the National Capital Area Public Access Network, the Washington D.C. Free-Net. University of Michigan (vienna.hh.lib.umich.edu) provides Telnet access to resources specializing in business and economics. The University of Maryland (info.umd.edu) maintains a database strong on federal government information. All of these sites have other information available as well.

Telnet Exploring Tips – Many colleges and universities offer, in addition to on-line library catalogs, collections of specialized documents that can be of great help to a journalist working a story. The on-line journalist would do well to invest 15-30 minutes a day "browsing" the network and taking notes along the way. This process is analogous to a reporter new to a beat building his sources book. The note-taking becomes especially important as you navigate multi-tiered levels of menu.

Theseus and the Minotaur: Self-defense tabs

On multi-tiered menuing systems, it is easy to move randomly about the computer site's menus browsing among information that is not of particular use to your story or even to your beat. However, when you do find something that you expect may be useful now or in the future, you will want to be able to get back to that information. Entering a Telnet session is much like entering a maze. Remember Theseus and the Minotaur. If you want to get back, unravel a ball of twine along the way. You do this with notes. Record the Telnet address. Then as you move down through menus, keep notes of which choices you selected. For example, your environmental or state government beat might get you into a story dealing with wastewater being dumped into the ocean along the Atlantic seaboard. Browsing through NCSU's "Happenings," you happen onto the menu shown in Figure 6-7, "Water Resources Research Institute News." Your eye catches items 8 and 9, "Options for Integrated Coastal Wastewater Management" and "Petition for Judicial Review of Permits in Virginia." You ascertain that items on the menu are regularly updated, and you expect that "Water Resources Research Institute News" is a network resource you would like to regularly monitor. If you were casually browsing without "unraveling your ball of twine," you might have a hard time finding those files again. Here's how we found them:

1. We connected to NCSU through telnet happenings.ncsu.edu (Figure 6-4).
2. At the "Happenings" main menu (Figure 6-5), we selected Item 14, "Newsletters and Journals."
3. From the "Newsletters and Journals" menu (Figure 6-6), we chose Item 8, "Water Resources Research Institute News."
4. To get the piece on coastal wastewater management from the "Water Resources Research Institute News" menu (Figure 6-7), we selected File 8, "Options for Integrated Coastal Wastewater Management."

A relatively standard shorthand for tracking network navigation would summarize our actions this way:

"Path = 1/14 Newsletters / 8 Water Resources / 8 Options"

meaning we started at the Top Menu (1) and chose Item 14, then Item 8, and then Item 8 again. The first word or two of each menu choice is kept with that choice's number as a security check. The path shorthand would be attached to the site address (happenings. ncsu.edu) in order to provide a full record of where we had been.

Keeping path shorthand becomes even more critical as you "surf" the Internet using tools such as Gopher and World Wide Web (Chapter 7), though each of those tools has built-in tracking devices. Telnet has no such devices. It is merely a program to connect two computers together so that the terminal (your personal computer) may access information from the host. A final word of caution: The Information Superhighway is under construction; things on the Internet – including resource locating – change frequently. You will want to keep regular tabs, especially on those sites of most interest to you.

Getting help, bailing out gracefully

One other area bears note-taking. When you first connect to a site, you don't know what kind of computer is at the other end or what kind of software they are running. You probably don't care, and generally speaking you don't need to know. However, it's nice to know how to get help and how to disconnect from the host site. Frequently that information is provided to you when you first connect. In Figure 6-3, the connect screen for NCSU's "Happenings," the second line of the screen says "Escape character is '^]'." What that means is that by typing Ctrl-] (holding the Control key down and hitting the right brace key), you can escape the program and disconnect from "Happenings."

That combination (Ctrl-]) is common on the Internet. Other common ways of leaving programs include:

- Typing "Q" or "QUIT"
- Typing "E," "X," "EXIT," or "Ctrl-X"
- Typing "Ctrl-Z"
- Typing "Bye," "Goodbye," or "G"

Getting help online is generally accomplished in one of three ways:
- Type "?"
- Type "H" or "HELP."
- Enter the number, letter, or name of a menu choice.

In the top menu of "Happenings," the help function is accessed by typing "99." Help screens generally summarize available commands. If you are accessing the network by telephone, be alert to the commands of your software program. For example, Ctrl-] is a common escape command we have noted. However, if you are using ProComm communications software, that key combination merely toggles on and off a status bar across the bottom of the screen.

Capturing a Telnet session with log utilities

When you bring files to your computer screen during a Telnet session, you are doing just so much reading unless you take advantage of a utility built in to nearly every communications program on the market – session logging. What session logging does is to take all text that passes your screen and write it to a disk file that you name. You then have the full text on your computer so that you can import quotes or text charts directly into your story without having to rekeyboard them.

If you are using a PC with ProComm in any of its incarnations (or work-alike programs such as WordPerfect's MTEZ), you start a log file by typing Alt-F1. If you are networked using DEC Pathworks, the command is Ctrl-F1. In either case, you are prompted to name the file you wish the session log to be stored in. Whatever your communications software, check your manual (or your systems guru) for the procedure to start a log file or to log a session. This may be listed under "recording" a session but is not the same as recording a script or recording a macro. Most programs allow you to suspend the log temporarily during a session. In ProComm, once a log file is started, it may be toggled into and out of suspension with the command Alt-F2. In Pathworks, the Ctrl-F1 combination is a toggle.

Hytelnet puts menu on public Telnet sites

Telnet has two down sides from the view of user friendliness. First, you have to know each site's log-in procedure to get connected. Second, each site has different menuing and commands. Hytelnet is a client program that helps solve those problems. Hytelnet puts a menuing interface on publicly accessible Telnet sites and gives you online help logging into remote sites. Library systems, campus-wide information systems, and Free-Nets are among the more interesting sites indexed by Hytelnet. Hytelnet can hand you off to WAIS and Archie servers (accessible by Telnet), but has no network searching engine of its own. Some Gopher sites (**liberty.uc.wlu.edu**, for example,

Fig. 6-9: The Hytelnet connect dialog provides information on how to get login and get the information you requested..

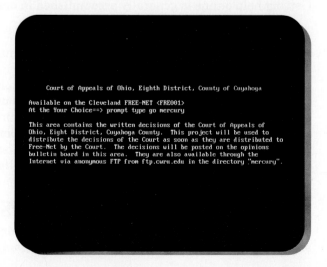

see Chapter 7 for Go-
pher) have programs
that search Hytelnet
indices and build you
a menu of Telnet sites
containing your
search term. How-
ever, within Hytelnet,
menus tend to get or-
ganized by subject,
and the journalist will
have to browse
through listings to
find sites that might

Hytelnet Commands

Down arrow	Select next Topic
Up arrow	Select previous Topic
Right arrow	Jump to next Topic
Left arrow	Return to previous Topic

hjkl (vi cursor keys) work as well

Enter	Chooses highlighted item
m	Return to the main menu
+ or space	Scroll down to the next page
- or b	Scroll up to the previous page
?	Help with commands
q	Quit Hytelnet

prove useful. That browsing can pay off.

If you or your Internet host do not have a Hytelnet client, you can access
Hytelnet clients by using Telnet to connect with **sdacs.ucsd.edu 7009**; or
red-dwarf.cit.cornell.edu 5000; or **info.ccit.arizona.edu 23**; or
hytelnet.cwis.uci.edu. These last two sites require you to log in as
"hytelnet." You can also start a Hytelnet session from a Gopher server (Chapter
7) such as the Library of Congress (marvel.loc.gov) where Hytelnet is under
the Internet Resources menu (Figure 7-9). Another Gopher source for Hytelnet
is **liberty.uc.wlu.edu**, again picking "Explore Internet Sources" from the
root menu, and "Hytelnet" from the Internet menu.

Beneath the top menu, different Hytelnet sites, often using different
versions of the software, provide some variation on menu choices. Again,
each journalist should take time on a regular basis to explore for a few minutes now and again what is available and keep log notes of Telnet sites you
visit using Hytelnet. During the writing of this book (which was pretty quick
as books go), we observed appreciable expansion and improvement of Hytelnet
offerings as potential sources for news stories. Hytelnet is especially strong
in providing access to the rapidly expanding world of Free-Nets.

On Hytelnet menus, terms in brackets < and > become selector items
and the cursor highlights one item at a time. When you choose a highlighted
item by pressing the Return/Enter key you either get a new menu, a text
document, or you begin the Telnet connect dialog. The connect dialog (Figure
6-9) in Hytelnet provides information about the site you have chosen. Usually it provides the Telnet address, log-in instructions, and a brief description of what you will find at the remote computer site. In Figure 6-9, the
Telnet address is not given because the destination site (Cleveland FreeNet)
is properly accessed through Hytelnet's Free-Net menus where it is choice
<FRE001>. The simple command structure for Hytelnet can be confusing at
first. It takes a little getting used to before you master the difference between the Left Arrow (previous topic) and the "-" or "b" key commands (which
take you up one page in the current document).

Chapter 4 outlines different kinds of connections to the Internet and discussed advantages of running your own client software for Internet programs. If you have direct access to the Internet through an Ethernet connection, or if you have SLIP or PPP connection by modem, you can take advantage of Hytelnet client software. It is available for both the Macintosh and IBM compatibles. You may get it by FTP from **access.usask.ca**. (See Chapter 8 for FTP.) The Macintosh version is hytelnet.mac.sea.hqx and resides in the pub/hytelnet/mac directory. The IBM-compatible version, which runs in the background and is called up by hot keys, is in the pub/hytelnet/pc directory and is called HYTELN##.ZIP. To GET the program, you will have to replace the ## with real numbers. To find out what they are, type either **ls <CR>** or **dir <CR>** to see a listing of the files in the directory. The current version of Hytelnet at book deadline was version 6.5. These are binary files, so you will have to use the binary command before GETting the files.

In general terms, the strongest areas of Hytelnet offerings are first, access to public libraries throughout the world; second, access to Freenets in the United States and Canada; third, cataloging of data bases, especially the listings of the National Aeronautics and Space Administration BBS offerings (about 16 systems); fourth, its friendly descriptions of the site and accounting of log-in procedures when you choose a site. The library connections should become more and more productive for journalists as libraries themselves come to grips with an age that is increasingly electronic. Already, universities and libraries have made available online the text to many classical pieces of literature (Shakespeare, Aesop's Fables, *Moby Dick* among them) as well as reference books including dictionaries, almanacs, the *CIA Fact Book*, and others. Finally, Hytelnet's ease of use speaks well for it.

The weakest areas of Hytelnet are that it has no built-in search capabilities and it is not very widely distributed. Hytelnet by its creator's own intent is limited in its offerings to Telnet sites. If information is not available by Telnet you won't find it under the Hytelnet umbrella. However, there is a lot of information on the Internet available by Telnet. Furthermore, Hytelnet's grouping of Telnet site offerings into broad subject categories can actually be helpful for journalists on projects where a broad context is important.

Ethical, legal issues using Telnet information

Some of the material reached by Telnet is copyrighted. All the applicable rules of copyright law must be assumed to apply. It is worth noting that many states have enacted laws making inaccessible government records which on paper were open to the public. The net legal result for journalists is to use the same kind of caution pulling files from the Internet that you would pulling files from traditional library sources. Among groups lobbying Congress and battling in the courts to assure that the Information Age is at least as open as the Gutenberg Age are The Electronic Frontier Foundation, The Reporters Committee for Freedom of the Press, and the Taxpayers' Assets Project.

On the ethical frontier, the same cautions issued for e-mail and mail lists apply to Telnet. Under normal circumstances the networking journalist really has no way of knowing who posted the information on the computer at the remote site. You don't know what that person's source(s) might have been. Every caution needs to be taken to verify information and to test the credibility of sources. Anybody can set up a computer, get an Internet address, and put information online. We expect that in the not-too-distant future we will read horror stories about reporters who included in their reports information taken from on-line sources set up for the purpose of misleading the media and the public in general.

Exploring Telnet further

Other Telnet sites are listed in Appendix C, organized by newsroom beats. Contributors to mail lists (Chapter 5) such as Journet, CARR-L, and Nit-Chron frequently have tips on network addresses of interest to journalists. So do newsgroups such as alt.journalism. Journalists across the country have generally been generous in sharing information about network resources with other journalists, and the place they do that is in the on-line places journalists gather.

This chapter began with an account of capturing information on the Northridge earthquake from a Telnet site in the California governor's Office of Emergency Services. If you didn't have the address of "oes1.oes.ca.gov 5501", you could have found out about it on CARR-L late on the day of the quake. But if you had even a fair index of Gopher systems, you could have let the little rodent from Minnesota lead you to the site. Gopher qualifies as a network finding tool, and we will describe the network tunneler in the next chapter.

Further reading

Books offering themselves as "Internet directories" are comprised primarily of address listings for network sites. Two of particular interest are:
1. Eric Braun. *The Internet Directory*, New York: Ballentine Books, 1994.
2. Harley Hahn and Rick Stout. *The Internet Yellow Pages*, Berkeley, California: Osborne McGraw-Hill, 1994.

Chapter

7

Gopher & World Wide Web

Journalists who connected to the California governor's Office of Emergency Services' Telnet site the morning of the Northridge earthquake reaped a rich harvest of both "official" agency statistics – constantly updated – and leads to an abundance of human interest stories. We shared much of that in Chapter 6. What we didn't share is that before 5:20 a.m. (Pacific time) on the day of the quake we didn't know the OES had a Telnet site, let alone its address. How does a journalist on deadline find networked information sources?

The Internet-connected journalist stares at a screen silently linked to thousands of independent networks. Each of those networks contains numbers of machines. In the aggregate, one confronts hundreds of millions of computer files. There are few road signs, fewer maps, and almost no traffic cops or welcome stations along the Information Superhighway in 1994. What maps are published soon become obsolete amid shifting electronic landscapes. Panning for gold in a metropolitan flood control channel seems easier than finding useful information in such a massive sea.

Fortunately, the journalist on assignment has at his or her disposal several tools to subdue the network beast. In this chapter, the online journalist will learn how to

- use Gopher to quickly navigate among network sites world wide and to bring useful data and information quickly into the journalist's personal computer.
- use Veronica and Jughead programs to locate data and information stored on Gopher servers.
- walk Hypertext pathways on the World Wide Web.
- Use Gopher and World Wide Web servers to launch other network programs.

Assumptions that this chapter makes are that the reader is already comfortable with using his or her communications program and has logged onto dial-up bulletin board systems (BBSes, Chapter 3). It would be helpful if the reader has successfully logged into remote computer systems using the Internet Telnet protocol (Chapter 6). As in other portions of this book, descriptions offered assume the simplest, most common kinds of connection and interface to the Internet. Although we discuss several Internet finding tools separately, they are in many ways interconnected. For example, Gopher and World Wide Web servers provide gateways to all the other tools.

The following account tells how Gopher helped find the OES bulletin board on the Internet the morning of the Northridge earthquake.

Gopher pointed the way to breaking story information

Los Angeles County shuddered amid the first few dozen aftershocks of the Northridge earthquake, and hundreds of thousands of residents surveyed their surroundings without benefit from electricity. News came slowly to the rest of the world as well as to the stunned victims themselves. Telephone communications were erratic. Hundreds of reporters trying to interview the small handful of public safety officials available at 5 a.m. could not possibly all get through. Conventional wisdom teaches that news operations removed from the quake area by hundreds of miles would just have to wait for the wire services to produce reports.

Not so.

The network-connected journalist needed only a little perseverance to strike news pay dirt. In Chapter 6 we described the news information offered online and regularly updated by the California Office of Emergency Services. Prior to the quake we did not know the OES had a Telnet site. Gopher helped us find the news information source.

Fig. 7-1: First page of the root menu for Oklahoma's Geological Survey Observatory Open Station contains the option (12) of connecting to seismic sites outside Oklahoma. Minutes after the Northridge earthquake this helped one of the authors locate the OES Telnet BBS service described in Chapter 6.

```
               Internet Gopher Information Client 2.0 pl10

               Root gopher server: wealaka.okgeosurvey1.gov

        1.  -----------------------------------------------------
        2.  !WELCOME! OKLAHOMA GEOLOGICAL SURVEY OBSERVATORY  OPEN STATION !.
        3.  !near real time continuous and event seismic and magnetic data !.
        4.  !Oklahoma earthquake and nuke test catalogs, nuke test treaties!.
        5.  -----------------------------------------------------
        6.  WAVEFORMS, last 9 days continuous waveforms + selected events/
        7.  OKLAHOMA EARTHQUAKE CATALOG v earthquakes seismicity/
        8.  OKLAHOMA GEOLOGICAL SURVEY WAVEFORM, CAL, STATION, AND MISC INFO/
        9.  OKGEOSURVEY POSTSCRIPT SEISMOGRAMS v seismogram earthquake earthqu.../
        10. CATALOG OF KNOWN NUCLEAR EXPLOSIONS v test tests/
        11. waveforms from other sites/
  --->  12. connect to seismic sites outside Oklahoma/
        13. NUCLEAR TESTING TREATIES, RELATED TREATIES, DOCUMENTS v treaty/
        14. Seismic bulletins, info, some grams.ps  from sites outside OK/
        15. VERONICA: BOOLEAN SEARCHES OF ALL GOPHERSPACE/
        16. MOTHER GOPHER, OMENET GOPHER, OTHER SELECTED GOPHERS/
        17. K12/
        18. OUTSIDE CONTRIBUTIONS/

Press ? for Help, q to Quit                              Page: 1/2
```

Fig. 7-2: Selecting a non-Gopher choice from a Gopher menu results in a warning. The warning screen gives you a chance to change your mind and it may offer "survival" tips or log-in instructions for the new site. The University of California Earthquake Gopher warns that you are leaving Gopher, entering a Telnet session.

Here's how. Earthquakes are studied/tracked by earth scientists, and so network sources under the "Science and Technology" beat (Appendix C) is where we find listings for network resources offering seismic information. We connected to the Gopher server run by the Oklahoma Geological Survey Observatory Open Station. We reached it by entering the command:

gopher wealaka.okgeosurvey1.gov

and were greeted with the menu shown in Figure 7-1. Because we sought information on an earthquake in California, we chose menu selection 12, "connect to seismic sites outside Oklahoma/."

Figure 7-1 shows the Gopher menu selector arrow pointing at item 12. You make choices on a Gopher menu by using your keyboard's Up and Down Arrows to move the menu pointer to the item you want to view (a document file), launch (a search routine or another network program), or move to (another directory). With the menu arrow pointing at 12, "connect to seismic sites outside Oklahoma/," you press either the Enter key or the Right Arrow key to retrieve a directory of sites outside Oklahoma. (Figure 7-5 gives a summary of Gopher commands.)

One of the sites "outside Oklahoma" was the Earthquake Information Gopher at the University of California at Berkeley. That Gopher in turn had a menu item titled "California OES Earthquake Program." From years as a reporter and editor in California, we knew that OES was an acronym for the state's Office of Emergency Services. If you did not know the meaning of OES, selecting that choice would take you to a menu that spelled out what the office is and does.

The OES Gopher offered us the opportunity to Telnet to the OES Emergency Digital Information Services (EDIS). That Telnet system in turn provided a steady stream of solid news information updated about every 13 minutes during the first hours after the quake and two to three times per hour in the days succeeding. From one electronic site the journalist could snag "official" information from several state public safety agencies, the governor's office, the Federal Emergency Management Agency, Caltrans (in charge of California's highway system), public utilities, the Red Cross, and others. (See Chapter 6 for a discussion of Telnet in general and what the OES site offered to journalists during the quake.) When you select a Telnet site from a Gopher menu, Gopher warns you that you are leaving the Gopher program. Frequently the warning message will provide information about logging into the Telnet site or suggestions about navigating the new site. Figure 7-2 shows the warning provided by the OES Gopher.

In the case of the EDIS bulletin board, the transition from Gopher to Telnet – and back again – is smooth. In fact, if it were not for the warning message, you might never know you had left Gopher. Because the Information Superhighway is still under construction, it is not unusual for some sites to dump you out to your system prompt just when you thought something else should have happened. Patience is warranted in "construction zones"; the payoff frequently is worth temporary inconveniences.

A simple, powerful Internet tool

Network tools with exotic sounding names like WAIS, Hytelnet, and World Wide Web are sensitive to changing electronic landscapes. They aid journalists in finding files containing information relevant to topics the journalist defines. Comic strip characters lend their names to a stable of network information-finding tools called Archie, Veronica, and Jughead. Anyone with Telnet access (Chapter 6) has at least some measure of access to all these tools, if only through Gopher.

No other commonly available network tool offers so much network power to a journalist for so little effort as Gopher. We will spend more time describing Gopher than any other single network finding tool. We do this in part because

- all other major network tools are accessible from Gopher servers.
- Gopher is easy to learn and to use.
- many Gopher commands perform the same functions in the Lynx World Wide Web browser.
- Gopher is well-suited to displaying text files and to moving files when necessary.
- Gopher is widely distributed and available in most of its power to a large number of users.

A product of the University of Minnesota, Gopher unites widely scattered computer sites and powerful information-gathering tools under the umbrella of one simple menu system. A journalist on the hunt for critical information simply dials up his favorite Gopher server and lets the Gopher program "tunnel through" Internet "Gopherspace" to the "Gopher hole" where desired information resides. The reporter then may read the information online or download it for inclusion in the story of the moment. Because it is menu driven and employs only two dozen commands, Gopher is not complicated to learn. Because it plays text files one screen at a time and executes file downloads with just a few keystrokes, Gopher scores high on ease of use. As long as you stay in Gopher, accessing other Gopher sites, you have no need to log in again. In fact, through most network navigating, Gopher does the tedious work of logging in for you. A journalist exploring the net who just happens to stumble on a great find of information relevant to her beat has a great friend in Gopher. You simply place a Gopher bookmark on the current directory or file. Any time you wish to return to the same "gopher hole," all that is necessary is to call up your bookmark list and select the mark in question. It is unnecessary to remember the desired Gopher's address or even to type it.

Gaining Gopher access

For the user, a Gopher session at first glance looks and behaves very much like a Telnet session (see Chapter 6). Once connected, the network user faces a menu of less than 20 choices. Figure 7-4 shows the Judiciary menu from the Library of Congress (LOC) Gopher. If the local host has a Gopher client (each journalist will have to ask the network access provider), one has considerably more freedom in moving around Gopherspace. Usually all that is necessary to start a Gopher session (if your host has a Gopher client) is to type the word "gopher" at the system prompt and then to hit Enter. Typing the word "gopher" followed by a Gopher server's address takes the journalist to the Gopher site she chooses. For example, one might access the Library of Congress Gopher by typing

gopher marvel.loc.gov <CR>

Another way to get to the Library of Congress Gopher from a local Gopher site would be first to launch the local Gopher, then to "point" the Gopher at a chosen destination site. Typing "o" (lower case) brings up a window (Figure 7-3) in which you are asked to enter the address of the destination Gopher (the one you want to connect to). In this case, you would type simply

marvel.loc.gov <CR>

Finally, one may access some public Gopher clients by using the Internet Telnet program (Chapter 6). Thus, typing the command

telnet marvel.loc.gov <CR>

launches a remote log-in to the Library of Congress. At the log-in request, you type "marvel <CR>" to start up the LOC Gopher. The "Great Mother Gopher" at the University of Minnesota is also accessible by Telnet at

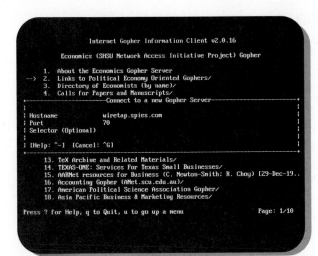

Fig. 7-3: At any Gopher menu you may connect to any other Gopher host by typing "o" and entering for the hostname the Internet address of the site you wish. Here, we have asked to connect to wiretap.spies.com, a server with strong civics and government resources.

consultant.micro.umn.edu. Some other public Telnet addresses that allow access to Gopher clients include **sunsite.unc.edu,** log in as "gopher"; **gopher.who.ch**, log in as "gopher"; **scilibx.ucsc.edu**, log in as "infoslug"; **panda.uiowa.edu**, log in as "panda"; **infopath.ucsd.edu**, log in as "infopath"; **gopher.ora.com**, a commercial site, log in as "gopher," specify VT100 terminal. If you tried out the Telnet addresses in Chapter 6, you already connected with one Gopher, **vienna.hh.lib.umich.edu**, log in "mlink."

Not all Gopher servers may be accessed via Telnet. Some may be reached only through another Gopher client or other network front end. If you have to Telnet to access Gopher, you will not be able to take advantage of Gopher's *Bookmarks* feature nor the *Save* (file) feature. But one great feature about Gopher that sets it apart from Telnet is that Gopher presents the same face and responds to the same commands wherever the Gopher server is. With Telnet, on the other hand, each site has its own "face" and responds to its own commands. Some, like the California OES site, are simple. Others are much more complex and sophisticated.

Some Gopher commands and conventions

The way Gopher lists menu items gives the user information about the menu listing. In Figure 7-4, lines 2-6 end with a slash mark (/), indicating that each is a directory that will have further choices if it is selected. You select a choice in one of two ways: 1) type the number of the choice and hit the Enter (Return) key, or 2) use the Up or Down Arrow keys to move the selector arrow to the number of the item desired and then hit the Enter key. The period at the end of choices 1, 7, 8, and 9 indicates those selections are text files. If you select one of them, the text displays on your screen. Some Gopher sites omit punctuation for menu choices that are text files only. The item selector arrow

Fig. 7-4: The Judiciary menu on the Library of Congress Gopher illustrates typical Gopher menu structure. Items 1, 7, 8, and 9 (all end in periods) are text files. Items 2-6 (end with slash marks) lead to new directories. Items 10 and 11 (question marks) will start user-defined searches.

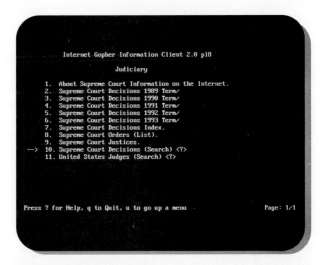

```
                Internet Gopher Information Client 2.0 p18

                              Judiciary

          1.  About Supreme Court Information on the Internet.
          2.  Supreme Court Decisions 1989 Term/
          3.  Supreme Court Decisions 1990 Term/
          4.  Supreme Court Decisions 1991 Term/
          5.  Supreme Court Decisions 1992 Term/
          6.  Supreme Court Decisions 1993 Term/
          7.  Supreme Court Decisions Index.
          8.  Supreme Court Orders (List).
          9.  Supreme Court Justices.
    -->  10.  Supreme Court Decisions (Search) <?>
         11.  United States Judges (Search) <?>




     Press ? for Help, q to Quit, u to go up a menu              Page: 1/1
```

in Figure 7-4 points to choice 10, which is an option to let the user employ key words to search for Supreme Court decisions. The bracketed question marks <?> at the end of lines 10 and 11 denote menu choices for which the user will be asked to provide searching parameters. You could search for all Supreme Court decisions affecting public schools. You would get a listing of the docket numbers, and then you could review the abstracts to ascertain whether you want the entire decision. Sometimes one finds a Gopher menu item labeled "under construction." This marks choices that may not be fully functional. In Gopher, as with other network programs and utilities, patience is indicated. It is not unusual to find Gopher menu choices for which no files, directories, or information is available. When such an item is selected, Gopher returns a message telling you that nothing is available. You might want to try that choice again at a later date. There are other kinds of temporary frustrations encountered on the network.

You move around in Gopherspace by selecting menu items to explore. The selector arrow points at the current choice. You move the selector arrow up and down the menu by using your keyboard cursor arrows. Hit your Return key (Enter key) or hit a Right Arrow key and Gopher goes to work retrieving the item in question. If it is a directory (items 2-6 in Figure 7-4), that directory will appear on the screen when it has been retrieved from its point of origin. The menu item in question may be on the currently logged computer or on another computer halfway around the world. While Gopher is working, a message in the lower right-hand corner of the computer screen reports "Retrieving xxxxxxxx /" where the xxxxxxxx may be a file or a directory, and the slash mark spins to show work in progress. When Gopher has retrieved the item in question, messages across the bottom of the screen report status and user options. Across the bottom of the Gopher menu screen runs a list of three basic commands:

- Entering "?" for help produces a list of Gopher commands and their results.
- Typing "u" moves the user up one level on the Gopher menu hierarchy.
- A "q" starts a dialog asking whether you really want to quit Gopher. (A capital "Q" quits without question.)

If you select a file from the menu, that file displays on your terminal one screen at a time. Across the bottom of the screen, a message reports what percentage of the file has been viewed. When all the file has been viewed, the last line on screen reminds you that pressing "D" starts a dialog that allows the selected file to be downloaded to the your personal computer.

A list of common Gopher commands is given in Figure 7-5. Gopher is case sensitive. If you are looking at a menu comprised of your bookmarks and you want to download a file you are pointing at, you would enter an upper case "D." However, if you enter a lower case "d" while you are pointing at a bookmark, you delete the bookmark. Another point worth noting about Gopher commands is that commands for moving around often have synonyms. To move down a screen, you could hit the Page Down key. However, if you are logged into a host system using a communications program that is command compatible with ProComm, Page Down starts the

Fig. 7-5: Internet Gopher commands are case sensitive ("D" starts a download while "d" deletes a bookmark). Four navigating actions may be invoked in multiple ways: Entering an item, exiting an item, viewing the previous page, viewing the next page.

Common Gopher Commands

Commands for moving around
Up Arrow .... : Move to previous line.
Down Arrow .... : Move to next line.
Right Arrow, Return ... : "Enter"/Display current item.
Left Arrow, u .... : "Exit" current item/Go up a level.
>, +, Pgdwn, space ..... : View next page.
<, -, Pgup, b .... : View previous page.
0-9 .... : Go to a specific line.
m .... : Go back to the main menu.
Bookmark commands
a .... : Add current item to the bookmark list.
A .... : Add current directory/search to bookmark list.
v .... : View bookmark list.
d .... : Delete a bookmark/directory entry.
Other commands
s .... : Save current item to a file.
D .... : Download a file.
q .... : Quit with prompt.
Q .... : Quit unconditionally.
= .... : Show Technical information about current item.
o .... : Open a new gopher server
O .... : Change Options
/ .... : Search for an item in the menu.
n .... : Find next search item.
^z ...... : Ends browsing of long text file.
!, $ ..... : Shell Escape (Unix) or Spawn subprocess

download process. You would want to use one of the other keys, such as the spacebar or the "+" key.

"U" for up or "b" for back?

Two actions that at first seem identical are not. These are the "u" key and the "b" key. Figure 7-1 and Figure 7-3 show the first pages of Gopher menus, which are several pages long. The bottom right hand corner of a Gopher menu screen tells you where you are in the current menu. In Figure 7-1 the whole menu is two pages (two screens) long. In Figure 7-3, the entire menu requires six screens. You could get to the second page (or subsequent pages) by pressing your Down Arrow key repeatedly. When the arrow moves below the last item on the current page, the next screen displays. A quicker way, however, is to use the Space Bar, which will take you to the next page. So will the "+" key, the ">" key, or the Page Down key (if that key is not intercepted by your communications program). This is where the "b" key becomes handy. If you are several pages into a Gopher menu, pressing the "b" key moves you back one page of the menu. Pressing "u" (up), however, takes you entirely out of your current menu and moves you up one level in the menu hierarchy.

Pressing the "=" key in Gopher brings to the screen a report that tells the networker where (what machine, in which directory) the selected item is physically located (Figure 7-6). Here is another distinction between Gopher and Telnet. When you use the Telnet protocol to access a distant computer, you are a captive of that site. With few exceptions (some large government sites especially offer gateways to other government sites), your menu choices do not connect you to computer networks other than the one you first connected to. In Gopher, however, you might start with a Root Menu

Fig. 7-6: Pressing the "=" key prompts Gopher to report the physical location of any menu item – here, Census data residing on a host Gopher at the University of Michigan.

that resides on a machine in your home town. You pick a menu choice that calls up a new menu/directory. That menu, and any number of items on it, may actually be called up from a machine in another state or even another country. In fact, it is possible that the 10 to 15 menu items on a typical Gopher directory could be located in 10 to 15 different places. You pick the menu selection by pointing the selector arrow at the piece you desire. Gopher "knows" where the requested file or directory resides and goes out and fetches it for display on your screen. Whether the requested file or directory comes from France or rests on a machine next door, you see the same dialog, the same kinds of displays. Again, pressing the "=" key will give you a report of where your menu choice really resides.

Gopher bookmarks

Because Gopher facilitates movement so easily from one menu to another and another and another and so on, it is very easy to lose track of where you are. Two Gopher features help keep track of where you are. The "=" sign already mentioned is available to anyone, even with only Telnet connections to Gopher.

Assume for a minute that you connected to Gopher by Telnet to **consultant.micro.umn.edu** or some other Telnet host. Browsing, you moved down through a series of menus until you happened onto a menu full of the very crime statistics you need. You suspect from signatures on some of the files that they are updated regularly, and you would like to get back to where you are, but you have not kept thorough notes. You could point at a file or a menu, press the "=" sign, and write down the host address and the path information provided. (See Chapter 6 for path shorthand.) The next time you want to get to your precious crime statistics you start by connecting to your usual Gopher. Once connected, you press "o" and type in the host address you recorded from the earlier dialog. That at least will get you to the right host, and with luck (or good path notes) you will again find the files you seek.

There is even a more graceful way of keeping track of where you are in Gopherspace. If the machine you use as your connection to the Internet houses a Gopher client, you may employ Gopher bookmarks. Placing bookmarks in Gopherspace is very easy. If you want to mark an item on a Gopher menu, just move the arrow selector to the item and press the letter "a" (lower case). A dialog box pops onto your screen highlighting a suggested name for the bookmark. This is the name that will appear on your bookmark menu when you recall your bookmarks. If you want to return to the menu now on your screen, you press "A" (upper case) and you will get the same kind of dialog box. If you accept the suggested name, you just hit the Enter key, and the bookmark is recorded. Otherwise, you may type in a name to suit your taste. The display given when you press "=" (Figure 7-6) is actually the information stored in your bookmark.

To recall your bookmarks, you press the "v" (for view) key. Gopher displays your list of bookmarks in menu format, replacing whatever menu was on the screen with your bookmark list. Again, just point your selector at the menu item (or type in its number), and hit the Enter key (or Right Arrow key) to call the item to your screen.

Dealing with network gridlock

Because the volume of Internet traffic has exploded since 1992, It is common to find more popular network sites more in demand than the existing network structure can manage. If you try to connect to a site where there is already too much traffic, you are likely to get one of three kinds of messages. The friendlier, more enlightening messages (less common) tell you something like "there are already too many people connected to 123.456.78" The second kind of message simply says something like "unable to connect to 123.456.78." Another common occurrence is that your computer screen just sits for several minutes with a message like "trying to connect" or "retrieving directory" and finally comes back with a message about being unable to connect because the connection process "timed out."

A journalist confronted with any of these situations – especially on deadline – might adopt the following strategy:

1. Try going to an alternative site for the same information. If you can choose an alternative from the same menu, do so. If you have to go to another Gopher or perhaps a Telnet site taken from Appendix C, do so.
2. If you got the message when you selected a menu item from Gopher, you might try asking Gopher for the address of the site (pressing the "=" key) and then connecting there directly from your system prompt if possible.
3. If the site is accessible by another method (Telnet, modem), try that method.
4. Just try again in a few minutes.

Viewing and capturing files with Gopher

If the Gopher selector arrow is pointed at a menu item that is a file (and not a directory or a search program for example), striking the Enter key tells Gopher to get the file and to display it on the screen. It does this one screen full (25 lines) at a time, reporting how much of the file has been displayed (e.g., 48 percent). You page down through the file a page at a time by hitting the Page Down key, the space bar or the "+" key. If you hit the Enter key, you scroll down one line at a time. If you have a large text file, and you want to get directly to the end of it, press Ctrl-Z.

At the end of the file, Gopher prompts you for some action. You are told that if you hit Return you will continue. This means you will be taken back to the menu from which you chose the current item. Your other choices include "m" to mail the document to someone, "D" to download the file, "s" to save it, and "p" to print it. If you use the mail option, you are prompted for an e-mail address. If you enter your own, the document is returned to you (in just a few minutes, generally) as e-mail. The download (capital D) command presumes you are accessing the network through a modem. Pressing "D" starts a dialog that asks you for the downloading protocol. If you have Zmodem protocol in your communications software, Gopher has the ability to start a dialog with your computer and automatically download; you need take no further action. If you select "s," Gopher will attempt to save the file on the computer where the Gopher client resides unless you reached the client by Telnet. A request to print the document "spools" the file out to the client. It may wind up just taking up disk space. Generally, you are better off not selecting the print option unless your systems people give you specific instructions on how to use it.

You have another option for seizing Gopher text. If you want to capture a text document on your computer, you may open a log file (capturing all the text that passes your screen) as we described in Chapter 6. You should open the log before you start reading the text. Mailing the file to yourself will work well, as will downloading. You may log the file, download it, save it, or mail it to yourself. Take the option which is most suitable to your circumstances.

Searching Gopherspace by group

When we wanted information on the Northridge earthquake, we went first to a Gopher server whose sole purpose on the Internet is to provide access to information on geological phenomena, among them earthquakes. Of the thousands of gopher sites on the network, a good many have some primary topic focus. People who set up Gopher sites often have a special interest in some topic; the information available through the gopher they establish reflects that interest. We probably first found out about the Oklahoma Geological Survey Observatory Gopher from some other source on the net. We tried the site, and logged its address into our notes as a good source for science and technology information. You have the benefit of our notes in Appendix C. In the meantime, you might want to try visiting some of the following Gopher holes, as Gopher servers are often called.

1. **peg.cwis.uci.edu.** From the root menu choose gopher.welcome/ peg/. This is a rich resource on politics and government, which includes, among other things, a searchable Congressional Directory.
2. **Niord.SHSU.edu.** This Gopher houses or is a gateway to a wide range of financial and economic data sources.

3. **gopher.tamu.edu.** From the root directory choose .dir/ freenet.dir. This provides Telnet windows to about 20 different FreeNet sites in the United States and Canada.

4. **gopher.rtpnc.epa.gov.** This is the Environmental Protection Agency's Gopher providing proposed rules, notifications, a library, and a window to other environmental sources on the Internet.

5. **igc.apc.org** will connect you to the Institute for Global Communication's Gopher, which includes material on environmental issues, labor and peace interests.

6. **nywork1.undp.org** is a United Nations Gopher.

7. **cwis.usc.edu** / Other Gophers/ Gopher-Jewels/ contains a live version of the topic-oriented Gopher Jewels document.

8. **gopher.austin.unimelb.edu.au** has online the world's country and area telephone codes (outside the U.S. and Canada) index.

In each case, the bold type gives the Internet address of the gopher described. You gain access by any of the methods described earlier in this chapter. The specialties are described here, and at least implied by the beat designation afforded in Appendix C. However, no matter how specialized a Gopher site is, it frequently has access to a wide array of information outside its chosen area of specialty.

Searching with Veronica and Jughead

Many Gopher sites offer as a menu choice something like "Search Gopherspace using Veronica." The menu listing will usually be followed by a bracketed question mark <?> because the user must provide search parameters. Such

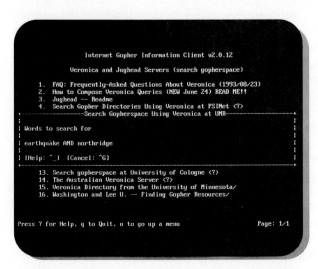

Fig. 7-7: The Veronica search dialog allows the use of Boolean logic in searches for information. Here, we have asked Veronica to find Gopher directories containing both the words Northridge AND earthquake.

Fig. 7-8: Veronica reports the results of a search by creating a Gopher menu from which you may choose any item.

a choice is offered on the Library of Congress Gopher, **marvel.loc.gov**. From the root menu choose "Internet Resources" (choice 11 at this writing) and then choose "Veronica and Jughead" (also 11 at this writing). You then will be asked to input the term(s) you want to search for. One of the strengths of Veronica is that it allows you to narrow your search using Boolean (AND, OR, NOT) logic.

Figure 7-7 displays a typical Veronica search dialog in which we have asked Veronica to find all the Gopher files and directories (wherever in the world they might be) that use both Northridge (the search is not case sensitive) AND earthquake in their names. When Veronica is done searching, she reports results of the search in Gopher menu format. That is, you are given a customized Gopher menu that looks like any other Gopher menu. It also works like any other Gopher menu. You select an item in any of the normal ways, and Gopher goes out and connects you to that site. In the first hours following the Northridge quake, the search we have entered here would have produced no findings. But as the magnitude of the quake became more clear, and more and more network resources addressed the problem of providing quake information, the results of such a search offered increasingly varied choices.

Figure 7-8 shows the results of a successful search of Gopher servers containing directories or files whose names contain both "Northridge" and "earthquake" (case insensitive) in them. Menu choices 2-5 have the appearance of being multiple occurrences of the same item. They could, however, represent Gopher directory choices with the same names but in different locations. To tell the difference, you have only to point at each item and press the "=" key to get Gopher's report on the item location. In this case, all four are the same. The reason you get duplicate listings is that Gopher administrators (the people who set up the server offerings) in four different locations elected to establish menu choices leading to the same place, a machine at the University of Minnesota. Because the same menu item occurred in multiple locations, Veronica reported once for each occurrence.

Jughead operates much the same way as Veronica. In fact, you could conduct precisely the same search with Jughead that we made in Veronica and get the same result. You would see no difference. There are, however, some subtle differences in search capabilities. At each Jughead and each Veronica site there are files describing search parameters of the respective programs. If you wish to become a Gopher guru, you will want to study each document. Most sites have short documents explaining how to do searches. Veronica has been out a little longer than Jughead and is more widely distributed.

Extending the reach and finding the limits of Gopher

We repeat the assertion made at the beginning of this chapter that of all the network tools and programs, Gopher offers the most return for your investment in time and learning energy. The Gopher menu and command structure are uniform world wide. Whole libraries of information are made easily available. Gopher administrators have grouped gateways to like information together in many instances, making it easier to find what you are looking for. Veronica and Jughead searching tools expand the finding capabilities for a journalist on the prowl for some particular kind of data.

One of the limitations to Gopher, however, is that there is a lot of information which is available on the network but may not be indexed to Gopher searching devices. There is even more information that is not stored at Gopher sites or under the Gopher umbrella. You might find pointers to some of that information if a Gopher menu happens to point to a Telnet site. But to get to the Telnet site, you must leave Gopher. And Veronica and Jughead

Fig. 7-9: The Internet Resources menu on the Library of Congress Gopher offers the user a full array of Internet searching tools: Among them Archie, Veronica, Jughead, other Gophers, Hytelnet, WAIS and World Wide Web.

won't tell you what is at the Telnet site other than what is on the Gopher menu pointing to that site.

However, many Gopher servers offer a menu choice something like "Internet Resources" or "Other Internet Resources." The Library of Congress Gopher server (marvel.loc.gov) has such a choice on its Root menu. Typically, selecting this menu choice brings up a new menu populated with several selections offering use of network tools that reach beyond the limits of Gopher. Figure 7-9 shows the Internet Resources menu from the Library of Congress Gopher. It offers access to Archie and FTP (Chapter 8), to university Campus Wide Information Systems, to Free-Net systems, Hytelnet (Chapter 6), WAIS servers (Chapter 8), to Veronica and Jughead servers. Menu choice 10 promises guides to Mail Lists (Chapter 5) and Usenet news groups (Chapter 9). By offering gateways to services that reach beyond Gopher, Gopher is enhancing its claim to be the only all-purpose, do-everything Internet navigating tool you'll ever need. It even offers a gateway to the other main claimant to the same distinction, World Wide Web.

World Wide Web: Hypertext and more

Many applaud Gopher as "the all-purpose" Internet information front end. Others commend World Wide Web as the ultimate Internet navigating tool. The Web, or WWW, as it is sometimes called, is the newest and most ambitious of the network navigating tools. As such it is very much still under construction. Different WWW clients have different looks and varying command "dialects." Web servers and public-access Web clients are not as numerous (yet) as corresponding Gopher clients and servers. The setup and management of information for a Web server is more complicated than that of a Gopher, and the way material is organized is not always friendly to deadline-bound journalists. That said, the potential of WWW is such that it has captured the attention of many who are otherwise partial to other, more traditional, network navigating and searching tools. Traffic on the Web and new Web offerings are growing rapidly, and already there is much on the Web that is worthwhile for journalists. Two things set the Web apart from other tools: graphics capabilities and information object linking.

Graphics Capabilities

One of the first things you notice when you log into many WWW sites is that some words in the menu choices appear in a different color (if you have a color monitor) and/or they are brighter than others, even with the most elementary (text-based) kinds of Internet connections and communications software. If you happen to have the right connection with the right client software, those words which appear in different colors or different brightness on your text-based screen appear not only in different colors (if you have color) but in different type faces and type sizes in the graphics environ-

Fig. 7-10: Graphical World Wide Web browsers such as Cello put a rather seductive look on Internet information servers. This is a portion of the Home Page of the U.S. Bureau of the Census World Wide Web server.

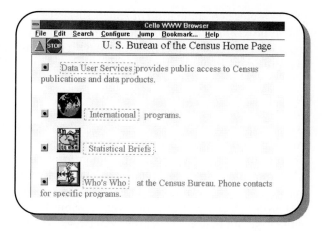

ment. Those words or expressions may be underlined or boxed. The text can even appear in a different text layout on your graphics-based terminal.

Furthermore, photographs, line drawings, and other art may accompany the text. In this respect, the Web can be sometimes more seductive than productive. It is easy to gape at all the exciting visual things that come your way and to forget what you are looking for on the network. Figure 7-10 shows the WWW "Home Page" for the U.S. Census Bureau Web server as it is seen using a graphics client called Cello. A Web Home Page is much like the Root menu of a Gopher server. It is the entry point for using that information source. Make selections from a Gopher menu and you get "taken" to another menu or a text document or an information-searching program dialog. When you view WWW documents, you select words or terms that are highlighted. Your selection opens a new document, which in turn may have other selection possibilities. The processes are similar, but underlying the process are different ways of organizing information. Other aspects of WWW bear comparison to Gopher. Some Web clients allow you to place bookmarks. Also, many of the commands used by the Lynx client (see Figure 7-11) are identical to Gopher commands. While many Gopher servers offer gateways to other Internet resources, so do many Web servers. Both programs are vying for position as the only tool you'll ever need for Internet navigating.

Information linking

Other network tools – Gopher, mail, and FTP among them – are capable of delivering text files as well as binary files, which might contain digital photos or other art, or even sound bites. In a World Wide Web document, all of those separate pieces of information – the text, the photo, and the sound – are linked by computer. They appear on screen and are sounded for you to experience when you select them from a WWW document. You might be writing a piece on some kind of space mission and want background on the shuttle program. You tie into a WWW document that describes the Challenger disaster, and it comes complete with photo images and a sound clip of then President Reagan. It is possible you logged into a Web site in New York that found the text file in Florida linked to image files in the National Archives in Washington, D.C., and sound files at the University of Southern California. They all appeared together at your computer through links, in a process commonly called "hypermedia." When text documents contain words linked to other text documents, the term hypertext is often used. Hytelnet (Chapter 6) uses an hypertext implementation for its network front end.

The scenario described above is technologically feasible at the writing of this book. In fact, journalist Adam Gaffin described in the January-February 1994 issue of *Internet World* "touring" the Smithsonian online. And announcements went out in March over many network venues that a new WWW server was online in Taiwan that delivered both audio and visual images along with text. Though the technology exists in 1994, we suspect it will be a few years before both the advanced capabilities and the kinds of network connections required to drive those capabilities are widely available. In the meantime, we will focus our discussion on the lowest common denominator – text-based, publicly available clients. As we found with Gopher, you will have capabilities if you have a local client that you won't have if you have to Telnet to use a public client. One of these capabilities, like Gopher, is that of placing bookmarks. Additionally, some Web clients publicly accessed through Telnet have "jump" capabilities turned off. This means that if you have a specific Internet address you want to go to, you will be unable to tell the client to take you there. A local client is better. You will want to ask your host people if your host site has a WWW client, and if so, how it is launched. If you can't get answers quickly enough, you might experiment. After you have logged in, from your system prompt, type one of the following commands: 1) "www" 2) "lynx" or 3) "w3" followed by a carriage return (Enter). If you get an error message at each try, chances are you will have to use Telnet to "walk" the World Wide Web.

Finding a WWW browser

World Wide Web clients are called "browsers" because their basic function on a text level is to help you read and move through a hypertext document. Let's start walking the Web.

If you have no local client, you may launch one by using Telnet to get to the home of the World Wide Web in Switzerland:

telnet info.cern.ch <CR>

which will return to you a menu (Figure 7-12) that looks more like a text file than a menu. That really is the idea of hypertext. The user sees a text

Fig. 7-11: The publicly accessible WWW browser at info.cern.ch tells visitors in its opening screen that Telnet (text only) servers "are very primitive."

```
                                          Welcome to the World-Wide Web
                    THE WORLD-WIDE WEB

This is just one of many access points to the web, the universe of
information available over networks. To follow references, just type the
number then hit the return (enter) key.

The features you have by connecting to this telnet server are very primitive
compared to the features you have when you run a W3 "client" program on your
own computer. If you possibly can, please pick up a client for your platform
to reduce the load on this service and  experience the web in its full
splendor.

For more information, select by number:

A list of available W3 client programs[1]
Everything about the W3 project[2]
Places to start exploring[3]
The First International WWW Conference[4]

This telnet service is provided by the WWW team at the European Particle
Physics Laboratory known as CERN[5]
      [End]
1-5, Up, Quit, or Help:
```

document that has certain words (or numbers) highlighted. You select the word (number) of your choosing by moving your cursor to the linked word or by typing the number associated with the word. The Web client responds by giving you a new text file linked to that word. The new document in turn may have highlighted or "linked" words. In the public access CERN WWW browser, numbers are used as the jump-off points, and you may type a number to select an item rather than moving the cursor to the number before selecting. Another public access WWW client that uses a numbering system is accessible at **www.njit.edu**, log-in: www. The NJIT client presents you with a screen divided into three sections including a document window, a commands section and a title line. NJIT's opening screen looks more like a menu because it has many choices laid out in table format. The basic command structure at NJIT more closely resembles that of Gopher or the Web client at University of Kansas (Figure 7-11). The Kansas public WWW client is Telnet accessible at **www.cc.ukans.edu**, log-in: www.

Other public access Web clients reachable by Telnet include **sunsite.unc.edu**, log-in: www; **www.law.cornell.edu**, log-in: www; **millbrook.lib.rmit.edu.au**; log-in: lynx; **info.rutgers.edu**, no log-in; **lanka.ccit.arizona.edu**, log-in: www. Unlike Gopher servers, which present pretty much the same face all around the world, each WWW client is pretty much its own individual. At the University of Arizona (lanka.ccit.arizona.edu), the Home Page welcome screen has all the appearance of a Telnet menuing system. As of this writing, the only apparent access to the rest of the world from the Arizona Web client is through Hytelnet and Gopher. Even though each Web access client has its own personality, several use the same client software. Rutgers (info.rutgers.edu), Millbrook (millbrook.lib.rmit.edu.au), and Kansas (www.cc.ukans.edu) use a text-based Web client called Lynx. The command structures for Lynx and for CERN's public browser are displayed in Figure 7-11.

Navigating (walking) the World Wide Web

Once you launch a Web client, you are taken to the top of the Home Page of the Web server at the client's home site. Text-based Home Pages such as that

---

Fig. 7-12: The command structure for two different World Wide Web clients shows a big difference in the program. The Lynx client responds to commands very much like Gopher.

WWW Commands from CERN

Top	Return to the first page of the document.
Up	Move up one page within the document
List	List the references from this document.
* <number>	Select a referenced document by number (from 1 to 4).
Recall	List visited documents.
Recall <number>	Return to a previously visited document as numbered in the recall list.
HOme	Return to the starting document.
Back	Move back to the last document.
Next	Take next link from last document.
Previous	Take previous link from last document.
REFresh	Refresh screen with current document
Go <address>	Go to document of given [relative] address
Verbose	Switch to verbose mode.
Help	Display this page.

WWW Commands from University of Kansas (Lynx)

MOVEMENT:	Down arrow	- Highlight next topic
	Up arrow	- Highlight previous topic
	Right arrow, Return, Enter	- Jump to highlighted topic
	Left arrow	- Return to previous topic
SCROLLING:	+ (or space)	- Scroll down to next page
	- (or b)	- Scroll up to previous page
OTHER:	? (or H)	- Help (this screen)
	a	- Add the current link to your bookmark file
	c	- Send a comment to the document owner
	d	- Download the current link
	e	- Edit the current file
	g	- Goto a user specified URL or file.
	i	- Show an index of documents
	m	- Return to main screen
	o	- Set your options
	p	- Print to a file, mail, printers, or other
	q	- Quit (Capital 'Q' for quick quit)
	/	- Search for a string within the current document
	s	- Enter a search string for an external search.
	n	- Go to the next search string
	v	- View your bookmark file
	z	- Cancel transfer in progress
	[backspace]	- Go to the history page
	=	- Show file and link info
	\	- Toggle document source/rendered view
	!	- Spawn your default shell
	CTRL-R	- Reload current file and refresh the screen
	CTRL-W	- Refresh the screen
	CTRL-U	- Erase input line
	CTRL-G	- Cancel input or transfer

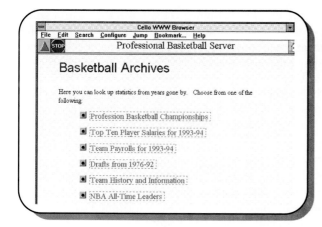

Fig. 7-13: The Sports Information Server at MIT offers latest NBA scores, schedules, as well as an archive of basketball statistics.

at Rutgers University will have some text highlighted. Highlighted words indicate words for which there are links. Cursor movement in a Lynx browser (client) is governed by Up and Down Arrow keys the same as it is in Gopher. As in Gopher, you select an item of interest in one of two ways: 1) move the cursor to the linked word and hit Enter (or Right Arrow) 2) type the number of highlighted word (if the Web site displays numbers) and hit Enter. That will then call up a document to which the highlighted word is linked. You may find another word or concept to follow in the new document, select it, and so on. The World Wide Web folks call this "browsing" or "walking" the Web. Again, it's wise to take notes on your pathway though the Web so that you can find your way back again. If you have a local client, you can always place bookmarks. If you are using Lynx, you can back up a page with the "b" or "-" keys (Gopher-compatible commands).

In Gopher, you have the option of "pointing" your Gopher to another Gopher site by typing "o" and then giving the Internet address of the Gopher server with which you wish to connect. On the World Wide Web (using Lynx), you type "g" and then the Universal Resource Locator (URL) of the object you want. Assuming you are logged into a Web client now, type "g" (generally you do not have to hit the Enter key). The client then asks for the URL you want. Type

http://riskweb.bus.utexas.edu/finweb.htm <CR>

and you will be taken to a Web server at the University of Texas to a location where a collection of financial documents reside. In Web parlance, you "jump" when you tell your client to fetch a particular document using a URL.

Let's try another jump. Interested in all the statistics on your favorite NBA team or player or the order of the NBA draft in 1992? Then jump (type "g" first) to

http://www.mit.edu:8001/services/sis/sports.html <CR>

where all those statistics are available. Figure 7-13 shows the Sports Information Server NBA choices as shown in the graphics WWW browser, Cello.

In each case, we jumped to a new site using URLs. Some WWW browsers (Cello for example) permit you to use URLs to read or download files at FTP (Chapter 8) sites, at Gopher servers, or at Telnet locations. The syntax of the URL is simple. The "word" to the left of the double slash tells the Web client what network protocol to use. That word is always followed by a colon. Thus "http:" indicates a WWW server. "Gopher:" would denote a Gopher server, "ftp:" an FTP site, and so forth. To the right of the double slash (//) is the Internet address, including relevant port information, for the machine housing the data. What then follows is the complete path (names of all the subdirectories between single slash marks) to get to the document. At the end of the URL is the name of the document (directory, Home Page) sought. Frequently it will be in the format of *name.extension*.

Some other interesting Web places to go include:

http://www.census.gov/	U.S. Bureau of the Census
http://www.ed.gov/	U.S. Department of Education
http://ds.internic.net/	InterNIC Directory & Database Service
http://cui_www.unige.ch/w3catalog/	A Web searching device like Veronica; when you get connected, hit "s" to start a search.

Two other Web searching engines are the WebCrawler at

http://www.biotech.washington.edu/WebCrawler/WebQuery.html

and the WWW Worm at

http://www.cs.colorado.edu/home/mcbryan/WWWW.html

The current edition of the World Wide Web FAQ is at

http://sunsite.unc.edu/boutell/faq/www_faq.html[1]

In parting, strengths and weaknesses of the Web

Computers – through programs like Telnet – make it possible for journalists to be two places at once. You sit at your desk in Ames, Iowa, while you browse through the National Archives in Washington D.C. and then you zip in just seconds to the Earthquake Gopher at the University of California. Hypertext, in one sense, allows one document to be in many places at once. In another sense, hypertext allows one document to "incorporate" many other documents scattered anywhere along a network. Online documents can be "virtually" several places at once. Contrast this to a book or report done by the Environmental Protection Agency. The EPA document reports on health risks to people who eat oysters taken from coastal areas subject to pollutants created by processes used in electroplating.

In a traditional library that document may sit on a shelf in only one place. Does it get filed under environmental concerns, government documents, medical/health reports, electronics, metallurgy, or maybe industrial pollution. Hypertext allows such a document to physically reside on one computer but through computer linking to be "incorporated" within or "annexed" to or accessed by other documents. Thus the report resides in the electronic library in multiple locations at once. Information at World Wide Web sites, is, as the name implies, "webbed" together with other information in a worldwide network. Theoretically, this webbing should give the network browser a better chance of finding any given document because that document can be approached from many directions.

Other strengths of the Web include its enthusiastic following and its graphical awareness for those who can take advantage of it (this will attract many new users). The ability of Web clients to use bookmarks and to use URLs for accessing information across many platforms strongly recommends Web software. Finally, many Web sites offer gateways to other Internet resources such as Gopher and Hytelnet, WAIS and Archie.

On the down side, World Wide Web browsers like Cello and Mosaic are the newest of the network tools, and like many other things on the Information Highway, many components are under construction; they don't always work as you expect them to. The number of sites with Web servers is limited, but growing rapidly. From a journalist's point of view, the organization of Web resources is sometimes obscure, not really connected well to some beats. But rapid expansion, especially in 1994, suggests the Web of the future may be a dynamic tool for journalists.

As we have used the network navigators Hytelnet, Gopher, and World Wide Web, we have run repeatedly into references to Archie, FTP, and WAIS. They will round out our stable of Internet tools in Chapter 8.

Further reading

An excellent all around Internet resource book is

> Paul Gilster. *The Internet Navigator*, New York: John Wiley & Sons, 1993.

Chapter **8**

Finding & fetching files

In Chapter 7, we used Veronica and Jughead to find information stored on Gopher servers. New tools are making key word searches feasible on the World Wide Web. That is fine if what you are looking for happens to reside on a Web or a Gopher server. Many resources are not so located, and if your aim is to do a thorough search, three more Internet tools are widely available: Archie, FTP, and WAIS. FTP (file transfer protocol) is used to go out and fetch the files that Archie finds, while WAIS does both the finding and the fetching. None of these programs has an especially user-friendly face. They are, however, fairly straightforward and easy to use.

In this chapter, you will learn how to

- find files and directories using Archie.
- fetch ASCII and binary files using FTP.
- conduct WAIS searches and use WAIS to retrieve the results.

What Archie finds, FTP fetches

Archie and FTP go together. Like his comic book cousins Veronica and Jughead, Archie is a network detective. Archie scours a constantly updated index of data bases and archives for any "hits" on key words you provide. What Archie comes back with is a list of directories and files whose names contain the word you have given. The listing of those files and directories is organized by host site (Figure 8-3). Below the name of each host site is a list of the directories and files whose names match your query. Archie tells you if the matching object is a file or a directory and then reports full path information for getting to the directory or retrieving the file by FTP.

If your host does not have an Archie client and you do not have one on your machine, you have two options for accessing a public Archie client. You could access Archie clients by using one of the network navigating tools: Hytelnet (Chapter 6), Gopher (Chapter 7), or World Wide Web (Chapter 7). At a general Gopher site or Hytelnet site, Archie access is generally found under an Internet Resources menu. The advantage of using Gopher is that you may not have to start a separate FTP session to fetch a file if you find one you would like. Some WWW clients also permit this. You also could use Telnet to connect to an Archie client. Some examples include: **archie.ans.net** (Advanced Network Services in Michigan); **archie.unl.edu** (University of Nebraska, Lincoln), log-in: archie (hit Return at password); **archie.doc.ic.ac.uk** (United Kingdom); **archie.sura.net** (a consortium of Southern universities); **quiche.cs.mcgill.ca** (McGill University in Montreal, the home of Archie). In all cases, the log-in word is "archie." Figure 8-1 lists addresses of Archie clients around the world. You should always use the client nearest you.

When you launch Archie at a remote site, you are given a brief message that tells you the default settings for searches at the site to which you are connected. You must take note of these settings; they determine whether Archie's search is case sensitive and whether Archie looks for whole words or reports a match when your search string shows up anywhere. This setting will impact heavily on the results of your search. Figure 8-2 reports that default search parameters are set at "sub," which means that the search is case insensitive and that anywhere Archie finds a match – whole word or partial – a match will be reported. This generally is the best kind of search for what journalists seek. We asked Archie to report to us the names and locations of files and directories containing the string "earthquake." We don't know ahead of time whether the name of a file is upper case or lower case; nor do we care, so long as it has useful information in the file. If Archie were looking only for whole word hits, it would not report back to us such files as "la-earthquake" or "earthquake.list".

Public Archie Clients

archie.unl.edu	USA (Nebraska)
archie.internic.net	USA (New Jersey)
archie.rutgers.edu	USA (New Jersey)
archie.ans.net	USA (New York)
archie.sura.net	USA (Maryland)
archie.doc.ic.ac.uk	United Kingdom
archie.edvz.uni-linz.ac.at	Austria
archie.univie.ac.at	Austria
archie.funet.fi	Finland
archie.th-darmstadt.de	Germany
archie.rediris.es	Spain
archie.luth.se	Sweden
archie.switch.ch	Switzerland
archie.unipi.it	Italy
archie.au	Australia
archie.uqam.ca	Canada
archie.ac.il	Israel
archie.wide.ad.jp	Japan
archie.kr	Korea
archie.sogang.ac.kr	Korea

Fig. 8-1: Addresses of publicly accessible Archie clients.

Other Archie search settings include *exact, regex,* and *subcase. Exact* will report only exact matches (same case, whole word). *Subcase* looks for matches in terms of case, but does not require whole word matches. *Regex* sets the search to look for strings in UNIX terms. If Archie tells you that the search type is anything but "sub" you may want to change the setting. You do that by typing the command

set search sub <CR>

Starting an Archie search

Once your search is set to "sub," the way that you launch an Archie search is by typing the word "prog" or the word "find" followed by a space and the string of characters you want to find. Hitting the Enter key starts the search. Figure 8-2 shows that we typed "prog earthquake." On the occasion we did so, the Archie server at Nebraska reported to us that 21 search requests were in line ahead of us: "Your queue position: 22." Then it estimated our wait in line at 17 minutes, 55 seconds. That is a long time, and indicative of heavy traffic at the UNL site. You may not want to wait that long. Or, if your computer can run communications programs in the background (Windows, Macintosh System 7, OS/2, Desqview all do this; see Chapter 3), you could send the Archie search to the background and work on something else, checking occasionally on the progress of the search. Your other options include taking a coffee break, opening your mail, or aborting the search and seeking another Archie server. If you are in a hurry, close to a deadline, finding files by Archie, retrieving by FTP, and then viewing the files may not be a wise strategy.

When Archie has completed the search, you get a list of files and directories matching your search terms. Figure 8-3 displays partial results of our

Fig. 8-2: The Archie startup dialog at University of Nebraska, Lincoln, reports default search settings. When you start your search, you are told your place in line and given a time estimate for your search.

```
Host stubbs.ucop.edu    (128.48.188.25)
Last updated 14:38 10 Mar 1994

    Location: /pub/dlabulletin/issue28
       FILE    -rw-rw-r--    7778 bytes  15:20 15 Feb 1994  earthquake.txt

Host calypso-2.oit.unc.edu    (198.86.40.81)
Last updated 15:02 10 Mar 1994

    Location: /pub/academic/communications/logs
       DIRECTORY    drwxr-xr-x    512 bytes  07:51 19 Jan 1994  94-earthquake

    Location: /pub/academic/communications/logs/.cap
       FILE    -rw-r--r--    75 bytes  12:03 24 Feb 1994  94-earthquake

    Location: /pub/academic/political-science/whitehouse-papers/1994/Feb
       FILE    -rw-r--r--    4976 bytes  22:13  1 Feb 1994  1994-02-01-President-
       FILE    -rw-r--r--    16560 bytes 21:44 27 Feb 1994  1994-02-23-President-

    Location: /pub/academic/political-science/whitehouse-papers/1994/Jan
       FILE    -rw-r--r--    7266 bytes  00:50 18 Jan 1994  1993-01-17-Presidents
       FILE    -rw-r--r--    16624 bytes 00:49 18 Jan 1994  1993-01-17-Press-Brie
       FILE    -rw-r--r--    1604 bytes  23:35 20 Jan 1994  1994-01-20-President-
       FILE    -rw-r--r--    838 bytes   16:55 24 Jan 1994  1994-01-24-Earthquake
       FILE    -rw-r--r--    17894 bytes 20:11 24 Jan 1994  1994-01-24-Earthquake
```

Fig. 8-3: When Archie completes your search, you get a report with files and directories grouped by host site. Our search on "earthquake" was several screens full, ending with these two sites.

search on "earthquake." The format of the report is in a three-tiered hanging indent. The first tier (all the way to the left of the screen) reports the anonymous FTP host site. Figure 8-3 shows two: "stubbs.ucop.edu" and "calypso-2.oit.unc.edu". In each case, the IP address (all numbers) of each site is also reported, and Archie tells you on the second line of the top tier the last date Archie updated its index on the site.

The second tier reports the "Location", which actually is the directory path leading to the object that registered the hit. In Figure 8-3, the top hit is at stubbs.ucop.edu. The location entry reads "/pub/dlabulletin/issue28". What this means is that on the computer at stubbs.ucop.edu there is first of all a directory called "pub". This is standard designation for a directory accessible to the public. Within the "pub" directory is another directory devoted to the "dlabulletin". And finally, within that directory is another directory called "issue28", which is where the file in question resides. This directory path is very much like the hierarchical menu structure we have already seen in Gopher and at some Telnet sites.

The third and final tier describes the object itself. In the case of the stubbs site, only one object was found, a file called "earthquake.txt." The name in this case tips you off that the file is a text file because it ends in ".txt," a standard designation for such files. Archie reports the size of the file (7,778 bytes), as well as the time (15:20 or 3:20 p.m.) and date (15 Feb. 1994) it was last revised. The time and date information can be of help if you are looking for information on a particular event. The size information will give you a sense of whether you're looking at a novel-length document or a one-page backgrounder.

As the Archie report results scroll past your screen, you can stop the scrolling by typing Ctrl-S. Once stopped, you start the scroll again with Ctrl-Q. If your communications program permits, you can of course create a log file and capture the Archie report as it passes. You also have the option of mailing the results to yourself. At the end of the search, you remain in the Archie program and have the option of issuing a number of commands. To mail the results of your search, you type

mail username@host.domain

where you would substitute your e-mail address for the string "username@host.domain."

When you are done with Archie, you type "q" for quit. Generally you will be released back to your host. The "qarchie" server at archie.sura.net (log-in: qarchie) accepts an abbreviated set of commands and does not drop you immediately back to your host.

Help, in Archie, is accessed by typing "help" just as it is in many of the Internet programs. When you ask for help, you are given a set of help topics upon which you may get further information. If you want to see a full set of Archie commands and what they do, you give Archie the command

manpage <CR>

and you will see an Archie manual which is about 20 typewritten pages long.

While journalists are generally more interested in finding text files on the Internet than they are in finding software, Archie and FTP are uniquely suited to finding and retrieving software archived at FTP sites around the world. Sometimes that software can be useful for developing stories. One of the mail lists at which journalists gather announced a program that calculates league standings and games behind leader for baseball clubs based on their won-loss records. The announcement said it was available over the net. Especially for the network newcomer it is not always easy to tell whether a file is a text file or a binary (program) file. Some naming conventions – discussed under FTP – provide clues. The Archie "whatis" command can also provide information about files. If you type

whatis baseball <CR>

for example, "whatis" searches the Archie Software Description Data Base for the string "baseball," ignoring case. In the data base are names and short descriptions of many software packages, documents, and data files on the Internet. When Archie finds a match, it will report proper file names and their descriptions. A "prog" or "find" search on the file names will then tell you where to get the files. That is a job for FTP.

Moving files with FTP (File Transfer Protocol)

You may have done a search using Archie and come up with a list of files that appear relevant to your story or your software needs. Or somebody may have given you a tip that there is some really hot information on a breakthrough in AIDS research. The information, you find, is stored not at a Gopher site nor a Telnet location, but it is available by "Anonymous FTP."

FTP stands for file transfer protocol. It's a name given by computer programmers to a series of conventions that enables one kind of computer operating under its own set of rules to send/receive files to/from another kind of computer operating under another set of rules. Thus a UNIX machine connected over a network passing through a VAX machine running VMS can exchange files with an IBM mainframe operating under still another set of rules and then pass the file on to your Macintosh/PC. Anonymous FTP is standard procedure for gaining entry to computer archives made available to the public. You log in as "anonymous." You are anything but anonymous, however. You input your e-mail address as your password. And for that matter, the FTP site doesn't really have to ask for your address; it knows already where the log-in request originated.

FTP is perhaps the least friendly of all the Internet protocols. It is "strictly business" and assumes you know the rules. Fortunately, there are only a few simple rules to learn. Those rules govern 1) connecting to and disconnecting from FTP sites, 2) getting and reading directories, 3) moving between directories, and 4) retrieving files with the proper protocol.

Making the FTP connection

FTP connections are made exactly the same way Telnet connections are. You know the address of a site that has a file you want. Assuming you have FTP

Fig. 8-4: The more commonly used FTP commands help you move through the remote server directory structure, get directory reports and retrieve files. Commands that turn features on, such as "hash," "bell," and "interactive," can be turned off by issuing the same command with "no" added to the front of the word. For example, "nobell" turns off the bell that sounds at completion of file transfer.

Basic FTP Commands

Command	Description
abort	Terminate current operation
ascii	Set file transfer mode to ascii
bget	Retrieve a file in binary mode
bput	Send a file in binary mode
bell	Ring bell when file transfer completes
binary	Set file transfer mode to binary
bye	Close the connection and exit
case	Toggle mapping of local filenames to lower case
cd	Change current working directory on remote host
cdup	Change working directory on remote host to parent directory; synonym = cd ..
dir	Display contents of a directory in long form
dis	Close the connection
get	Retrieve a file from remote host
hash	Print # for each packet sent or received
help	Display help messages for all ftp commands
interactive	Prompt with each filename for mget, mput and mdelete commands
ls	Display contents of a directory in short form
mget	Retrieve a group of files from the remote host
open	Open a connection to a remote host
put	Transfer a file from local host to the remote host
pwd	Print remote host's current working directory
quiet	Do not display transfer statistics
remotehelp	Display list of FTP commands implemented by the server
stat	Display contents of a directory in short form
show	Show current status
verbose	Display server replies & transfer stats

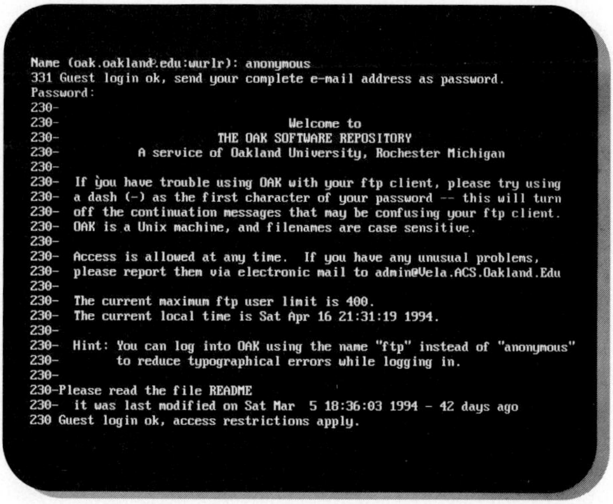

Fig. 8-5: The Oak
Software Depository
FTP site greets you
with one of the more
friendly messages for
all remote log-ins. It
helps you log in and
provides hints for
dealing with common
problems.

```
Name (oak.oakland.edu:wurlr): anonymous
331 Guest login ok, send your complete e-mail address as password.
Password:
230-
230-                              Welcome to
230-                      THE OAK SOFTWARE REPOSITORY
230-               A service of Oakland University, Rochester Michigan
230-
230-  If you have trouble using OAK with your ftp client, please try using
230-  a dash (-) as the first character of your password -- this will turn
230-  off the continuation messages that may be confusing your ftp client.
230-  OAK is a Unix machine, and filenames are case sensitive.
230-
230-  Access is allowed at any time.  If you have any unusual problems,
230-  please report them via electronic mail to admin@Vela.ACS.Oakland.Edu
230-
230-  The current maximum ftp user limit is 400.
230-  The current local time is Sat Apr 16 21:31:19 1994.
230-
230-  Hint: You can log into OAK using the name "ftp" instead of "anonymous"
230-        to reduce typographical errors while logging in.
230-
230-Please read the file README
230-  it was last modified on Sat Mar  5 18:36:03 1994 - 42 days ago
230 Guest login ok, access restrictions apply.
```

client software at your host, you could make your FTP connection in one
motion by typing

ftp oak.oakland.edu <CR>

to connect to the site of Oakland University software repository in Roches-
ter, Michigan. As an alternative, you can launch the FTP client first and
then from its prompt (typically "ftp>"), type

open oak.oakland.edu <CR>

and get the same results. In either case you are greeted by the dialog shown
in Figure 8-5. At the log-in prompt you type "anonymous", and when you are
asked for the password, you enter your complete e-mail address. This process of logging in with the username "anonymous" and your e-mail address
as your password is known as *Anonymous FTP*.

Anonymous FTP is the way to get the text of Federal Communications
Commission rules and proposed rules, the text of Supreme Court decisions,
National Institutes of Health data files, Securities and Exchange Commission filings, and Commerce Department data. Also available by Anonymous
FTP are U.S. Navy policy and strategy documents, immigration information, NASA documents on and graphic images from space missions, and
gigabytes of software for all kinds of different computers.

Because anybody can log in using Anonymous FTP, host sites grant limited or "restricted" access to people doing so. The FTP greeting screen at
Oakland University Software Repository (Figure 8-5) – which is just about
as friendly as FTP gets – concludes with the line "Guest login ok, access
restrictions apply." If you have an account with the host site, you would give
your assigned username and chosen password. You then presumably would
have more liberal access than people logging in anonymously. In either case,
each site is limited in the number of persons who can log in at one time.

Fig. 8-6: The FTP "dir" command produces a detailed directory. At the far left is a listing of descriptors that tell you whether the object is a file or a directory. At the far right is the object's name.

Again, the Oakland University site greeting screen says that its limit is 400 users. Other sites handle considerably fewer.

You should try logging in to the Oakland University FTP server using one of the command sequences above. Once you are logged in you are staring at a command line prompt (here an asterisk) with no menu. Typing the command

   dir <CR>

produces a detailed directory. Figure 8-6 shows the results of asking for a directory immediately after logging into the Oakland University FTP site anonymously. FTP reports back that the "PORT" command was successful, that an ASCII (text) "file" is being opened (the file is actually the directory), and that the transfer of information from the distant server to your local host is complete. Before displaying the list of files and directories, FTP reports that there are 10 files and directories.

The first two listed in Figure 8-6 are files including a README file, which you are encouraged to read. The remaining objects listed are all directories. You know this because the first two characters in the 10-character string at the left of the lines describing those items are "dr". The leftmost characters on the line describing the README file are "-r". Near the end of the directory in Figure 8-6 are two directories labeled "pub" and "pub2." These are standard designations for publicly accessible directories. You change to the pub directory by using the "cd" (for change directory) command:

   cd pub <CR>

being very careful to observe differences in upper- and lower-case letters because many FTP sites are case sensitive. FTP will report back to you

Fig. 8-7: The FTP "ls" command produces an abbreviated directory. The names of files and directories are all that are reported, and there is no sure way to tell which is which. This "ls" report describes the same directory as Fig. 8-6.

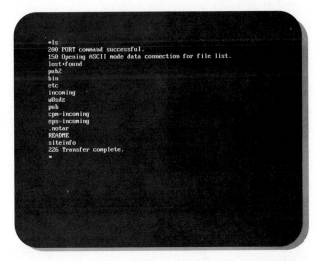

```
*ls
200 PORT command successful.
150 Opening ASCII mode data connection for file list.
lost+found
pub2
bin
etc
incoming
w8sdz
pub
cpm-incoming
eps-incoming
.notar
README
siteinfo
226 Transfer complete.
*
```

that the PORT command was successful if you typed it properly. Below the "pub" directory are several other directories occupied by still other directories in a hierarchical fashion. At the Oakland University software repository, software for Macintosh computers, CP/M machines, UNIX, and other computers is actually kept under the "pub2" directory. But if you have entered the "dir" command from within the "pub" directory, you will see several entries with names like "macintosh", "cpm", and "unix-c" that have descriptions a little different from the ones we saw in the root directory. The entry taking us to Macintosh files is

lrwxr-xr-x 1 root   oak 17 Feb 16 08:54 macintosh -> ../pub2/macintosh

The leftmost character is an "l" indicating neither a directory nor a file. Instead, it is a list entry placed there by the Oak site administrators, anticipating people who would instinctively go first to the "pub" directory, then look for "mac" or "macintosh" directories. The "l" indicates a listing that actually takes you to another directory hierarchy. The end of the line, "macintosh -> ../pub2/macintosh" says that if you "cd" to "macintosh" you will actually be rerouted to the "pub2" directory and then to the "macintosh" subdirectory.

We began this session by using the "dir" command to give us a list of available files and directories. A close relative of the "dir" command is "ls" for "list." The "ls" command gives you a short directory, listing only the names files and no other information about them (Figure 8-7). The "ls" command tends to give you results more quickly than the "dir" command, but you have less information reported. Consequently you don't know if an item in the list is a directory leading to files or if it is a file. Still, if all you need to know is the exact name of a file so that you can "get" or "bget" it, then "ls" does the trick.

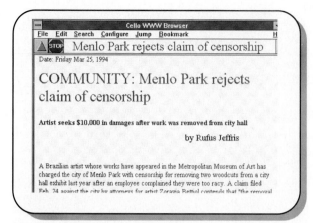

Fig. 8-8: Magazines and newspapers are now publishing electronically. The *Palo Alto Weekly*, for example, takes advantage of the graphical capabilities of World Wide Web to give its electronic "paper" a more traditional look and feel. Software to create such documents is available by FTP.

A file Getting (Bgetting) session

Usually the reason for using FTP is to retrieve a file you already know something about. FTP is not an especially friendly or efficient browsing tool. You know, for example, that the most recent set of Supreme Court rulings are at ftp.cwru.edu or that data from the National Archives are at nih.gov. If you've done an Archie search, you have full path information. So you know where you are going and what you want to do ahead of time. For an example of FTP in action, we will download a piece of software to help us publish electronically. "Html Write" will help us take ordinary computer-based text and give that text the look and feel of paper-produced magazines when our readers tap into our server.

In 1993 and 1994 many newspaper companies began offering some form of information in an electronic package. One format getting much attention is the hypertext environment supported by the World Wide Web (see Chapter 7). Graphical WWW browsers like Mosaic and Cello present online information with different size (and color) headlines, subheads, body text, and captions. Photographs and line drawings can be part of any hypertext document, giving the whole experience much more of a traditional newspaper or magazine "feel" than the text-only experience of "Videotex" ventures of the 1980s. Two publications offering online versions of their products in mid-1994 were *Palo Alto Weekly* and *Wired* magazine (see Figure 8-8). We found out by monitoring a journalism mailing list that the program "Html Write" had been placed on an FTP server at Brigham Young University late in April of 1994.

Using the same procedure described earlier, we "opened" ftp.byu.edu and moved to the "/tmp" directory. Because "Html Write" is a program file and not a text file (for reading by human beings), it is binary. Figure 8-9 shows our dialog with the FTP server as we retrieved the file. First, after we used "cd" to get to the /tmp directory, we issued the "dir" command to

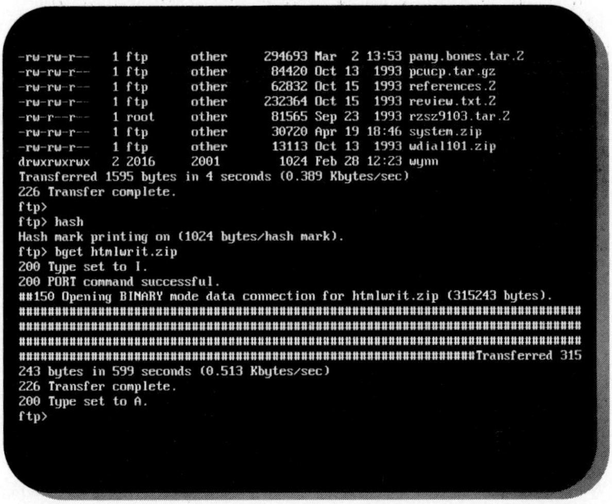

Fig. 8-9: The entire
process of download-
ing a binary file using
FTP marked by hash
marks (#) is shown.
We asked for a
directory, issued the
"hash" command, and
then "bget
htmlwrit.zip." The
FTP server acknowl-
edged our commands
and reported on its
progress in sending
the file.

```
-rw-rw-r--  1 ftp     other      294693 Mar  2 13:53 pany.bones.tar.Z
-rw-rw-r--  1 ftp     other       84420 Oct 13  1993 pcucp.tar.gz
-rw-rw-r--  1 ftp     other       62832 Oct 15  1993 references.Z
-rw-rw-r--  1 ftp     other      232364 Oct 15  1993 review.txt.Z
-rw-r--r--  1 root    other       81565 Sep 23  1993 rzsz9103.tar.Z
-rw-rw-r--  1 ftp     other       30720 Apr 19 18:46 system.zip
-rw-rw-r--  1 ftp     other       13113 Oct 13  1993 wdial101.zip
drwxrwxrwx  2 2016    2001         1024 Feb 28 12:23 wynn
Transferred 1595 bytes in 4 seconds (0.389 Kbytes/sec)
226 Transfer complete.
ftp>
ftp> hash
Hash mark printing on (1024 bytes/hash mark).
ftp> bget htmlwrit.zip
200 Type set to I.
200 PORT command successful.
##150 Opening BINARY mode data connection for htmlwrit.zip (315243 bytes).
############################################################################
############################################################################
############################################################################
###########################################################Transferred 315
243 bytes in 599 seconds (0.513 Kbytes/sec)
226 Transfer complete.
200 Type set to A.
ftp>
```

- confirm that the file was where it had been reported.
- get the exact name of the file, noting case of letters.
- ascertain the approximate size of the file.

The "ls" command would have answered our first two questions but would
have provided no insight on the file size.

Because the file was more than just a few bytes, we entered the FTP
"hash" command, which tells the FTP server to report to us the progress of
the file transfer. It does so by sending "#" marks to the screen for each "packet"
of file data it sends out to our machine. After entering the hash command,
we were ready to begin the transfer. There are two common command sequences for retrieving binary files. We used the one-step process of issuing
the command

    bget htmlwrit.zip <CR>

which tells the server that we want to "get" a file in binary mode. We might
just as well have done this in two steps

    binary <CR>

    get htmlwrit.zip <CR>

following the FTP command structure given in Figure 8-4. In either case, we
need to tell the remote host that we want to move a file in binary mode and
we need to identify the file.

If the file you want is a text-only (ASCII) file with no special formatting
commands or any other programming code, you can use FTP in the ASCII
mode, which is its default generally. In that case, we would have used the
"get" command rather than "bget." As a note, you may successfully transfer
text files in binary mode, but you may not move binary files in ASCII mode.

Users of Macintosh computers have a further consideration. Popular Macintosh client programs such as NCSA/BYU Telnet permit you to take an extra step in transferring binary files to your computer over the network. "MacBinary" (under the File menu) must be enabled for you to transfer some files successfully. It is generally advisable to enable MacBinary at each FTP session. FTP must also be enabled, but that can generally be set as a default. When the server is done moving the file, it reports the time required (599 seconds here) and the rate of transfer. The rate reported in our example (0.513 Kbytes/sec) is fairly slow by Internet standards, reflecting the weekday traffic, which often is very busy during business hours.

We noted earlier that some file-naming conventions provide clues to the nature of the file. The name of the file we downloaded ended with the extension ".zip" and that was a clue to us that the file had been compressed and archived using a program such as PKzip. In order to use the program we would have to "unzip" it. PKunzip and PKzip are IBM-compatible shareware programs widely available on bulletin boards. The unzip program would unpack the software we had just retrieved. Other compression/archiving schemes use the extensions "hqx" (Macintosh), "arc" (IBM), and "lzh" (IBM). All such files must be moved in binary. Other common file extension names requiring binary are "sea" (Macintosh self-extracting archive), "ps" (PostScript), "exe" (an IBM executable file), as well as graphics files with extensions such as "tif," "pnt," "pcx," "gif," "cgm," and "mac." Some FTP sites will tell you in their welcoming screens about other compression schemes that the host site can uncompress "on the fly" if you follow instructions. The most common file name extension for ASCII (text) files is "txt."

When you get a file with FTP, the file is moved from the host machine to the machine where the client software resides. If you are dialing in with a modem to access a host machine that has the FTP client you use, FTP brings the file to your disk space on the local host. You then will have to download the program to your computer using Kermit, Zmodem, or some other protocol your host recognizes. If, on the other hand, you are directly connected to the Internet with a network card and hard wire, or if your dial-in host provides SLIP access, then the file moves directly to your personal computer.

The opposite of "get" and "bget" commands are "put" and "bput", which allow you to upload files to another computer. It is not likely you will have need to use the put commands much unless you really get involved in network activity.

FTP without an FTP client

If you do not have access to an FTP client, you still may bring files by FTP to your desk. You have two methods of doing this. First is mail. There are two ways of getting FTP server files delivered to you by mail. Both of these require that you know the precise name of the file and its exact location. But there are ways of finding that out even through mail. The FTP mail "Gatekeeper" service operated by Digital Equipment Corporation acts as an FTP-mail go-between. It is described in greater detail in Chapter 9 under advanced mail considerations.

If you have access to a Gopher client either on your host machine or at your desktop, you can use Gopher's FTP interface to bring files to you. Several Gopher servers that have an "Internet Resources" directory offer connections to both Archie for finding files and to FTP for retrieving them.

- At the University of Illinois Urbana-Champaign – **gopher vixen.cso.uiuc.edu** – Choice 13 on the root menu is "Internet File Server (ftp) sites."
- At Texas Tech University – **gopher gopher.ttu.edu** – Choice 9 on the root menu is "Information and Services From Around the World," which brings you a menu offering "Popular FTP sites" as Choice 6.
- The "Mother Gopher" at the University of Minnesota – **gopher gopher.tc.umn.edu** – offers from its Root menu (Choice 5) "Internet file server (ftp) sites."
- The Library of Congress Gopher – **gopher marvel.loc.gov** – under "Internet Resources" (Choice 11) extends a menu the first choice of which is another menu, "Archie and FTP."

Gopher sites offering the FTP option allow you to transfer a file by merely selecting it from a menu. This makes the transfer process feel easier, but using Gopher for FTP restricts your mobility and your control over the FTP process.

Whatever way you bring software "down from the net," remember that most of it is copyrighted. Shareware programs put you on your honor to pay for them if you decide after a reasonable trial period that you like a program well enough to use it. Freeware is, as the name implies, free, but is still copyrighted. Other programs are in the public domain, and still others available in Internet archives are programs in some state of testing. During testing periods, users are encouraged to report software bugs to the authors in exchange for free use of the program. Whatever the case, it's up to you legally and ethically to know the terms under which the software is distributed. Generally there is some kind of notice provided with each program. Notice may be in a "README" file or in the program's opening screen.

Some FTP sites of particular interest to journalists include

town.hall.org	SEC's Edgar data base filings on specific companies. In /Edgar directory, Get "general.txt" to provide operating instructions
ftp.cwru.edu	U.S. Supreme Court decisions archived. Change to the "hermes" directory and get the index file first.

ftp.cu.nih.gov	National Institutes of Health archives. Use "guest" as password instead of e-mail address when logging in
ftp.fcc.gov	Federal Communications Commission rulings, proposed rule makings, and announcements. Get the README and index.txt files for guidelines
nctamslant.navy.mil	U.S. Navy policy, strategy; documents from *Joint Forces Quarterly*; speeches and announcements
ra.msstate.edu	Fine Art Forum at Mississippi State University; lists Internet arts resources; try cd pub/archive/ fineart_online/Online_Directory

Other FTP sites are listed in Appendix C.

Retrieving with WAIS

Many higher level Gopher menus offer a choice with a title something akin to "Internet Resources." On the Library of Congress' Gopher, for example, the choice would be selection 11 from the Root menu. Select it, and you get the menu shown in Figure 7-9. Among the 14 menu choices are all the Internet searching and navigating tools we deal with in Chapters 6, 7, and 8: Archie, Veronica, Jughead, other Gophers, Hytelnet, World Wide Web, and WAIS (pronounced WAYZ). In many respects WAIS is the most powerful of the Internet searching tools. You may give to your WAIS client a single word, a pair of words, or a phrase to locate. You tell WAIS what data bases to search (from a list of more than 600) and the word(s) or phrase you are trying to locate. With great speed, WAIS scours documents in the data bases you designate and gives you a report of "hits" that are ranked in order of the closeness to your search terms. Each hit is given a score from 1 to 1,000. Theoretically, a perfect match is 1,000. However, WAIS will give 1,000 to the best match, and score others in comparison.

WAIS (Wide Area Information Servers) searches report network information which volunteers have indexed around predefined topics. Some commercial database services, such as Dow Jones Information Services, use WAIS searching programs; you pay for the commercial services. For "free" information on the Internet, most of the indexing is done by volunteers who have a special interest in the material being cataloged. WAIS information is organized into data base "libraries" and you have to preselect the library (subject area) you want to search. At this writing there are 600 WAIS libraries. You implement a WAIS search by first marking the data bases (libraries) you want to search. Let's do a simple search first.

If you do not have a WAIS client on your personal computer or your Internet host, you will have to borrow one. You might choose WAIS from a Gopher menu or you might use Telnet to get to a WAIS site and then log in as "wais" or "swais." If your Internet host has a WAIS client available, you may launch the program by typing "wais" or "swais" from the system prompt .

Fig. 8-10: WAIS
searches require you
to choose beforehand
which data bases you
want to scan for
relevant information.
WAIS tells you the
cost of access and the
name of the data base.
This screen indicates
597 source data bases:
all are arranged
alphabetically by the
name of the data base.

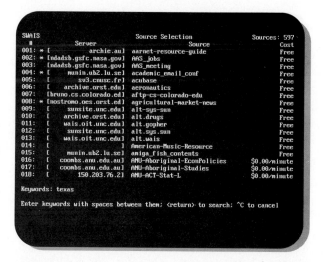

WAIS clients that reside on your personal computer require the right
connection: SLIP, PPP, or direct connection by Ethernet or some similar hard
wiring scheme (Chapter 4 describes the different connections). For those
who need to use Telnet for accessing WAIS, a few WAIS server (Telnet) addresses follow: **sunsite.unc.edu 23,** log in as "swais;" **hub.nnsc.nsf.net
23,** log in as "wais"; **quake.think.com**, log in as "wais." This last site is the
home of Thinking Machines Corporation who played a major role in the development of WAIS. Because at this writing the folks at quake.think.com
are experimenting with their search organization, we will describe their system last.

For our first search, we connect to sunsite.unc.edu and log in as "swais."
You have to tell the sunsite server what terminal you have; the default is
VT100 (see Chapter 6 for terminal emulation). The screen in Figure 8-10
shows that we have taken the first steps toward launching a simple search.
The top of the screen says there are 597 sources (database libraries) to choose
from. We have marked four – indicated by asterisks. When you are at the
sources screen in WAIS, you move a highlight bar down through the sources
listing until the bar marks the desired source. To mark a data base for searching, you hit the space bar. For the purpose of demonstrating a simple search
we marked four data base sources (aarnet-resource-guide, AAS_jobs,
academic_email_conf, and agricultural-market-news) located at four different servers. Having marked the data bases, we typed "w" (for word) so that
we could give WAIS a key word to search for. We typed in "Texas" and hit
enter.

Once a search is started as we have done, WAIS attempts to connect to
each of the server sites and retrieve the documents. Incidentally, we marked
a server in Australia, one in Sweden, a U.S. government (NASA) site, and a
university in the U.S. WAIS reports across the bottom of the screen the
progress it is making. If it cannot make a connection, it tells you so. When

```
SWAIS                           Search Results                    Items: 10
  #    Score    Source                        Title                        Lines
001:  [1000] (academic_email_) Copyright 1994 by Diane K. Kovacs, The D 21763
002:  [ 462] (academic_email_) tx-firearms      Contact: tx-firearms-re    10
003:  [ 385] (academic_email_) BIRDEAST%ARIZVM1.BITNET@CORNELLC.CIT.COR   106
004:  [ 385] (academic_email_) CADUCEUS@Beach.Gal.UTexas                   15
005:  [ 385] (academic_email_) FedTax-L@SHSU.BITNET                        41
006:  [ 385] (academic_email_) FICTION on LISTSERV@PSUVM.PSU.EDU           28
007:  [ 385] (academic_email_) INFO-TI-EXPLORER@SUMEX-AIM.STANFORD         19
008:  [ 385] (academic_email_) comp.sys.ti           Discussion about Texas I
009:  [ 385] (academic_email_) comp.sys.ti.explorer   The Texas Instrumen
010:  [   0] (ANU-Demography-) Search produced no result. Here's the Ca   105




<space> selects, arrows move, w for keywords, s for sources, ? for help
```

Fig. 8-11: Reply to our WAIS search for information on Texas using four databases produced this listing. Two of the data bases were not available during the search and did not show up. The top listing scored a perfect 1,000 rating.

the search is ended, WAIS tells you how many items it found, listing them together with the scores each item tallied. Our search for "Texas" produced 19 reported hits, but only 18 displayed. Figure 8-11 shows the results of the search. Each located source is given a score. The top two items scored perfect 1,000 marks. WAIS reports scores, the name of the source, the title of the document containing the match, and the length of the document in lines.

On our Texas search, WAIS found matching documents from news group archives, Bitnet mail lists, agricultural data bases and others. You can view the documents WAIS uncovers, you can save them to the machine on which your client software resides (if it is your personal computer or the host site where you have an account), or you can have the document mailed to you. WAIS most often turns up text files, but it may just as well find video or

Fig. 8-12: One of the replies to a WAIS search on information about earthquakes produced a document describing the California Office of Emergency Services' EDIS service. The EDIS Telnet service was invaluable as a source of hard news information during the Northridge earthquake of 1994.

```
SWAIS                          Document Display                    Page:   1
(:source
  :version  3
  :ip-address "152.2.22.81"
  :ip-name "calypso.oit.unc.edu"
  :tcp-port 210
  :database-name "Health-Security-Act"
  :cost 0.00
  :cost-unit :free
  :maintainer "root@calypso.oit.unc.edu"
  :description "Server created with WAIS release 8 b5 on Oct 28 13:17:10 1993
by root@calypso

The Health Security Act of 1993 holds the promise of a new era
of security for every American -- an era in which our nation
finally guarantees its citizens comprehensive health care
benefits that can never be taken away.


Today, America boasts the world's best health care
professionals, the finest medical schools and hospitals, the
most advanced research and the most sophisticated technology.
Press any key to continue, 'q' to quit.
```

Fig. 8-13: WAIS keyboard commands are case sensitive. If any of these commands do not work, try asking for help with either a question mark or a lower case "h."

WAIS Keyboard Commands

```
j, ^N ................. Move Down one item
k, ^P ................. Move Up one item
J ....................... Move Down one screen
K ....................... Move Up one screen
R ....................... Show relevant documents
S ....................... Save current item to a file
m ...................... Mail current item to an address
## ..................... Position to item number ##
/sss ................... Position to item beginning sss
<space> ........... Display current item
<return> ........... Display current item
| ........................ Pipe current item into a unix command
v ....................... View current item information
r ........................ Make current item a relevant document
s ....................... Specify new sources to search
u ....................... Use it; add it to the list of sources
w ...................... Make another search with new keywords
o ....................... Set and show swais options
h ....................... Show this help display
H ...................... Display program history
q ....................... Leave this program
```

audio segments. If your document is text, you may view it by positioning the selector bar over the item in question and hitting the Enter key. Figure 8-12 shows a portion of one such document, retrieved during a WAIS search for earthquake information.

In Chapter 6 we reported that a Telnet site in California provided timely hard news material on the Northridge earthquake. In Chapter 7 we explained that we found the site by using Gopher. Had we performed a WAIS search on "earthquake," we could have discovered that the Office of Emergency Services in California operated its Emergency Digital Information Service and what the purpose of the service was, what it costs, and a little about accessing it.

Like Gopher and some Web clients, WAIS clients offer minimal help commands on screen continuously. A full list of commands, such as those given in Figure 8-13, is available by typing a lower case "h." Also like Gopher and Web servers, the number of WAIS servers is expanding rapidly. When we started writing this book in the middle of 1993, there were fewer than 500 database libraries covered by WAIS. By the time this manuscript was in the editors' hands there were more than 600. The proliferation of data base sources for WAIS brings both good news and bad news to journalists. The good news is that more data bases means a greater likelihood of finding useful information. But the bad news in the short term is that a longer list of data bases means the first step of the WAIS search – choosing data bases to search – takes longer.

Probably the most difficult part of using WAIS from a journalist's point of view is that first step. Traditionally there has been no convenient way to browse for information by topic or to know whether any given data base has information of use to you. What you must do is read through screen after screen of alphabetical data base listings (more than 600 if you want to get all of them) and mark (with the space bar) the ones you think might pertain to

Fig. 8-14: An experimental approach to WAIS searches uses only the directory of servers as a first source. We have entered the terms "politics clinton health plan."

your topic. You do have the option of having the list of data bases mailed to your e-mail box. In theory you could print the list and choose ahead of time which data bases to mark. Because the list is growing rapidly, you would need to go through the mail and print sequence every few weeks to stay current. At press time for this book, the folks at Thinking Machines had adopted a new "top" strategy for doing WAIS searches.

A new approach and a more advanced WAIS search

If you used Telnet to access the WAIS client at quake.think.com during the first part of 1994, you got a message that acknowledged that the growing number of sources was making the first stage of a WAIS search more difficult. To address the problem, the site presented WAIS users with only one source: the directory of servers. The welcome message read in part:

> To find additional sources, just select the directory-of-server.src source, and ask it a question. If you know the name of the source you want, use it for the keywords, and you should get that source as one of the results. If you don't know what source you want, then just ask a question that has something to do with what you're looking for, and see what you get.

What this meant was that instead of getting a list of 600 potential sources to browse through and mark, you got one. Give it something to search for and if it turns up sources you like, you can mark them for use.

We'll see how this works as we give WAIS a more complicated search. The real power and promise of WAIS is in its ability to track down phrases. Our first search was a single word affair, looking for the word "Texas" in a small group of almost randomly chosen data bases. Let's get more realistic. Let's see if we can find anything on the politics of President Clinton's National Health Care Initiative. We select the one source we have at quake.think.com and then offer as our key words "politics clinton health plan" (see Figure 8-14). Because WAIS does not respond to Boolean searches the way Veronica and Jughead do, we have merely entered the words, adding no qualifying conjunctions.

In scoring its finds, WAIS considers the whole collection of terms. One of its finds (Figure 8-11) scored 1,000. Scores dropped off rapidly in this test case. If we liked the document WAIS found the first time and wanted more like it, we could mark it with a "u" ("use") and ask WAIS to search again. This time WAIS will take the marked document as its example and look for other documents that use a lot of the same words.

The WAIS searches and retrievals we have been describing are "interactive" WAIS searches and presume you have access to at least Telnet. If all you have is e-mail access to the Internet, you can do some limited WAIS searching and retrieval by mail. That process will be described more fully in the advanced mail section of Chapter 9.

A WAIS review

The WAIS search involves several steps:

1.   Select the data bases you want to search.
2.   Tell WAIS the key words you want to locate.
3.   WAIS goes out to all the data bases you have selected and searches for matching documents.
4.   WAIS scores matching documents and displays a list of them on the screen with their scores, the name of the server, the title of the matching document, and its relative size.
5.   You may view documents thus listed, mail them, or use them as starting points for new searches.

The WAIS interface is nowhere near as clear and easy to understand or to use as the Gopher menuing system so it scores lower than Gopher in that regard. Nor is WAIS nearly so accessible. Though there are clients available for personal computers, the number of WAIS clients available by Telnet can be counted on your fingers.

WAIS indices appear to be strongest in uncovering information on computer sciences (and anything else related to computers), biology, and other traditional sciences. In any case, WAIS requires some patience, good instinct, and a fair amount of luck for it to become a tool useful to a journalist on deadline. A good strategy would be to take good notes as you go – especially with regard to the list of data bases if you find some that seem useful. If you browse a few minutes now and then, you will develop a feel for those data bases that are most relevant to your beat. Having done that first, you have a better chance of using WAIS fruitfully as an "on deadline tool." Most of the time, WAIS is more suited to use on major projects where you want to uncover everything you can. Another good strategy would be to return to WAIS now and then as you get more experience on the Internet; some of those source names take on new meaning as you encounter them from other directions.

The power of WAIS for journalists is twofold. First, WAIS will find many things other network finders do not. Second, WAIS has the ability to handle phrases, which can greatly assist you in finding what you seek. Third, by using documents returned in one search as new sources you can do recursive searching that may produce extremely beneficial results.

WAIS has in its list of sources a number of Bitnet mail list and Usenet news group archives. That is one way to get at those materials. In Chapter 9, we will explore some advanced mail listserv searching functions and other person-to-person Internet tools.

Further reading

Archie, FTP, and WAIS are described in

1. Ed Krol. *The Whole Internet User's Guide & Catalog*, 2 ed. Sebastopol, Calif.: O'Reilly & Associates, 1994.
2. Daniel P. Dern. *The Internet Guide for New Users*, New York: McGraw-Hill, 1994.
3. John R. Levine and Carol Baroudi. *The Internet for Dummies*, San Mateo, Calif.: IDG Books Worldwide, Inc., 1993.

Chapter **9**

News groups & relay chat

For the past 150 years, the mass media have been the primary source of information about most major news stories. Readers depended on reporters to inform them about important and interesting events happening around the world. Reporters, in turn, often had to rely on official, government sources for the information they reported.

With the development of the Internet and other global communication networks, however, journalists' monopoly on the ability to disseminate news around the world in a timely fashion to a large number of people has begun to break down. At the same time, monopolies that government officials and other "official" sources have held on information have begun to break down. Journalists now have many more alternatives for obtaining important information about breaking news events as well as ongoing news stories.

For example, in 1991, the body of a young girl who had been hacked to pieces and placed in blocks of concrete was discovered at the bottom of a lake in southern Ontario, Canada. In the spring of 1992, a 15-year-old girl was abducted in the same general area. Two weeks later her naked, mutilated body was discovered by the side of the road.

In 1993, a husband and wife, Paul Bernardo and Karla Homolka, were arrested and charged with the crimes. Less than two months later, Homolka pleaded guilty to manslaughter and was sentenced to 12 years in prison, leaving her husband Paul to face two charges of first-degree murder as well as 53 other related and unrelated charges.

After Homolka pleaded guilty, a Canadian court banned publication of any details of her trial until the trial of her husband was completed, arguing that Bernardo's right to a fair trial outweighed freedom of the press in this case. The judge was particularly worried that the American press just across the border would violate the ban, so he excluded foreign media from the courtroom and forbade anyone to publish any circumstances of the deaths mentioned in Homolka's trial until the conclusion of the Bernardo case.

The judge's ban could not stop the flow of information about the trial to mass audiences in the United States and around the world. Soon after Bernardo was arrested, several electronic bulletin boards containing facts and rumors about the affair were launched. On July 14, Justin Wells and Ken Chasse set up a Usenet news group about the trial on Chasse's Sonic Interzone BBS, a public access bulletin board in Toronto. The Usenet news group, which was named alt.fan.karla-homolka, distributed information around the world about the trial, in defiance of the publication ban.

Consider the news coverage of the Persian Gulf War in 1991. In January of 1991, people of the United States could witness the launch of Operation Desert Storm, the war against Iraq through the eyes of Bernard Shaw, the anchor of Cable News Network, who was posted in Teheran at the time. In a display of telecommunications prowess, live pictures were transmitted via satellite to viewers around the world, while Shaw narrated what he could see and hear.

Still, throughout the entire month-long operation, the information that reached the public via the mass media was strictly controlled either by the U.S. military or by the Iraqi government. To a large degree, reporters could only see and hear what the military command wanted them to see and hear. They knew only what the officials running the operation wanted them to know.

But there was a back channel of information. People using what was called Internet Relay Chat interactively communicated with each other in real time, sharing what they knew and what they had heard about the activities in the Gulf War. People on Internet Relay Chat did not have to rely exclusively on the U.S. news media and the U.S. military command for their information about Operation Desert Storm.

In this chapter we will discuss

- Usenet news groups. You will learn what Usenet is, how news groups are organized, and how to access network news.
- The basics of Internet Relay Chat. You will learn how to access and use Internet Relay Chat.
- The promises and pitfalls these services hold for reporters.

Usenet news groups

Usenet news groups, which are sometimes referred to collectively as network news, make up a huge distributed conference system in which people with common interests interact with each other. In many ways, Usenet is like the forums on CompuServe, America Online and other commercial information services, and the electronic bulletin boards described in Chapter 3. People post and read messages on boards or in news groups organized around topics of common interest.

While Usenet news groups appear to be like Internet discussion lists discussed in Chapter 5, they operate differently. Internet discussion lists work via electronic mail. Once you subscribe to a discussion list, every message posted to the list is sent to your account as electronic mail.

Messages to Usenet news groups are posted to servers that communicate with each other through bilateral arrangements of the system administrators. When one server receives news group postings from another, that is known as a news feed. When you read the messages posted to a news group, you are reading messages that are located on a server, not in your own account. In the same way, when you post a message, the message is posted to a server. It is not automatically distributed to thousands of people.

Technically, Usenet news groups are not part of the Internet. Usenet is the name given to the network of servers whose system administrators have agreed to feed news to each other adhering to a specific communication protocol. Consequently, it is a very informal network with no governing body and few specific usage rules. Each system administrator controls the traffic at his or her particular site. If you know of a news group (such as "alt.journalism") that your news site does not carry, you can ask to have it included. Some Usenet sites also have Internet connections, which is how some network news gets to the Internet. Similarly, many Internet host sites and gateways offer Usenet access.

The structure of the network news has some advantages over listserv-oriented, mailing list-based discussion groups. Because the messages are not actually sent to an account but reside on a central server, people who are reading news group postings do not find their mail boxes filled with mail if a discussion gets lively. Nor do they have to suspend mail if they plan to go on vacation or cannot monitor their computer account for a couple of weeks.

On the other hand, not everybody with Internet access can conveniently access Usenet news groups. As noted later, people whose system administrators opt not to receive a news feed will have to access public systems. Also, most Usenet news groups do not archive their messages. That means you can only access current discussions.

Another concern for journalists is that the quality of the information communicated in these groups is very uneven. Some information is excellent. Some is just wrong. And sometimes it is hard to tell which is which. Nonetheless, the amount of information circulated through network news is enormous. By some estimates, there are now as many as 6,000 network news groups involving more than 100,000 computer sites. An estimated 10 million people have accounts on computers carrying Usenet, and 2.6 million people read Usenet news at least occasionally. In 1994, one expert estimated that approximately 370,000 articles per week were copied world-wide through Usenet. This traffic represented roughly 20,000 printed pages per day of announcements, questions and answers, advice and bits of program code, and other information. A typical server subscribes to about 1,500 news groups and may receive as much as 10 megabytes of information a day.

Network news hierarchies

Network news groups are organized according to hierarchies going from the general to the specific. The name of each news group is divided from its parent and various subgroupings by a period. For example, the news group alt.fan.karla-homolka was initially placed in the hierarchy of news groups reserved for discussion of alternative and controversial material. All news groups in this hierarchy begin with "alt."

The second element in the news group name "fan" designates fan clubs. Other fan clubs listed that begin with alt.fan. range from the Addams Family to Madonna to Dan Quayle. In fact, the Homolka murder case is not the only crime to have its own fan club. The highly publicized Amy Fisher-Joey Buttafucco attempted manslaughter case in which a teenage girl shot the wife of her purported lover was also the subject of a news group under the alt.fan hierarchy.

Traditionally, Usenet news groups have fallen into seven categories listed in Figure 9-1.

But news groups can also be created locally. And because system administrators can arrange for news feeds for any group that is of interest, many locally created groups gain as wide a distribution as standard network news groups and are generally considered part of the Usenet news group family.

The most popular designation for the locally created news groups is the alt prefix discussed above. Many of the wild and wooly discussions about risque topics take place in news groups with the alt designation. Some other common designations include bionet for topics of interest to biologists and biz for business related subjects.

Fig. 9-1: Traditional Top-level domains for naming of news groups. Others include "alt," "biz," and "bionet."

Seven Major News Categories

comp .... Computer science and related topics
news .... Network news itself
rec .... Hobbies, recreational activities
sci .... Scientific research and applications
soc .... Social issues, either political or simply social
talk .... Forum for debate on controversial subjects
misc .... Anything that doesn't fit into the categories above.

Although it seems as if much of the publicity given to Usenet news groups in the media has focused on groups talking about topics like bestiality or bondage, the range of discussion is extensive. Perhaps as many as 300 or more news groups discuss issues of interest to scientists in different disciplines.

There are news groups about major political events and leaders in both the alt and social hierarchies. The soc.politics designation includes politically oriented news groups. Soc.rights.human is a news group that discusses human rights issues. Finally, most major professional sports teams as well as many entertainment activities and industries are the topics for news groups in both the alt and rec hierarchies. For example, in the rec hierarchy there is rec.sport.baseball, rec.music.bluenote for discussions about jazz and the blues, and rec.mag for discussion about magazines.

Getting access

The easiest and most efficient way to access Usenet news groups is for the system administrator to arrange for a news feed to your local system and to mount news reader software (i.e., a news client) for you to use. Two of the most common news readers in the Unix environment are called nn and rn. To see if you already have access to network news enter "nn," "rn" or "trn" (an updated version of rn) at your system prompt. If not, you might also try "news" (which on some systems gives you news only for the system), "unews", "usenet", or "netnews". You can also consult your system administrator.

NN and rn are only two of the news readers available for reading network news. Other popular programs include Trumpet for MS DOS, Nuntius for the Macintosh, and NNR and VMS News for VMS. Like other client software described earlier, news readers organize the information on the servers on which the news groups are stored in ways that meet your needs. For example, messages on similar topics will be linked together in what are called threads, which can then be read in sequence. News readers also help you post messages to news groups.

Alternative access to news groups

Many system administrators, do not want to support a network news feed. They fear the large volume of message traffic strains their system resources, and they deem other tasks are more important than reading network news. For you to configure a news reader to access a different network news server on your own is possible, but it can be a complicated and frustrating process. However, if the system you use is not running network news locally, you can access news groups via other publicly available avenues.

```
Main Menu

1. Network News
2. Electronic mail
3. On-line Information Systems (LIBTEL)
4. Topical document search (WAIS)
5. Download files
6. Find user
7. User Options
8. Pherrit - gopher client
9. Lynx - WWW client
10. Triangle Free-Net experimental gopher

(? or h)elp, (q)uit.
```

Fig. 9-2: The Main Menu at the University of North Carolina's Launchpad offers "Network News" as an option.

Many Gopher sites provide access to Usenet news. One public access service is the Launchpad at the University of North Carolina. Launchpad provides users with electronic mail accounts and client software for several advanced Internet applications as well as access to network news (Figure 9-2).

You access Launchpad by using Telnet to connect to lambada.oit.unc.edu. To log in, you type "launch" and that will take you to the Launchpad service. You will then be instructed how to set up an account. You should first select the user options choice from the menu and read the Launchpad frequently asked questions (FAQ) to see what Launchpad has to offer.

If you select option 1 from the main menu, you will see the menu in Figure 9-3.

Launchpad runs a news reader call RN. It has its own list of commands and you will have to invest some time in learning how to maneuver through the system. Once you do, you will be able to read the news groups you wish, although there may be some limitations on where and how you can post messages.

Another avenue to access network news is through Campus Wide Information Systems like the law library system at Washington and Lee University. To access this system, you Telnet to 137.113.10.35 and log in as "lawlib". Your log-in launches a Gopher client and you will then see the menu in Figure 9-4.

If you select number 13, you will be able to use the Usenet news readers at Washington and Lee University itself as well as those at selected other sites. The Internet is always changing, however, and some news readers may not be publicly available. Others may allow use only during restricted hours. On the other hand, the news reader at the Danish Academic Net-

Fig. 9-3: The Network News Menu from University of North Carolina's Launchpad.

```
Network News
1. trn - threaded rn
2. trn - won't prompt for new groups
3. rn - line-oriented news reader
4. rn - won't prompt for new groups
5. pnews - post news
6. Download news articles
7. Manipulate .newsrc file

(b)ackup to previous menu, (? or h)elp, (q)uit.
```

work, which is item 9 on the Washington and Lee Usenet news reader menu provides search indexes as well as reading news.

Another Gopher/Usenet gateway appears as item 6, "News and Weather," at Michigan State University (gopher.msu.edu). It offers public access to a wide range of information. Item 13 on that menu provides a news reader for network news.

The problem with these public alternatives is that traffic can get heavy. Launchpad, for example, services 2,600 users a day. More than 12,000 people have free accounts. Consequently, its performance can be slow. Moreover, from time to time all the ports on public access servers will be full and you will be denied access.

A fourth option for accessing Usenet news is a gateway between Usenet and Bitnet, which is the network on which most listserv-mailing lists operate. Those news groups that take advantage of the Usenet/Bitnet gateway can be accessed via e-mail using the same processes associated with a standard discussion list described in Chapter 5.

Most Usenet news groups, however, do not correspond to mailing lists, and they cannot be accessed by e-mail. For people who don't have easy access to Usenet, the "List of Active News groups" can be retrieved from archives at MIT and UUNET using the procedures described under "Finding the Right News Group" later in this chapter. For a list of news groups that have a gateway to listserv discussion groups, see the "List of Active News groups" posting in news.announce.newusers. To do that, you need to know how to navigate the Usenet.

Organizing your news groups

Before you begin to read messages, your first task when you access network news is to designate which news groups you want to follow. Local

Fig. 9-4: The Washington and Lee University Gopher, accessed through Telnet, provides a Usenet Newsreader directory option. Several Gopher sites offer this option.

servers may offer access from 1,500 to 3,000 news groups. When you first begin to read network news, the system assumes that you may want to read all the news from all the news groups. Consequently, the process of eliminating news groups can be time consuming.

Most news readers, however, have features that allow you to eliminate news groups according to major designations and categories. For example, you may not be interested in anything that has to do with computer science, so often you can exclude all news groups that begin with the comp. prefix.

If you have a local news feed and local reader software, the specific commands you need should be available in the help files.

News readers keep a log of the news groups to which you subscribe and which articles within that group you have already read. That way, when you select that group again, you are brought directly to messages that have been posted since you last read the postings.

This information is stored in a file frequently called "NEWS.RC" on the machine where the news reading client resides. If the client is your Internet host, it is stored in the space you are allocated on the host. If you have a client on your personal computer, the file (or its equivalent) will be stored there. If you are using public access to Usenet through a Telnet or Gopher connection, you do not have the benefit of the NEWS.RC file tracking. If you are accessing Usenet from a BBS or commercial service, you must ask your service provider about this kind of tracking.

A word of caution regarding the NEWS.RC file and the way you exit from your Usenet reader. Both "quit" and "exit" commands may take you out of the news reader. However, when you "quit" from some programs, the reader does not update your NEWS.RC file. When you "exit," it does.

Fig. 9-5: A portion of the news group listings from a Usenet News server. To select a group, you point to it with the cursor pointer (here on group 1992) and hit the Enter key.

```
VMS NEWS v1.24 --- Newsgroups [TOTAL] 2818 (Posting OK)
==> 1992 info.sun-nets                                -     2
    1993 info.sysadmin                                -     1
    1994 info.theorynt                                -   448
    1995 info.wisenet                                 -  3071
    1996 junk                                         - 659693
    1997 k12.chat.teacher                             -   590
    1998 la.eats                                      -  2181
    1999 la.general                                   -  3744
    2000 la.news                                      -   221
    2001 la.seminars                                  -   247
    2002 la.slug                                      -    44
    2003 la.test                                      -    77
    2004 misc.activism.progressive                    - 13780 Mod
    2005 misc.answers                                 -   621 Mod
    2006 misc.auto                                    -     8
    2007 misc.books.technical                         -  2703
    2008 misc.comp.forsale                            -    65
    2009 misc.computers.forsale                       -   232
    2010 misc.consumers                               - 32466
    2011 misc.consumers.house                         - 31720
NEWS:
%NEWS-I-GRPSEL, Newsgroup news.answers with 1319 articles selected
%CLI-W-IVVERB, unrecognized command verb - check validity and spelling
```

Thus if you "quit" the reader keeps no record of what you have read or your subscription list.

Navigating Usenet levels

When you read Usenet news, you enter a program that functions on three tiers: 1) a group listing/directory level, 2) an article listing/directory level, and 3) an article reading level. Additionally, you may be in screen mode or command mode at either directory level.

When you first launch the news reading program, you enter at the group directory level. Figure 9-5 illustrates a directory of news groups. The message across the top of the screen indicates that this particular news carries 2,818 news groups. The directory lists 20 groups to a screen. The top line also tells us the news reading program we are using (VMS News) and the version (1.24). Beside the number of the news group is the news group's name. The top domain categories for the groups shown here are "info," a broad information category; "junk," an active, nondescript category; "k12," a grouping for teachers and students in elementary and secondary schools; "la," a grouping for subjects about Los Angeles; and the ubiquitous "misc" category. Only this last category is one of the seven traditional top domains of Usenet news.

In the news group directory, to the right of the news group's name, is a number that corresponds to the number of the last article posted to the group. The group "k12.chat.teacher" has had 512 postings to it, and "la.general" has had 3,744. The first two groups in the "misc" domain have the word "Mod" to the right of the posting number. This indicates these groups are moderated. In such a group, a moderator screens all incoming messages before posting them for all readers to see. In unmoderated groups, people can post just about anything they please. The vast majority of Usenet news groups are unmoderated.

Using your cursor keys, you move the news group selector arrow through the list, in order to choose the group you want. Or you can also enter a number, and the news reader will take your cursor to that number. Because group numbers change, they are not reliable bookmarks for getting to the group you want. If you know the name of the group you want, you can enter the command Group followed by the group's name to send your cursor to that group. A shortcut for Group in the VMS News reader is simply "g." Thus if we wanted to read messages in the group "misc.consumers," we could enter the command

g misc.consumers <CR>

and our cursor arrow would point to that group. Having chosen the group we want, we get a listing of the articles available by hitting the Enter key while the cursor arrow is pointing at the chosen group.

While the examples here are taken from the news reader VMS News, other readers have similar – often identical – commands. In any case, you will understand how the news reading and posting process works and what commands to look for when you issue the "help" command to your reader.

You can scroll through the list of news groups a screen at a time by entering the command "down" to go down 20 groups or "up" to go up 20 groups. If you aren't sure of the exact name of a group, you may search for matches using the asterisk wildcard. Thus, if you want to find a group aimed at consumer interests you could enter the command

g *consumer* <CR>

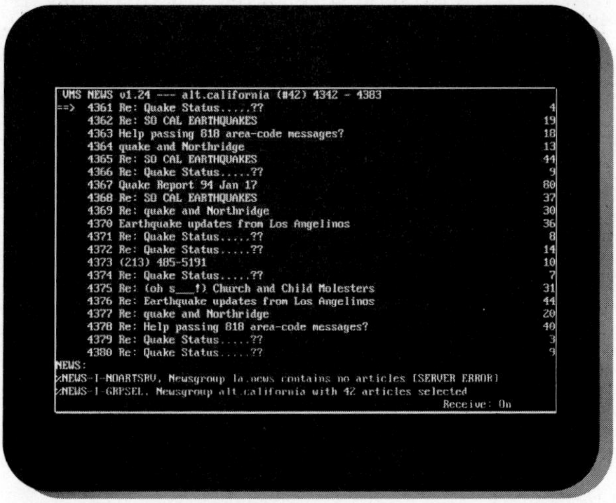

Fig 9-6: A listing of article postings to the news group "alt.california" on the day of the Jan. 17, 1994 earthquake in Northridge. News of the quake dominated the group as it did other groups affiliated with the Los Angeles area.

and the news reader program will take your cursor to the next group that has "consumer" in its name. If what you get is not the group you wanted, you may repeat the command until you find the right group.

Figure 9-6 shows a listing at the article directory level of the group "alt.california" on the day of the Northridge earthquake. You select articles in a fashion similar to the way you select news groups. You move the cursor pointer to the article you want and hit the Enter key. As an alternative, you can use the "Go" command followed by the number of the article to move your cursor to that article. When you are in the article directory, you must type the whole word; the "g" shortcut only works in groups.

In both of the directory levels, you are automatically placed in *screen mode* until you type something other than a number, a Return key, or a cursor arrow key. As soon as you type a letter (or hit the space bar), you are taken into the *command mode*. In command mode, your Up and Down Arrows do not move the cursor. Neither does the Return (Enter) key select anything; instead, a Return signals to the news reader completion of a command. Most of the time this screen mode vs. command mode is fairly intuitive, and it goes on unnoticed. But if you find peculiar things going on at one of the directory levels, you might wish to note whether you are in screen or command mode.

Once you select an article to read, you can scroll through the article one line at a time by using your Down Arrow, or you can scroll a screen at a time by typing the command "down." The "Dir" command and its shortcut "d" move you up a level in Usenet news. If you are reading an article, the "d" command takes you out of reading the article into the article directory. If you are in the article directory when you type the "d" command, you are taken to the group directory.

When you select news group messages to read, what you see on screen has all the appearance of an e-mail message or a message posting to a bulletin board. If you wish to respond, you have the option to write a "followup" message, which then will be displayed to the network. Or you can "reply," which will send a mail message privately to the originator of the message. See Figure 9-7 for a summary of commonly used news reader commands.

If you choose the "followup" or the "post" command, you start a header dialog that has a few more options than a mail header. Figure 9-8 shows a posting header dialog. The "Distribution" field demands special attention. What you put in the Distribution field governs how far your message will be disbursed. If you select "world," your posting or followup will go out world wide. If you select "local," it will generally stay at the site you post to. Other acceptable distribution categories are

CA, OH, NY, TX, etc. = specified state
can   = Canada only

eunet = European sites only
na   = North American destinations
usa   = United States based servers

An important restriction on distribution codes is that your site must be included within the zone you designate. If you post from Canada, you

---

Fig. 9-7: Some of the more commonly used Usenet news commands appear here in their VMS News incarnation. Other news readers will have similar commands. It is wise to invoke "Help" to get instructions specific to your program.

Basic Usenet News Commands

Bottom	Moves cursor to the bottom of the display. Goes to last entry in the group or article list
Directory	Displays a directory of news groups or news items within a group. Moves up one level in tier structure. Synonyms = "Dir" and "d"
Down	Moves down one screen. In directory levels, moves cursor down generally 20 items. In article reading level, scrolls to end of article or down one screen, whichever is first.
Exit	Leaves the news reader program, updating your NEWS.RC file.
Extract	Saves the current news article in an output file which you name on the same command as "extract." Thus "extract filename" Synonym = "Save"
Followup	Starts a dialog that posts to an entire news group your reply to news item.
Go	Selects (goes to) an article or news group specified by the number which follows the word "go."
Group	Selects (goes to) the news group named following the word "group." Accepts wild cards (*). Synonym = "g"
Help	Calls up the help facility, from which you may gain more detailed instructions.
Mail	Starts program to mail message to individual, not the group.
Mark	Marks specified articles as read/unread by user.
Next	Only in article reading level, this command takes you to the next article in the group. Synonym = "n"
Post	Initiates process of posting an article to the news system.
Reply	Posts a mail message directly to the sender of a news item without putting the message out to the whole net.
Scan	Command is followed by a pattern to search for. Works in Article reading level. Useful for finding a string in large articles. Example: Scan "*searchterm*" (quotes necessary).
Subscribe	Marks a group as one you want to monitor, so the news reader program keeps track of what you have read.
Top	Moves cursor to the top of the display.
Unsubscribe	Reverses Subscribe command.
Up	Opposite of Down; moves up one screen.

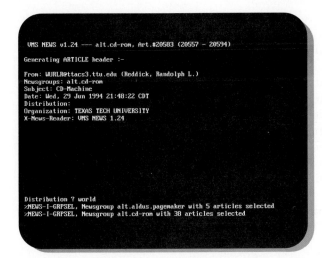

Fig. 9-8: The Article Header dialog in Usenet News. When you issue the "post" or the "followup" command, the news reader asks you for header information, suggesting default values for you. For some fields you have no options. Here, we are defining the scope of distribution as world wide.

may not specify "eunet" distribution. If you post from Florida, you may not specify "PA," but you may specify "usa."

Most news readers track what you have read through a system of marking files. When you are in the article directory level, you are reading articles that are described by a one-line subject tag. You may know that you don't want to read certain articles. By issuing the "mark" (or "skip" in some systems) command, you tell the news reader to treat the article as if it had been read.

Most simply, the mark (skip) command marks the article at which your cursor is pointing. You can also add qualifiers (or arguments) to the command. Thus "mark /all" will mark all of the current postings as if they have been read. More commonly, you would give the command, "mark *num1-num2*," where you would substitute the actual numbers of the articles you want to skip.

Finding the right news groups

For journalists, network news can serve many functions. Reporters may want to monitor beat-related news groups to stay current on specific topics and to find potential story ideas. In that case, the reporter may have the time to select several news groups and monitor the messages on them for several days to see if the information is relevant.

In other cases, however, you will be on deadline and looking for precise information about well defined topics. You won't be able to leisurely survey 20 news groups to find what you need.

In those cases, you can start by reading the FAQ or "Frequently Asked Questions" posting, which generally describes the news group and its charter. The FAQ also often contains other valuable information and leads about the topic in question. Most news groups routinely repost their FAQs.

FAQs are also available via FTP (Chapter 8). Perhaps the most comprehensive listing of FAQs is at Massachusetts Institute of Technology. Connect to rtfm.mit.edu using FTP and do a standard anonymous FTP log-on (Chapter 8). Then change directories using the CD command to / pub/usenet/news.answers. At that point, type a directory command (DIR) and the list of news groups for which the site has an FAQ will scroll by. When you see the name of a news group in which you may be interested, write it down.

Most of the FAQs listed at the MIT FTP site are made up of multiple files. Consequently, you will want to run the list command (ls) and the name of the news group in which you are interested. For example, if you are interested in the FAQ for the news group alt.baldspot, enter the command

ls alt.baldspot.

This will list all the FAQ files associated with that news group. Once you see the individual files, you can retrieve the one you want using standard FTP commands.

Because of the amount of information contained in the FAQ archives, some of the FAQs may be compressed. If they are, their names may end with a *.Z.* Some FTP servers will automatically decompress files if you omit the *.Z* when you ask for a local file name in the retrieval process. If the archive is busy, however, the decompress function may be disabled.

The site at MIT is often very busy and you may not be able to get on the system. But there are several other good FAQ archives available. They include

FAQ Archives

N. America:	ftp.uu.net	/usenet/news.answers
Europe:	ftp.uni-paderborn.de	/pub/FAQ
	ftp.Germany.EU.net	/pub/newsarchive/news.answers
	grasp1.univ-lyon1.fr	/pub/faq
	ftp.win.tue.nl	/pub/usenet/news.answers
Asia:	nctuccca.edu.tw	/USENET/FAQ
	hwarang.postech.ac.kr	/pub/usenet/news.answers

Another alternative for retrieving any of the mentioned FAQs is to request it from the e-mail server at MIT. To find out how to use the server to get what you want, send mail to "mail-server@rtfm.mit.edu". In the body of your message include simply the word "help." The server will return a mail message to you explaining how to get the documents you want.

Finally, you can often locate an FAQ you may wish by using one of the search tools described in Chapters 7 and 8. An FAQ is simply a file stored on the Internet. Using Gopher or other more sophisticated search tools can help you find the FAQ you need.

Archived Usenet information

Most news readers retain Usenet news group messages for a limited period of time. The quantity of messages being posted daily makes it impossible to save everything. Consequently, when you read a news group, you will only be able to read the messages that have been posted within that specified period.

Old news group messages are generally not saved anywhere. There are often good reasons for this. First, to save all Usenet news group messages would be similar to saving a record of all telephone conversations. It represents a lot of data. Secondly, as the Usenet FAQ puts it, the signal-to-noise ratio, i.e. the amount of good, useful information compared to the amount of useless information on many news groups is very low. In other words, the information is not worth saving in many cases.

The information from some news groups are archived, however. The Sunsite server at the University of North Carolina, for example, archives the messages from many of the news groups carried by the Launchpad service discussed earlier. To make use of the archive, you can FTP to sunsite.unc.edu. The system administrators there, however, recommend you use WAIS, which was described in Chapter 8, to search the archives for the information you want. They apparently are experimenting with description-based searches and downloads from the archive with WAIS. To find out more, you should FTP to sunsite.unc.edu and get and read the file /pub/wais/ftp-wais.readme.

If you don't have a WAIS or Gopher client, you can Telnet to Sunsite (sunsite.unc.edu) and log on as "swais" to test out a sample WAIS client or log on as "gopher" to test out a sample Gopher client. If you send e-mail to info@sunsite.unc.edu in the same manner as we describe for the MIT site (the body of your message reads "help"), you will be sent help information about how to use the different services the Sunsite server provides.

Key word searches and news filtering

Negotiating Usenet news groups can be a pressure-packed process for journalists on deadline, and the payoff in good, solid leads or reportable information is uncertain. A useful alternative for journalists is a filtering service for network news provided by the Database Group at Stanford University. You send key words in an e-mail message to a server at Stanford University. A search is conducted overnight, and results consisting of several lines from each matching message are returned by e-mail. You send the message to netnews@db.stanford.edu. In the body of the message, you write "subscribe" followed by the key words for which you wish to search.

In addition to the subscribe command, the service has several other commands to manage your subscription. The first three are "period", "expire", and "threshold". They can be included as additional lines in the initial subscribe message. These additional commands must begin on new lines in the message with no initial indentations or spaces. "Period" determines the number of days between notifications of matches. If you do not include a period command, you will receive notification every day. "Expire" sets the number of days for which your subscription is active. If you do not specify an expiration date, the subscription will run for 9,999 days. The "threshold" command determines how closely matched what the news filter finds must be to your key words for the information to be returned to you. As with WAIS, information is scored according to how well it fits to what you said you were looking for. If you do not specify a threshold score, it will return anything that has a score of 60.

Let's say you are working on a story about global warming. Your deadline is in one month, and you think you will only be able to check your e-mail every other day. Moreover, you are not sure that the term "global warming" captures all the issues you want to explore. Because you are not an environmental reporter, when the story is finished, you will not need information on global warming on a regular basis.

Your subscription message to the news filter service could look like this:

```
$mail send
To: IN%"netnews@db.stanford.edu"
Subject:
subscribe global warming
period 2
expire 30
threshold 50
end
```

The results will be a list of articles with about 20 lines each that scored 50 or more in the matching process. The results will be sent to you every two days, and your subscription will expire in 30 days.

After receiving notifications of articles that may be relevant to your interests, you may decide to see an article in its entirety. You can get the whole article with the GET command by sending a message: GET article articlename. You will get the articles that are specified by their article IDs. For example

```
get news.announce.conferences.3670
```

Once you have received several articles, you can fine tune your search using the "feedback" command to tell the service to look for articles like others that you have received. A feedback message could look like the following:

```
feedback 1
like news.announce.conferences.3670
```

The "1" after the "feedback" command is your subscription number, a number assigned when you send the original "subscribe" message to the Stanford server. Following the "like" command on the second line is the article that you want the service to use as a model for future searches.

You can update your subscription, changing the period, expiration or threshold number using the "update" command. You enter "update" and the subscription identification number on the first line. On the following lines you then must enter the parameters you want updated. You can also change the key words associated with the subscription by using the update command. On the second line you enter the command "profile" followed by the new key words.

To cancel your subscription, you send a message with "cancel," followed by your subscription ID number. The "list" command reports all the subscriptions you have.

The news filtering service is geared to finding contemporary messages. It can also search recent archives of Usenet news group messages using the "search" command. The body of your message reads "search," followed by the key words for which you are looking. You may want to include a threshold command on the second line. You should end every series of commands with the command "end" particularly if a signature file is routinely appended to your e-mail.

While not 100 percent efficient or inclusive, this service is a helpful way to identify network news groups that may be discussing issues relevant to stories on which you are working. It is also a good method to receive appropriate articles without having to read a host of news groups regularly.

Proper Usenet behavior

Like other groups of people interacting, people communicating with each other via news groups have developed their own rules of etiquette. If you begin to assert yourself in a group without understanding how to behave, at least some people in the group are bound to get mad at you. While you might think that might not make a difference, boorish behavior may mean that you will miss a good lead or contact.

Rules of Usenet Netiquette

Never forget that the person on the other side is human.
Don't blame system administrators for their users' behavior.
Never assume that a person is speaking for their organization.
Be careful what you say about others.
Be brief.
Your postings reflect upon you; be proud of them.
Use descriptive titles
Think about your audience.
Be careful with humor and sarcasm.
Only post a message once.
Please rotate material with questionable content.
Summarize what you are following up.
Use mail, don't post a follow-up.
Read all follow-ups and don't repeat what has already been said.
Double-check follow-up newsgroups and distributions.
Be careful about copyrights and licenses.
Cite appropriate references.
When summarizing, summarize.
Mark or rotate answers or spoilers.
Spelling flames considered harmful.
Don't overdo signatures.
Limit line length and avoid control characters.
Please do not use Usenet as a resource for homework assignments.
Please do not use Usenet as an advertising medium.
Avoid posting to multiple newsgroups.

Fig. 9-9: Primer for Usenet users by Chuq Von Rospach, posted to the news.answers news group. The primer stands as a rules of net news etiquette, or "netiquette," for people who post to news groups.

People just starting to read network news should probably read several of the FAQs about Usenet itself aimed at new users. The news.answers news group carries most of the relevant FAQs for new users, including what to do if you have questions about network news. A primer for new Usenet users written by Chuq Von Rospach available in the news.answers news group summarizes the rules for working with the Usenet community is shown in Figure 9-9.

As a journalist, you may not find yourself fully participating in the discussions in a particular news groups. More commonly, you will monitor the traffic – which is called "lurking" in online jargon – to identify people with whom you may want to be in touch outside the context of the news group or to discover leads to other sources of information.

You can think of a news group as any other kind of public forum. As a reporter, if you attended a community meeting, you probably would not grab the microphone and begin interviewing a person who you thought made an interesting comment. Instead, you would try to take them aside, identify yourself as a journalist, and talk to them privately to elaborate on their remarks. You should follow the same process with a news group.

On the other hand, it certainly is not impolite to inform the group of the reason for your participation and invite people to get in touch with you via e-mail if they have information they wish to share.

Internet Relay Chat: Real time interaction

Network news is not an e-mail system. On the other hand, although people can be interacting with each other in almost real time if they are posting the server at nearly the same time, news groups do not necessarily have the feel of an interactive conversation either. When you access a news group, you see a list of messages, and you choose the messages you want to read and to respond to.

Live, real time conversation is available over the Internet through a service called Internet Relay Chat (IRC). Originally written by Jarkko Oikarinen in Finland in 1988, it has been used in more than 60 countries around the world. It is a multiuser chat system, where people convene on "channels" to talk in groups, publicly or privately. Channels are generally defined by the topics that are being discussed at that moment.

IRC has emerged as an interesting back channel of communication during several major, breaking news stories. In the first few hours following the Northridge earthquake in 1994, IRC was more reliable than telephone communications. During the police freeway pursuit and subsequent arrest of O.J. Simpson, Los Angeles residents, joined by fans and other interested folks, gathered in IRC channels like "#OJ" set up spontaneously to discuss the matter. When other, more traditional means of communication have been blocked or interrupted during the progress of a major news event, IRC has proved a viable alternative.

But you should be aware that Internet Relay Chat is also fraught with many shortcomings. IRC clients are not as widely distributed as some other Internet tools. Conversation can be difficult to follow, especially in active channels when many people are chatting simultaneously. IRC forces people to communicate under assumed nicknames, which encourages artificial conversation, use of jargon, and complicates the process of verifying information.

Using IRC

When you launch Internet Relay Chat, you are greeted by your site's Message of the Day, which in IRC jargon is abbreviated simply "MOTD." The MOTD usually provides information about the site as well as current IRC traffic throughout the network. Figure 9-10 shows the MOTD at Texas A&M University's IRC client site. You are asked for a nickname or "handle" you want to be known as while you are using IRC. If you have a local client, you can make your nickname permanent so you don't have to fill it in each time.

Once you log onto an IRC client and enter a nickname, you may automatically start on an active channel called #chatzone or you may simply be staring at an inactive screen. All IRC channel names start with the # sign. All IRC commands are initiated with a slash mark. Most of the commands are logical.

To become a part of a chat session, you need to know the name of the channel. You can get a list of the different channels that are in use at that particular moment and the number of people talking on them. You do this by typing the "/list" command.

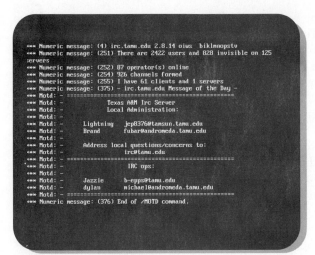

Fig. 9-10: The welcome screen and Message of the Day from the IRC client at Texas A&M University. The screen reports the number of users (2,422), the number of active channels (926), operators (87), servers from the site (1), and clients (87).

Don't do this if you are in a hurry. The greeting screen in Figure 9-10 reports 926 active channels. If you enter the "/list"command with no qualifying description, hundreds of channels will scroll past your screen. You can pause the scrolling by typing Ctrl-S and restart the scrolling by typing Ctrl-Q, but you are going to have a long scroll regardless.

Instead, you could do a search for channels on your topic by using a key word and wild card marks. If the topic is "earthquake," you could give the command

/list *quake* <CR>

and hope to turn up the channel. You might try other combinations to find a relevant channel.

You join a conversation by issuing the command "/join" followed by #(channel name). When you first join a channel, IRC announces that you have joined to everyone else on the channel and gives you a list of the nicknames of all those currently in the channel.

IRC can support both public and private conversations. When you are participating in a public conversation, everything you write is seen immediately by everybody who is participating on that channel. The action can be fast and furious if a lot of people have a lot to say at the same time.

The conversation on most IRC channels is pretty mundane, not the stuff of which news is. Several people typically are online getting to know each other. In many ways it is like a party line telephone conversation without the $2 a minute charge and frequently with an international flavor. So in many cases, while it may be fun for participants, it may not be an important tool for journalists.

But when a major news story breaks, IRC can be very useful. In the same way that people run to the telephone to spread information about

Fig. 9-11: Text stream from the IRC channel #earthquake on the afternoon of Jan. 17, 1994. Each line of dialog is preceded by the sender's nick-name in parenthesis. Channel status changes are preceded by a series of three asterisks.

```
*** Signoff: doc
(APNews) Michale Jordan is going to play for Chicago WhiteSox?
*** Change: moo-man has left this Channel
*** Change: m80 has joined this Channel (#earthquake)
*** Change: serra has left this Channel
(APNews) BBC on 15.260mHz.
(Corax) I've been relaying this to several bbs talk channels in the UK. They
say thanks, to all the news guys.
*** Signoff: abb3w
(Taner) APNews: KhZ
(Corax) *xanaduu* has san bernardino been affected?  i dont know exactly where it is
(KNBC_News) thanx
(Corax) +in relation to the quake and the damage
*** Change: VisionC has left this Channel
(Newswire) Many victims of the Southern California earthquake may
(Taner) kHz - not MHz
(Newswire) face staggering repair bills since they lack insurance that will pay
(Newswire) for fixing their homes.
(Newswire)   People will be able to claim fire damage under standard homeowner
(Newswire) policies, insurance experts said. But many residents will not be
(Newswire) covered if their homes collapsed or had other structural damage due to
*** Signoff: bmca
(Newswire) the quake.
*** Change: GoldDrake has joined this Channel (#earthquake)
*** Change: hoyt has joined this Channel (#earthquake)
(Newswire)   Even those who bought special earthquake insurance may face steep
(Newswire) bills, because earthquake insurance policies typically require
(Newswire) customers to cover 5% to 10% of the damage themselves.
(Newswire)   Therefore, a couple with a $150,000 home, and quake insurance, might
*** Signoff: ScurvyDog
*** Signoff: peacelady
(Newswire) have to pay for the first $15,000 of damage out of their own pockets.
*** Change: pyd040 is now known as StarHawk
(Newswire)   ''I think there's quite a number of people who don't have the
*** Change: ellie has joined this Channel (#earthquake)
*** Change: DeadCupid has joined this Channel (#earthquake)
(Newswire) coverage,'' said Rock Jenkins, a spokesman for State Farm Insurance,
(Newswire) the biggest provider of homeowners' insurance in California.
(Newswire)   The Insurance Information Institute estimates that 25% of all
```

breaking news, some people now log onto IRC to chat. Moreover, the Internet was designed to withstand physical disruptions to any one part of the network and still continue to function. Therefore, even if the long distance telephone network is overburdened with calls or down for some other reason, IRC may still be functioning.

That was the case on Jan. 17, 1994, when the Northridge earthquake hit. The command to join the #earthquake discussion on that day was

/join #earthquake <CR>

One hundred sixty people were listed as participants in the #earthquake channel. If all 160 people who had joined #earthquake tried to chat at once, the resulting cacophony would have defeated all human communication processes. Less than a dozen – generally affiliated with news organizations – had posting privileges.

As it was, much of the discussion was interrupted by reports of channel traffic – people entering and leaving the channel. Figure 9-11 shows a small section of #earthquake chat from the day of the Northridge quake. The conversation is dominated by "Newswire" reporting on the insurance uncertainties quake victims would be facing. The two or three paragraphs of the Newswire statement are interrupted repeatedly both by channel traffic reporting and by others authorized to use the channel for chat.

Even with fewer than 12 people allowed to chat, the conversation can be hard to follow, especially if scores of other folks are drifting in and out of the channel. Still, IRC provided an alternative tool for reporters not on the scene in Los Angeles.

Moreover, during coup attempts and other major political upheavals, government officials may easily take over traditional means of mass communication such as broadcast stations. But it is very difficult to shut down the computer communications infrastructure in an entire country on short notice. During the demonstrations in Beijing in 1989, Chinese officials had no problem pulling the plug on CNN. Information still flowed out of the country via fax machines, however. IRC now can function in much the same way.

IRC access

As with other Internet services, users of IRC run a client program that connects to a server somewhere in the Internet. IRC is most convenient if you have a local client. To see if you do, type IRC at the system prompt. If you do not have a local client installed, you should try to cajole your systems people to install one. As with most Internet client programs, the software for the client is in the public domain.

There are several public access sites for IRC, but they tend to be crowded and can be unreliable from time to time. To reach a public access IRC client, you Telnet to the address. You must include the port number in the Telnet address. If you don't, you will not be able to log onto the remote computer. Here are addresses of some public access clients:

    sci.dixie.edu 6677
    exuokmas.ecn.uoknor.edu 6677
    obelix.wu-wien.ac.at 6996
    irc.tuzvo.sk 6668
    irc.nsysu.edu.tw 6668
    tiger.itc.univie.ac.at 6668

Public access sites allow a very limited number of users. For example, sci.dixie.edu (at the Dixie College Center for Excellence in Southern Utah) will allow only eight users at any one time. Of the systems listed, irc.tuzvo.sk allows the most public access users at any one time – 32 – but is not a great site either. It is located in Slovakia; not only is the message of the day in Slovakian, but communication is very slow.

Only the first two addresses in the list are in the United States. Obelix.wu-wien.ac.at and tiger.itc.unvie.ac.at are in Austria, and irc.nsysu.edu.tw is in Taiwan.

Usenet, IRC, and journalism

Both network news and Internet Relay Chat are fun to use. They represent ways to communicate with people around the world about topics of interest. By talking to people, journalists can get interesting ideas for stories as well as interesting leads to information.

But you have to keep in mind that just because somebody is computer savvy enough to be participating in a news group or an IRC channel, does not mean he or she knows anything about the issue. Many news groups are filled with rumors and mistakes, particularly about current affairs. Information gathered there has to be carefully checked out and verified.

Fig. 9-12: Common commands for Internet Relay Chat appear below. All IRC commands start with a slash mark. If you don't use the slash, whatever you type is sent as dialog into the current IRC channel.

Some Basic IRC Commands

/Bye	Leaves not only the channel, but IRC altogether. Synonyms = / exit and /quit.
/Ch	Followed by a channel name, takes you into the channel. If the channel does not exist, /Ch creates the channel. For example, "/ Ch #ozone" enters or creates a channel called "#ozone."
/Help	Invokes the help facility, which explains IRC commands.
/Ignore	Followed by a nickname or an Internet mail address, effectively blocks communication from the named individual.
/Join	Followed by a channel name, joins an existing channel. Unlike the /Ch command, /Join will not create a channel.
/List	Gives you a list of the active IRC channels. You may give arguments, using the wildcard * to limit the number of channels reported.
/Log	Followed by a file name starts a log file of your IRC session.
/Msg	Followed by the nickname of someone on the channel, and by the text of a message, sends a private message to that person. If you are in a channel with restricted posting access, you can message a person who has channel privileges, and ask for the right to post.
/Names	Shows the nicknames of all users on the channel.
/Nick	Followed by a new nickname changes your nickname.
/Part	Gets you off the current channel but leaves you in IRC.
/Quit	Same as /Exit or /Bye, takes you out of IRC.
/Who	Followed by the channel name tells you who is on a given channel, including their nickname, user name and host, and real name.
/Whois	Followed by a person's nickname shows the true identity of the person.

With IRC, the information you will see is even less trustworthy than with news groups. Everybody participating on IRC is using a nickname. Being anonymous is part of the fun; it lowers inhibitions and often increases sociability. But once people assume another identity, you can never tell if what they are telling you is the truth. You have to be very careful before you believe and report information obtained through IRC. Indeed, some people believe that as many as 80 percent of the people who identify themselves as women in the interactive games played on the Internet are, in fact, men. This same kind of deception can occur in other forums of Internet communication as well.

And while it seems that a good argument can be made that people who are participating in a news group or on IRC are participating in a public forum, they often do not know that a reporter is present and that they are on the record. Consequently, online journalists repeatedly debate when you can and ought to use information somebody posts to a news group. You should carefully consider all the ramifications of your actions including how much confidence you have in the accuracy of the information, how necessary the information is to your story, who will or could be hurt by the quote, and other issues before you make a decision.

On the other hand, Usenet news groups and Internet Relay Chat offer an intriguing new possibility for journalists: the opportunity to include the views of informed non-experts in stories. As has been widely noted, in many cases the information reporters use comes from a narrow slice of elite and expert opinion.

Though there are many reasons for that, one is that it was hard for journalists to identify and interview non-experts whose opinions may be significant. With the emergence of Usenet news groups concerned with professional sports teams, sports reporters could include information from fans as well as the usual quotes from the players and management in their stories. The alt.fan discussion groups on Usenet give reporters easy access to loyal fans for all teams. Not surprisingly, the baseball strike in the summer of 1994 was a hot topic of discussion for some news groups.

Usenet and IRC can provide journalists with access to people who may not be experts on a subject or part of the elite but yet are interested and have informed opinions. How that access is and should be managed and made to work for reporters has not yet been worked out. Over time, however, it could change the flavor and sourcing of many different types of reporting. And even today, Usenet and IRC are viable was for reporters to gather information and leads when more traditional means are cut off.

Further reading

While many of the standard Internet books talk about Internet Relay Chat, few give even the sparse details we have given. What they do give may help you understand something we have not been clear on. The Krol, Gilster, and Dern books all mention IRC in passing. Network news, however, is well documented in many books. You might also consider:

1. Howard Rheingold, *The Virtual Community: Homesteading on the Electronic Frontier*, (Reading, Massachusetts; Addison-Wesley, 1993).
2. Peter Rutten, Albert F. Bayers III, and Kelly Maloni, *Net Guide,* (New York: Random House, 1994).
3. Eric Braun, *The Internet Directory,* (New York: Ballentine, 1994).

Magazines that deal with network news include:
1. *Internet World* published by Meckler Media.
2. *Wired* Magazine, published by Wired Ventures, Ltd.

Chapter **10**

Putting online tools to work

In 1994, live network news coverage reached new saturation levels. One Friday night in June, people flipping through the channels of their television sets watched as the Los Angeles Police Department chased and apprehended former football star O.J. Simpson, a suspect in the murder of Nicole Brown Simpson and her friend, Ronald Goldman.

For months, the story seized extensive coverage by every media outlet from NBC to the National Enquirer. Reporters covered the investigation, Simpson's prior record of spousal abuse, the pretrial hearing, Simpson's financial situation, police forensic techniques, the efficiency of DNA testing, and most conceivable aspects of the case. In less than a month, several book-length biographies of Simpson appeared and a made-for-television movie was in the works. As could be expected, as many as half a dozen network news groups were formed on the Internet to discuss the case, including alt.oj.die.die.

In many ways, the O.J. Simpson story resembled an information monsoon. The public was drenched with information. And, unfortunately, a lot of what was reported was inaccurate or misleading.

The Simpson case represents one of the challenges journalists face as more information becomes more accessible through new technology. While the essence of contemporary journalism – collecting information about events, people, and trends; placing that information within an appropriate context, and then crafting an accurate and interesting story – should remain relatively unchanged, each task will become much more complicated. As the sources for information multiply, as the channels through which reporters can communicate with people grow, and as the potential contexts within which information can be understood increase, journalists will have to work smarter and more efficiently to successfully do their work.

This chapter will cover three areas.

- It will suggest a strategy for using computer-based network tools to strengthen reporting.
- It will offer two case studies in which network tools were used. The first example concerns breaking news; the second is an enterprise article. The case studies present a realistic picture of the of the Internet in journalism. The steps the reporters took in those articles can be followed by anybody with access to the Internet.
- The chapter will close with some words of caution about online reporting.

The reporting process

Good reporters learn how to develop research strategies that will produce thorough, accurate information. They learn to dig, poke, prod and peruse; to pore over documents in court houses, libraries and other repositories. They learn to ask tough questions in interviews, to play one source of information against another, to do whatever it takes to shed light on the issue under examination.

But they don't do so blindly. The best reporters relentlessly and systematically gather information.

Reporting a story can be broken into five steps. Every story starts with an idea. A reporter, an editor, a source or a reader has an idea that the public should know something. For example, Ralph Nader felt the American people should know about the safety performance of the General Motors Corvair. The result was his book, *Unsafe at Any Speed,* which placed automotive safety on the public agenda.

The next step is research. Traditionally, for newspaper reporters research has meant a trip to the clip morgue. Enterprising reporters typically conduct more extensive research. By reading what other reporters have written, you can learn whether you have an original idea. You will also identify potential sources of information including experts and documentary records.

The third step is self education. This process usually involves locating and studying books, articles, documents and reports – or sections of those kinds of publications – which have not yet received widespread publicity. By doing homework, you will be able to formulate insightful questions for the people who you will eventually interview.

Interviewing people is the fourth part of the process. By and large journalists report on the activities of people. That generally requires reporters to communicate with people involved with the story directly to elicit the most appropriate, interesting information for your article.

The final step in reporting is checking the accuracy of information. If reporters have questions about facts, they look for additional sources to verify or contradict the information they have. Sometimes, they will check back with a source to be sure they correctly understood what they were told or what they read.

The reporting process is not linear. For example, although journalists may start with one idea for a story, as information is gathered, the focus can change. In the mid-1980s, James Steele and Donald Barlett of the *Philadelphia Inquirer* wanted to learn what happened to people laid off from factory jobs. They finished with an award-winning series about the policies that led to a growing gap between the rich and the poor during the presidency of Ronald Reagan.

As you gather information, you have to be ready to pursue new leads; you have to be ready to return to do more research and you have to be prepared to talk to more people. During the Watergate investigation, lawyers from the special prosecutor's office through an offhand question to a midranking official learned that President Richard Nixon had taped every conversation in the White House. His answer led to the information that eventually resulted in Nixon's resignation. Good reporters complete many iterations of those steps before they consider the story complete.

Of course, not every assignment requires the same kind of reporting. Many routine or ongoing stories do not require a reporter to read clips or access obscure documents. But even stories for which reporters rely on a single source and stories that they know quite a bit about already can sometimes be improved through better reporting practices.

Online tools and reporting

Many journalists believe that conscientious reporting is the soul of good journalism. In the future, the methods reporters use to collect information will be one of the ways to distinguish journalists from other types of information professionals.

Consequently, the ways in which you use the Internet and other electronic resources in reporting is very significant. Computer-based networks can help you in every aspect of reporting. They can be a source of good story ideas. Online resources can be used to survey public records and to identify other sources. The Internet and other networks provide gateways to documentary sources of information such as government and university data bases that were once inaccessible to reporters who lived far away or were not experts in a given subject area. Computer-based communication can be used to communicate with individuals privately. And, electronic networks can help facilitate fact checking.

A suggested story development strategy

In a typical scenario, a reporter could monitor discussion lists and network news groups trolling for new story ideas. It is like listening in on conversations among people who are deeply interested in a specific subject.

Next, you can review newspaper articles that may bear on your story idea. With CompuServe, Dow Jones News Retrieval and other commercial information services, you can set up a clipping service to save appropriate articles from selected news wires such as AP, UPI or Reuters. With Internet access, you can use Telnet to use the public access catalog set up by the Colorado Alliance of Research Libraries (pac.carl.org) to use the National News Index. The National News Index uses key word searches to locate articles published since 1989 in five newspapers including the *Washington Post, New York Times,* and *Wall Street Journal.*

For more in-depth and less publicized information, you can use search tools such as Gopher, WAIS and the World Wide Web to locate relevant documents. Using these search tools or Telnet, you can search vast repositories of online information. E-mail is used to communicate directly with people. Or you can set up a private, online interview with Internet Relay Chat.

Finally, you can check your information by circulating it to people you have identified through the discussion lists and network news groups. Moreover, you can easily check technical information using e-mail.

Clearly, computer network-based tools can contribute to every part of the reporting process. But they should not be the sole tools reporters use to gather their information. These new tools must be integrated with the traditional ways reporters work. The following case studies demonstrate the way we used the Internet and other electronic sources to complete our assignments. The first case study looks at the experience of Randy Reddick, who used the Internet to report on a breaking news story. The second looks at the way Elliot King used online resources for an enterprise reporting assignment.

Case 1: The Northridge earthquake of 1994

At 4:31 a.m. on Monday, Jan. 17, 1994, the ground in California's San Fernando Valley shook with a violence that produced the most costly natural disaster in U.S. history. An earthquake registering 6.7 on the Richter scale jolted a densely populated suburb northwest of Los Angeles. Apartment buildings collapsed. Water mains and gas lines broke. Sections of the freeway buckled and fires erupted throughout the valley. In all, 57 people died and 20,000 lost their homes in the Northridge earthquake.

The quake was a major news story. But in the predawn hours, there was no way to know how serious the quake was. News people and public safety officials at the scene had difficulty sizing up the damage. Complicating matters, electrical power and telecommunications networks had been interrupted, making communication with the rest of the world slow and erratic. People in Los Angeles knew little about what had really happened. People not in L.A. knew less.

Within half an hour of the initial shock, Los Angeles television stations were on the air with reports of significant damage at least in isolated areas. But details were slow in coming and updates were sporadic.

I am based in Texas and decided to see if I could use the Internet as an alternative source of information. I only faced one problem. Where to begin?

Locating official information

I started my search using Veronica and Jughead, search tools described in Chapter 7. I also knew that there are several Gopher projects that offer subject-oriented searchable lists of Internet resources. One of these is "Gopher Jewels," a list of gopher servers that maintain archives and pointers to other archives focused upon specialty topics. Ironically, the Gopher site which contains the "live" version of Gopher Jewels is located at the University of Southern California (cwis.usc.edu) and was knocked off the network for five hours following the earthquake.

A static version of the Gopher Jewels list – that is, one that lists the resources but does not automatically log you onto different servers – from Rice University contained the address of a Gopher server at the Oklahoma Geological Survey open station (wealaka.okgeosurvey1.gov). Its Root menu appears in Figure 10-1. I used menu selection 12 to connect to other seismic sites outside Oklahoma, hoping to find information about the events in California.

My first choice, the USGS's U.S. National Earthquake Information Gopher in Golden, Colo., proved fruitless. The files were several days to several weeks old. One of the "outside Oklahoma" sites listed on the Oklahoma Gopher was the Earthquake Information Gopher at the University of California at Berkeley. I selected that Gopher, which had a menu item titled "California OES Earthquake Program." I had been a reporter in California earlier in my career and I knew that OES is an acronym for the state's Office of Emergency Services. But even reporters without an understanding of the

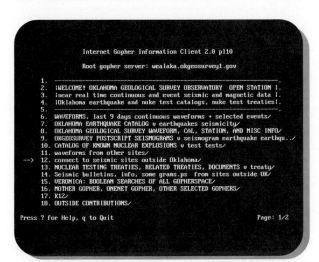

Fig. 10-1: First page of the Root menu for Oklahoma's Geological Survey Observatory Open Station contains the option (12) of connecting to seismic sites outside Oklahoma. This option ultimately led to sites in California rich with earthquake information.

acronym had only to select the menu item to gather its meaning. The OES program offers the option to Telnet (Figure 10-2) to the OES Emergency Digital Information Services (EDIS).

Operated by the governor's Office of Emergency Services, EDIS is a simple Telnet (Chapter 5) site. On Jan. 17, it offered a menu of the 14 latest messages from EDIS. Each message is numbered and one line of information about the message gives a headline, select code, date and time the message was posted and the source. A line across the bottom of the screen instructs the user to either enter a message number or leave the line blank to exit. When I first logged on, half the messages were more than three days old or indicated that they were system tests rather than newsworthy information (Figure 10-3).

But the latest message on the screen, number 0393, had the headline "Urgent News Release." It had been posted on Jan. 17 at 5:25 a.m., 54 minutes after the quake had struck. I knew I was in business.

The first message posted to the EDIS site on Jan. 17 gave minimal quake statistics and ended with a plea and a promise to the media. It asked that the media not telephone OES at that time and promised to provide additional information as soon as it was available.

OES kept its promise. It provided updated information approximately every 12 minutes for the first six hours following the quake. Morning postings included information from Caltrans (the state's highway department) listing highway closures and damage as well as Red Cross relief efforts, disaster declarations, the activities of the Federal Emergency Management Agency (FEMA), reports on structural damage and evacuations, the locations of relief shelters, and the number of deaths. Press releases and media advisories were regularly posted. There were reports of oil spills, a spill of hydrochloric acid, and a derailed train spilling 5,000 gallons of sulfuric acid. The postings contained accounts of the U.S. Air Force flying surveillance missions, the

Fig. 10-2: The OES Earthquake Program Gopher launches a Telnet session with a warning. The Telnet address for the Emergency Digital Information Service is provided in the warning. The EDIS Telnet site was a major center for "official" information during the Northridge earthquake.

California Conservation Corps assembling resource lists, National Guard deployments, and public safety officials coming from neighboring counties.

From this one site, I was able to obtain "official" information from several government agencies including the Federal Emergency Management Agency, Caltrans, the office of the Governor of California, and several public utilities as well as the Red Cross and other groups on the scene. I was able to get information via the Internet that would take other reporters much more time to track down by telephone. Or they would have to attend endless press conferences, if they could get to the scene themselves.

Live sources

But I wanted to get more than just documentary sources. At the time, I knew of three discussion lists that cater to journalists: Journet, CARR-L and NIT-Chron (see appendix for addresses). While official sources were busy gathering official information, reporters were hard at work as well. At 7:54 a.m., a woman from Pasadena posted a message about the quake to CARR-L. She attached her e-mail address and she consented to be interviewed.

As time passed, more people began to post to the discussion list and reporters began to share sources of information they had found on the network. In the three days after the temblor first struck, more than 20 messages were posted to the journalists' CARR-L list directing people to Internet resources relevant to the earthquake, including Quake-L, an established list that focuses on earthquake information.

At 9:35 a.m. on the first day, Adam Gaffin of Framingham, Mass., posted a notice that an Internet Relay Chat (see Chapter 9) channel called #Earthquake had been established to share news about the quake. Actually two channels were set up; one to distribute news and the other to discuss events.

```
          State of California - Governor's Office of Emergency Services
                 EMERGENCY DIGITAL INFORMATION SERVICE (EDIS)
                              Latest Messages

     Number  Headline                        Select  Date/Time    Source
     0380    NEWS RELEASE.................    c2bp-   Jan 13 16:29  bfd
     0381    TEST MESSAGE.................    d0-p-   Jan 14 05:47  fema
     0382    TEST MESSAGE.................    d6cp-   Jan 14 09:24  sdsd
     0383    TEST MESSAGE.................    d6cp-   Jan 14 09:31  sdsd
     0384    TEST MESSAGE.................    d6cp-   Jan 14 09:43  sdsd
     0385    EDIS SYSTEM TEST.............    d0-o-   Jan 14 10:00  OES
     0386    TEST MESSAGE.................    d2bp-   Jan 14 13:59  sfoes
     0387    EDIS SYSTEM TEST.............    d0-o-   Jan 15 10:00  OES
     0388    EDIS SYSTEM TEST.............    d0-o-   Jan 15 16:16  OES
     0389    TEST MESSAGE.................    d0-p-   Jan 15 16:19  edis
     0390    EARTHQUAKE INFORMATION.......    c0-q-   Jan 15 19:13  NWS
     0391    TEST MESSAGE.................    d2bp-   Jan 15 21:46  sonsar
     0392    EDIS SYSTEM TEST.............    d0-o-   Jan 16 10:00  OES
     0393    URGENT NEWS RELEASE..........    b0-p-   Jan 17 05:25  edis

     Enter Message Number (blank to exit): 0393
```

Fig. 10-3: The Emergency Digital Information Service (EDIS) is Telnet offering of California's Office of Emergency Services. On the morning of the Northridge earthquake, the first OES release on the quake appeared as item 0393 (bottom of the menu) at 5:25 a.m.

The IRC #Earthquake channel was dominated by people representing news agencies in the Los Angeles area including the television stations KNBC and KTLA, as well as AP News. Figure 9-11 shows an edited transcript of #Earthquake at 3 p.m. on the day of the quake. On a very active channel, IRC is often hard to follow because every incoming message interrupts what is being displayed on the screen.

In addition to IRC, the participants in three network news groups, la.general, alt.current-events.la-quake, and alt.california, began sharing information about the quake. On the day of the quake Kurt Foss of Madison, Wisc. noticed that Calvin Ogawa had posted a notice in alt.california five days earlier, observing, "a swarm of minor earthquakes, ranging from 2.0 to 4.0 (on the Richter scale)" in the Los Angeles Area concentrated over three days. Ogawa predicted in his network message, "I think we're in for a sizable one, if not the big one." The *Los Angeles Times* ran a story about the prediction on January 19, two days after the quake occurred.

The final piece of the puzzle was background information. How significant were the events at Northridge? To answer that question, I used an Archie search to look for files with relevant earthquake information on FTP servers. The search returned "hits" at 12 different host computers bearing 18 files as well as four directories with the word "earthquake" in the name. In this group I found historical information about earthquakes.

I also conducted a Veronica search of Gopher servers. This search identified 1,095 leads, including the USGS-U.S. National Earthquake Information Service Gopher in Golden, Colo. One file contained information about the most destructive earthquakes in the world; another outlined the 10 largest quakes in the U.S. (both including and not including earthquakes in Alaska). A third classified earthquakes by magnitude. There were also several documents with general information about earthquakes of interest to the general reader as well as maps, graphs and technical data.

In the final analysis, Internet resources proved to be a productive source of news for this breaking story. Even though I was in Lubbock, Texas, I was able to get all the "hard" data provided by official sources in a timely fashion without relying on a wire service or uncertain telephone communications. Moreover, the accurate information could be "pasted" into a story without having to transcribe it. Furthermore, I was able to access background information and even communicate with some people who were present at the scene.

On the other hand, a "virtual" press conference is not the same as a real press conference. I was not able to ask official questions or to probe for information that may have been of interest to me. Furthermore, the number of individuals with whom I could communicate directly was limited. That limited the amount of information I had to set the scene or describe the actual events.

Case 2: New technologies fight against AIDS

As opposed to the coverage of breaking events, enterprise reporting for magazine and longer newspaper articles often starts with an insight and a series of questions. The insight is that a particular angle or aspect of a public issue has never been fully and openly explored. The questions follow from there.

I am the editor of a monthly magazine that reports on the use of new technology in science. In the course of that work, I regularly cover federal initiatives including the Human Genome Project (a multibillion dollar foray into molecular biology), the $8 billion supercollider project for advanced research into particle physics, and the Hubble Telescope, which has led to breakthrough research in astronomy.

Each of those projects involved the development of new technology for science. Indeed, long before the first computer ENIAC was developed with funding from the Department of Defense, the federal government had been a prime sponsor of technological development in science and engineering. And, as NASA officials have frequently pointed out, the technologies developed through these efforts often have spin-off applications with uses well beyond the scope of the initial project. The Internet is a primary example.

In 1993, I began to wonder about the potential technological spin-offs from the fight against AIDS. AIDS had been a priority public health problem for nearly a decade, and the administration of President Bill Clinton had increased federal funding for AIDS research, treatment and education to $1.3 billion a year.

I knew that when the federal government heavily funds an effort in a specific area, it has several effects. First, scientists who rely on federal grants to support their work will tackle issues that they believe will be able to tap into the available source of funds. Second, if the problem is seen as a national priority, often riskier, more experimental science will win funding. In these cases, the peer review process generally used to issue grants will be modified in ways designed to move work forward more quickly.

As far as I knew, nobody had ever looked at AIDS as a large-scale federal science project. Instead of looking at how devastating the problem was, the state of drug development, how community education programs were or were not working, new populations of people at risk or any other of the more commonly reported issues, I wanted to find out the impact the multibillion dollar investment in the fight against AIDS was having on the technological infrastructure of the medical and biomedical community.

The story promised to be very intriguing. For many good reasons, biologists have been relatively slow to embrace computer technology. Many of the methods and procedures biologists use do not map easily onto computer-based techniques. Moreover, unlike physics and some other disciplines, biology labs historically have not been the sites of large-scale investment in technology, and, consequently, graduate students in the past were not well-trained in computing and automation technology. In many ways, the current generation in biology represents the pioneering generation for advanced technology.

Given that context, I suspected that the availability of federal funding coupled with the urgency associated with fighting AIDS could accelerate the introduction of new technology into many sites. First, medical research is under pressure to find a response to AIDS quickly. To do so, scientists have to turn to new tools to help them. Secondly, scientists who could show that advanced technology could have an impact on their work would have an easier time getting funds to invest. The thrust of the article was to find out if I was right. Was there a technological silver lining to the AIDS cloud?

Working within constraints

The magazine *Scientific Computing & Automation,* which I edit, and for which I planned to write the article, is a monthly with a circulation of 75,000 scientists and engineers. We have an editorial staff of one full-time and one part-time person.

Most of our articles are contributed by working scientists and engineers, so we have no provisions for the editors to do a lot of reporting. Therefore, I could not be freed from my other editorial responsibilities – to say nothing of my responsibilities as a professor at Loyola College – to investigate this article for weeks on end. At best, I could hope to find a few hours here and a few hours there during the month preceding my deadline.

Time constraints, of course, are a constant factor in journalism. Few journalists have the luxury of devoting as much time as they would like to a enterprise story. But I faced another problem as well. I didn't know much about AIDS. While I knew what people could read in the newspapers, I didn't personally know people with AIDS or many people on the front line fighting AIDS. I had no idea where AIDS research was being conducted. I did not have established contacts either in the AIDS community or in the federal, state or local health establishment.

The third constraint was the technology I had at my disposal. I have an account at CompuServe and access to Dow Jones News Retrieval. Through Loyola, I have access to the Internet. At the time, however, Loyola only had basic Internet functions such as FTP, Gopher and Telnet. It did not yet have interfaces like Lynx or Mosaic. Nor did the way I was connected to the VAX computer system at Loyola allow me to use them. I also did not have easy access to Usenet network news.

In other words, all I had was what I thought was a good idea for a story. I had little time to do it, no leads to start, and fairly basic technology at my disposal. Nevertheless, I was undeterred.

The reporting process

In the weeks before I actually started reporting, I clipped anything I came across having to do with AIDS. Neither my magazine nor Loyola has access to Lexis/Nexis; but through the CARL library system at Loyola, I am able to access an index for the *New York Times, Washington Post, Wall Street Journal* and other newspapers at the Montgomery County (Md.) library, about 50 miles away. I also used the Dow Jones News Service to retrieve clips about AIDS and I set up an electronic clipping file on CompuServe.

While only a few of the articles gave me concrete leads, over those weeks I was able to better educate myself about AIDS. At the same time, I mentioned the story to everybody I talked to in the course of my work. As the editor of *Scientific Computing & Automation,* I interact with companies that sell advanced technology to scientists. I asked those people if they knew any of their customers who were working in AIDS research. Several of them did, providing me with a handful of initial leads.

Searching the net

As my deadline approached, I began to step up my reporting activities. I knew that I wanted to identify as many sources using the Internet as possible. My first step was to send a private e-mail message to a scientist I knew at the University of North Carolina. He was not an AIDS researcher but was knowledgeable about scientific resources available on the Internet. He sent a list of several discussion lists that he thought could be appropriate.

He also sent me the FAQ of sci.med.aids. Sci.med.aids is a Usenet news group that discusses AIDS and HIV. It brings together health care professionals, researchers, people with AIDS, partners of people with AIDS and others around the world with an interest in discussing AIDS-related issues. The group estimates that it is read by approximately 40,000 people worldwide.

It is a moderated news group, which means messages are read by a moderator for appropriateness before they are posted to the entire group. Fortunately, the news group has a gateway to a listserv discussion group, so I was able to subscribe to the list even though I did not have easy access to Usenet.

Curiously, the same day my colleague sent me a copy of the sci.med.aids FAQ, I had located it myself using a Veronica search. Using Gopher, I had logged onto the New York Education and Research Network (NYSERNet). One of the menu choices there is "Searching the Internet." I chose it and was offered a selection of half a dozen Veronica servers. I used NYSERNet's Veronica server to enter the key words AIDS FAQ and received the FAQ.

At the same time, I entered the words "AIDS COMPUTERS" which bore directly on my article. Nothing was returned. Later, however, I used the same key words for a Veronica search at the University of Pisa in Italy and I received a list of National Institutes of Health grants that went to several medical centers in the United States. Unfortunately, I did not know where the medical centers were located.

The sci.med.aids FAQ offered a wealth of information. Not only did it tell me how to subscribe to the AIDS discussion list, there was a directory of AIDS-related electronic bulletin boards and other relevant material. Eventually, I talked to a person who ran an AIDS related bulletin board and included that information as an illustration of one of the uses of new technology in this area.

After subscribing to the list and reading it for two days, I posted a message telling people what I was doing and asking them to get in touch with me privately if they were engaged in an activity relevant to my story or knew of other people who were. I received about a dozen responses over the next three days or so. About half a dozen were from people who were using new technology in the fight against AIDS. Several were leads to other scientists who could be good sources. The remainder were people who asked to receive a copy of the article when it was finished.

I responded by e-mail to each of the people who had been in touch. For those who could be sources for the article, I gave them my telephone number and also asked for their telephone numbers and for a convenient time to call them for a telephone interview. I also asked five short questions – such as who they were, how they were involved with AIDS work and when they began their efforts. I thanked the others for their information.

Through the news group, I received 10 solid leads, as well as pointers to articles in easily available medical journals. Perhaps the lead that I would have been least likely to have received in any other way was a from researcher in Denmark working on ways to insure confidentiality for people diagnosed with HIV while notifying the people with whom the person had contact who were now at risk. We exchanged e-mail, and he sent me a preprint of a scholarly article scheduled to be published later in the year.

I received another paper from a computer science major who had taken a course about sexually transmitted diseases. Her term project was about computer-accessible information about AIDS.

In all, with the leads from sci.med.aids, the newspaper sources, and through networking through the magazine, I identified about 20 people who were doing relevant work. For the context within which I was working, I believed that would be enough. I eventually conducted telephone interviews with approximately 15 people about their use of new technology in the fight against AIDS. The applications ranged from designing software to allow scientists to model molecular behavior on computers as part of efforts to design therapeutic drugs, to tracking and testing blood, to providing timely information to doctors treating AIDS patients, to developing computer simulations for predicting the spread of AIDS in different populations given different public policy scenarios.

Several important themes emerged as I interviewed more people. First, every aspect of the AIDS problem is difficult, and computers are part of the effort in every aspect of the problem. Nevertheless, not only were researchers not close to a cure, they still don't know which road will lead to a cure. Much of the proposed public policy probably will not work, and there are no obvious answers to any of the questions raised by AIDS.

Secondly, the idea with which I started the article – that the urgency of and funding for AIDS was accelerating the diffusion of advanced technology in the biomedical community and that there would be ancillary benefits from that process – was only partly correct. Yes, many of the innovative ways computing and automation technology were being used to fight AIDS would be useful in other situations in the future. But, many researchers believed that if AIDS had not been the focal point, another disease or public health problem would have been. Many of the techniques used in biotechnology today, one researcher pointed out, were developed in the concerted federal fight against cancer in the 1970s.

At this point, I knew I had an interesting article. Still, I felt I was lacking context. I wanted to have up-to-date statistics about the scope of the AIDS epidemic and the federal funding efforts. To get those statistics, I again used Gopher to access the computers at the National Institutes of Health and the National Institute for Allergies and Infectious Diseases (Figure 10-4), which has specific responsibility for AIDS research. On the NIAID gopher, I found the latest Surgeon General's Report on AIDS, which, at the time, was approximately six months old.

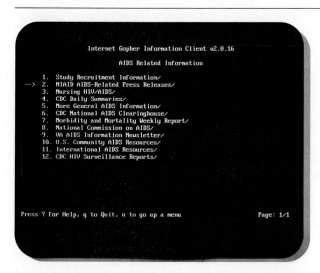

Fig. 10-4: Menu of the AIDS-related section of the NIAID Gopher server. The Surgeon General's report was in the press release section (menu item 2).

I also downloaded all the recent press releases about AIDS subjects issued by NIAID for the past several months. As it turns out, the NIH grants I had come across before had gone to eight Centers for AIDS Research (CFAR) around the country. Through the press releases, I was able to locate each one and the amount of money each received. The NIAID gopher also had a wealth of additional information and additional leads for information.

Now faced with a tight deadline, I could not pursue all of the leads I had. I had to write the story.

While I was writing the story, one of my sources asked me to send him a copy of his quotes to make sure they were accurate. Since I am not an expert in many of the areas on which I report, I often allow sources to check quotes for accuracy. I have found over the years that checking with the source generally improves the quality of the story. Scientists want to be clear, precise, and accurate; and so do I.

I sent him a copy of his direct quotes by e-mail with the proviso that if I did not hear back from him within a specified time limit, I would assume that the quotes were accurate. He did respond and I forwarded his very legitimate changes to the article's copy editor.

Some cautionary words

The case studies above demonstrate that the Internet and other online resources aid reporting both for breaking news and enterprise articles. In fact, the new resources allow reporters to tackle assignments that would have been impossible in the past. As the use and availability of online information grows, the constraints time and place impose on reporters is diminishing.

But online reporting is only one tool. It cannot replace the standard tools used by reporters, particularly, one-on-one interviews with human sources. It is through the one-on-one interview that people's stories come alive.

For example, Ben Barnes operates a computer bulletin board based in Chicago for people with AIDS. It was not difficult to access the board to describe it. Also, he answered several questions via e-mail. But only in a telephone interview did information about his partner who had passed away come to the fore. Only in a telephone interview could you feel his pain and sympathy for AIDS patients confined to hospital beds and who have no visitors. Only at that point could you understand his passion to establish a way for them to communicate with each other and with people who care about them.

While extremely useful, at this point using online resources will only take you so far in the reporting process. Online resources can stimulate story ideas. They will help you educate yourself about a topic. They can be used to prepare you for interviews and can aid you in checking your facts. But, in the end, reporters still have to talk to people, one to one, to get the whole story.

Further Reading

This chapter gives two case study examples of how multiple Internet tools can be brought to bear on one story. The early portions of the chapter also suggest something of a strategy for researching and writing stories. Other resources for guiding journalists in developing research strategies are

1. Lauren Kessler and Duncan McDonald. *The Search: Information Gathering for the Mass Media,* Belmont, CA: Wadsworth, 1992.
2. Jean Ward and Kathleen A. Hansen. *Search Strategies in Mass Communication,* New York: Longman, 1993.

Chapter **11**

Law, ethics and the Internet

In the spring of 1994, Brock Meeks read a notice on the Internet from a company called Electronic Postal Service. The company offered people money for receiving electronic mail, promising that people who signed up could earn between $200 and $500 a year and would receive full Internet access as well.

Meeks, a reporter for *Communications Daily* and publisher of his own Internet news wire (CyberWire Dispatch), asked for more information. The information did not come, he says, but Meeks later received a mailing from a company called Suarez Corporation Industries offering him a business opportunity, which the company claimed could generate from $30,000 to $1 million a year.

Investigating, Meeks discovered that the Electronic Postal Service was an account registered to Suarez Corporation Industries. Moreover, federal and state agencies had brought suits against Suarez for their direct mail practices. Armed with this information, Meeks wrote a story, which he circulated via CyberWire Dispatch expressing his disapproval of Suarez's business practices.

Suarez Industries then sued Meeks for defamation. It alleged that the article disparaged the company's products and interfered with its ability to develop EPS. Suarez filed the suit in Ohio, where it is headquartered. Meeks is based in Washington, D.C.

Meeks is not the first person to be sued for libel based on information circulated on the Internet, but his case has been well publicized. While he vigorously denied that he libeled Suarez, he faced more than $25,000 in legal fees, fees for which he was obligated personally because he wrote the story for his own news wire.

Clearly, the Internet and other electronic networks are not outside the boundaries that generally govern speech and communications media in

America. In the long run, reporters who use new computer-based media may face more restrictions than print journalists, who generally have enjoyed the greatest degree of First Amendment protection.

In the past, in cases such as *Joseph Burstyn, Inc. v. Wilson* the Supreme Court has indicated that different media enjoy different levels of First Amendment protection. The Internet and other communication networks represent a new media of expression. Because messages are usually written, computer-based communication functions like print. Because information can be widely distributed via a network providing one-to-many communication, conceptually it functions to some degree like cable television.

Because some messages appear to be private and because the federal government has played a large role in establishing the network infrastructure, the Internet itself can be seen as something akin to the telephone system before it was deregulated. Because information can appear on people's computers in their homes without them requesting it, some computer networks resemble broadcast networks. And because children can access and use computer-based networks relatively freely, they may face added scrutiny from the courts, which have a special mandate to protect children from certain categories of speech including indecent language.

Taken together, computer-based communications represent uncharted legal territory. The legal and ethical rules are not yet established. This chapter will

- look at six categories of speech with which reporters are traditionally concerned – libel, copyright, confidentiality, obscenity, speech codes, open meeting laws and freedom of information.
- briefly review other free speech issues raised by the growth of computer-based networks.
- examine some of the ethical dilemmas reporters using electronic communications resources may face.

The objective in this chapter is not to issue definitive legal or ethical opinions. Those will be worked out in practice and in court. Instead, it is intended to raise some of the key questions journalists and lawyers confront as reporters incorporate this new communication media into their daily work routines.

Libel

Libel laws are perhaps the most significant set of laws for journalists. The overwhelming majority of news reports about people. Sometimes published information contains false information that may damage the reputation of the people. Libel laws specify when journalists can be punished for publishing false information that may hurt other people.

In 1964, the U.S. Supreme Court issued its landmark ruling *New York Times V. Sullivan*. The court ruled that the news media could not be punished for libel for reporting false information about public officials unless plaintiffs demonstrated that the journalists had acted with "actual malice." The court defined actual malice as a reckless disregard for the truth. The court reasoned that American democracy depended in part on a vigorous press, but a vigorous press was bound to make mistakes from time to time. Therefore, the press needed "breathing room" in which it could make mistakes without being punished.

Since then, the court has issued a series of rulings in which it refined the *Sullivan* decision. In *Gertz v. Robert Welch Inc.* (1973), it ruled that the *Sullivan* standard applied to public figures who had thrust themselves into the forefront of public controversies or had involuntarily been thrust to the forefront. The Sullivan standard did not apply to private figures who had neither thrust themselves nor had been thrust into the public arena. For private people, the states are free to develop their own standards for libel as long as they do not impose liability without fault.

In the 1989 *Harte-Hanks Communications v. Connaught* decision, the court opined that the media exhibited "actual malice" if the reporters or editors most likely knew that the information they planned to publish was false, and they deliberately avoided acquiring the knowledge that would have confirmed the probable falsity of the information. In 1990, the court decided, in *Milkovich v. Lorain Journal Co.*, that "opinion" did not necessarily fall into a separate category regarding First Amendment protection. If an opinion column contained information that was demonstrably false and damaging to a person's reputation, the reporter and publication or broadcast could be punished for libel.

Finally, in 1977, the Second Circuit Court of Appeals decided in *Edwards v. Audubon Society* that reporters and publications could not be punished for libel if they published attributed information from sources which they thought were reliable and credible, even if that information ultimately proved to be false and harmful.

The rules of libel, of course, apply to all journalists. But reporters using the Internet and other electronic communication networks have to be particularly sensitive to potential problems. The first potential pitfall is the notion of a public figure.

What is a public figure?

In some ways, computer-based discussion lists and network news groups are new types of public forums – public forums in which individuals can be as vocal as they choose. Unlike other types of public forums, people on computer networks do not need a particular expertise to be recognized by people with authority, such as the moderator of a public meeting, to express their views.

As you monitor discussion lists and news groups looking for leads or sources of information, the names of people who regularly participate may quickly become very familiar to you, more familiar than perhaps other well known individuals. People who aggressively post to an online discussion may become a source or a subject of a story for you.

It is not clear, however, that people become public figures simply because they are active in online discussion groups. From one vantage point they have clearly thrust themselves into public view (at least regarding the issues they are discussing). From another perspective, they have not. Legally, it is still not clear if even the Internet should be considered a public forum. The status of commercial information services like Prodigy and CompuServe is even murkier. Because being active online may not make a person a public figure, reporter should not believe they are protected by the *Sullivan* rule if they choose to report on people they have encountered online.

Does net culture encourage libel?

The question about who is a public figure is more vexing because of the developing culture of the computer networks themselves. In many online discussions, despite admonitions against it, many participants will "flame" (violently disagree with) other people's messages using intemperate, hostile, and vituperative terms. As noted in Chapter 9, the majority of news groups are unmoderated. That means anybody can post anything. Moreover, from time to time, "flames" may be reposted to other discussion lists, to news groups, and may even be stored in databases.

While people who "flame" others may believe they are exercising their right to free speech, what they post could be libelous. That is, the flames could consist of *verifiably false information* that damages the reputation of the person who has been flamed. Unless there are very compelling reasons, reporters generally should not look at flames as useable, legitimate information.

In most cases, reporters looking for information will monitor the discussion lists and news groups looking for leads and then contact people privately. Nevertheless, they should be aware that almost all individuals participating in those discussions should treated as if they are private individuals for the purposes of libel. Consequently, if reporters choose to include information from or about people they have identified online, they should act accordingly. Because different states have different libel standards for private individuals, reporters must be even more careful to avoid reporting damaging, false information.

The best defense against accusations of libel is *provable* truth. Reporters should treat information they find online, particularly information about people, as critically as they treat information they receive from other sources. Veteran computer users have a long-standing rule of thumb: Garbage in, garbage out. That applies to information found in the Internet and other places as well.

Copyright

Copyright law is often poorly understood by journalists. In short, copyright law is intended to give holders of the copyright the exclusive right of use to what they have created. Generally, that copyright covers the expression of an idea via one of several media. The federal Copyright Act of 1976 created seven categories of authorship including literary works; musical works; dramatic works; sound recordings; audiovisual works; pantomime and choreographies; and pictorial, graphic and sculptural works. An infringement of copyright is judged by three factors: the originality of the work, the proof of access to the copyrighted work and the similarity between the works compared.

Works falling into most of the categories outlined by the Copyright Act can be distributed via computer networks. Because most journalists attribute the information they publish to a source, the key questions are when reporters can quote verbatim material they have found and how much of the work can they use.

A common scenario for online journalists comes when they see an interesting message in a network news group or discussion list and want to quote it directly, crediting the source. Many journalists see news groups and discussion lists as analogous to public meetings. If persons speak during business sessions of a public agency at a public meeting, of course, reporters can quote them. But postings to discussion groups are not spoken words; they are original works of authorship fixed in a tangible medium of expression – in this case electronic – which can be perceived, reproduced or communicated either directly or with the aid of a device, to use language close to that of the copyright statute.

Consequently, when somebody posts something to a list or news group, that posting is presumed to have copyright protection. The person who holds the copyright legally controls how that posting can be used. If the person does not want you to quote the posting, he or she legally may be able to prevent you from doing so.

Copyright infringement is not the only danger you may face in using material you find published via computer-based networks. If you do not directly quote information you find electronically but just use the facts contained, you may be able to avoid copyright infringement. But you may still be guilty of what is called misappropriation.

Misappropriation

Misappropriation is the legal expression of the notion that people should not be allowed to compete unfairly by using the work of others, particularly if they claim the purloined work is their own. The 1918 Supreme Court case

International News Service v. Associated Press is a classic example of misappropriation.

William Randolph Hearst, who owned the International News Service (INS), admitted that he pirated stories from the Associated Press using a variety of tactics. Sometimes INS editors would rewrite the stories – sometimes they wouldn't – before transmitting them to its clients. Hearst claimed that because AP did not copyright the story (the copyright law was somewhat different then) and nobody can copyright the news itself, the information was in the public domain. The Supreme Court decided that although AP did not have copyright protection the INS actions unfairly interfered with AP's operation at precisely the moment when it would reap the profit from efforts.

Misappropriation could emerge as a significant issue for people using online services. On the Internet, for example, many people now publish their own "news services." There are many, perhaps hundreds, of electronic journals circulating, and some print magazines are publishing electronic versions on computer networks. If journalists use these news wires and journals as sources of information, they have to be very careful about how they report the information. It is very easy, and tempting, to download information in an electronic form and cut and paste it into an article. That could open the reporter up to claims of infringement or misappropriation.

The Fair Use doctrine

Copyright laws and the notion of misappropriation, however, do not mean you can never quote information from the Internet. The 1976 copyright law also included provisions for what is known as "fair use" of copyrighted material. The "fair use" provisions allow for others to use portions of copyrighted material without the permission of the copyright holder under certain conditions. The criteria by which "fair use" is evaluated include the purpose and character of the use, including whether the material is used for non-profit educational purposes or for for-profit ventures; the nature of the copyrighted work itself; the amount of material used relative to the total amount of material; and the effect of the use upon the market value of the copyrighted work.

Perhaps the two most important criteria are the nature of the copyrighted work itself and the effect of the use on the market value of the material. In one episode, *Nation* magazine published an excerpt of the memoirs of former President Gerald Ford without permission of Harper & Row, who held the copyright. In the 1984 case *Harper & Row v. Nation Inc.*, the U.S. Supreme Court pointed out that a critical element of the work is whether it is published or not. The scope of "fair use" is considerably narrower for unpublished works.

In 1991, the Second Circuit Court of Appeals underscored the importance of protecting a creator's right to control the first public appearance of the expression of a work in *Wright v. Warner Books Inc*. Nevertheless, it allowed Warner Books to publish a biography of novelist Richard Wright even though it included small portions of his letters and journals stored at the Yale University library and not yet published. Because posting something on a discussion list that may be read by thousands of people is like publishing, the scope of fair use for material found in electronic sources is broader than for things like unpublished personal letters. Electronic messages that have been publicly circulated are probably open for fair use.

A work's market value

The second criterion that should help protect journalists if they choose to quote from news groups or discussion lists is the impact on the potential market value of the material. In *Salinger v. Random House* (1987), the Second Circuit Court of Appeals decided that biographer Ian Hamilton's use of unpublished letters in a biography of the novelist J.D. Salinger was not allowed because, in part, appearing in Hamilton's book could have an impact on the future commercial value of the letters. The panel ruled, however, that the biographer could use the factual content of the letters.

This ruling is significant because most of the postings on discussion lists and news groups probably have no future market value. News group postings are often not archived at all; they simply vanish. Consequently, journalists usually will not have to worry about hurting the market value of the postings they quote from electronic sources.

Nevertheless, if you want to quote material directly from the electronic sources, you should keep these limitations in mind. Nearly all of the information you find via electronic sources has copyright protection. Electronic journals, news wires and electronic versions of print material have the same copyright protection as material that has been traditionally published. You should also work under the assumption that information posted to news groups and discussion lists is copyrighted.

Therefore, you should limit the amount of material you quote directly as much as possible, particularly if you think that information either has not been published (you have been forwarded a copy of a private e-mail message, for example) or if you think the material may have market value in the future. The best alternative is to secure the permission of the creator of the work you wish to quote.

Some observers believe the need to secure permission from copyright holders to use specific material can have a chilling effect on robust debate in America. Nevertheless, in *Harper & Row v. Nation Inc.*, the Supreme Court specifically ruled out a First Amendment defense for copyright infringement. In that decision, Justice Sandra Day O'Conner declared that the *Nation's* interest in reporting the news as quickly as possible did not outweigh President Ford's right to control the first publication of his memoirs.

Journalists must keep in mind that if copyrighted material is posted to a computer bulletin board, the copyright itself has not been affected. In 1994, the federal government launched an effort to review intellectual property right laws, of which copyright is a part. Online services such as American Online were working to make sure that the revisions indicated that the services themselves would not be responsible for copyrighted information illegally posted to them. Instead, the infringers would bear the full brunt of the violation.

Confidentiality and speech codes

Journalists working online must also be aware that they are working in a new media. Some of the protections they may enjoy using traditional methods may not apply when they are online. Two of the most important ways in which online communication differs from other media is in the confidentiality of the information journalists gather and store electronically and in the emergence of speech codes governing online behavior in some settings.

Reporters have long fought to establish the principle that they can keep confidential the information they gather and the names of the sources from whom they gather it. The reasoning is that without that protection, sources may not be willing to share with reporters important information that the public should know.

The U.S. Supreme Court, however, has not accepted journalists' arguments about the need for a shield from law enforcement. In *Branzberg v. Hayes* (1972), the court decided 5-4 that the First Amendment did not absolve journalists of their responsibilities for testifying before grand juries and responding to relevant questions. Since then, some states have passed what are called shield laws to limit the way law enforcement officials can force journalists to disclose information; some state courts have recognized a limited privilege for reporters based on the First Amendment; and several U.S. Circuit courts have acknowledged that information gathered by reporters should have some limited protection against being snatched up by law enforcement. Still, there is no federal shield law rooted in the First Amendment. Nor has Congress chosen to pass a federal shield law.

The lack of a shield law could be more problematic for journalists working online. Typically, if police believe that a reporter has information relevant to a case, they subpoena the reporter to testify and to produce her notebooks. If need be, the police will issue a search warrant and physically gather notebooks and other information. In *Zurcher v. Stanford Daily* in 1978, the U.S. Supreme Court ruled that searching newsrooms for evidence did not violate the Fourth Amendment of the Constitution, which prohibits unlawful searches and seizure.

In those kinds of situations, journalists working with what they knew was sensitive information could take precautions against being forced to disclose it. They may not tell their editors the names of their sources. They may hide their notebooks or not write down important facts. And they can take a principled position and refuse to testify when called before the grand jury or into court. Several reporters have gone to jail rather than disclose confidential information. In many cases, their news organizations have supported them legally and financially in their efforts.

Online journalists do not have the same kind of control over their information; nor can they necessarily count on the support of the computer system or company they access to gather information online. By definition, online journalists initially gather information in an electronic format. Inevitably, at some point that information is stored electronically on a hard disk or tape.

As Oliver North (former National Security Council aide to President Ronald Reagan) found out, just because you delete something from a hard disk does not mean the information has been removed. When you do delete something, the information itself does not disappear until new information is written over it. Several software programs available can retrieve deleted files.

Not surprisingly, law enforcement officials know that computer hard disks can still retain information that the user intended to delete. Hard disks are now subpoenaed in the course of criminal investigations.

But law enforcement officials are not so sophisticated that they will examine a hard disk and only copy or take the information they need. Instead, they will often confiscate the entire hard disk with all the information on it.

Consequently, if you capture or store sensitive information that you do not wish to disclose, you should not store it at any time on a hard disk. Moreover, if you do store sensitive information on a hard disk that is shared with other users, you are putting all the information on that disk at risk. A law enforcement agency could conceivably confiscate the entire disk and there would be little that an individual reporter could do about it. People accessing the Internet through a university based connection could not even rely on the support of the university if law enforcement agencies demanded the information. A university might be disinclined to lose an entire hard disk full of information used by many users to support your interpretation of the demands of a free press.

Of course, many reporters never are asked to surrender confidential information to law enforcement agencies because it is relevant to a criminal or civil proceeding. But this extreme case raises a more common and troubling issue for online journalists. The information stored on a shared hard disk is not private or secure. In almost all cases, if you are accessing electronic information through a network, the system administrator can gain access to your files and can monitor your e-mail traffic. You have to conduct yourself accordingly.

For commercial services such as Prodigy and CompuServe, the rules and regulations are even more stringent. These services are owned by companies that reserve the right to define the limits of free discussion enjoyed by those using those services. For example, Prodigy has policies in place to forbid the use of hate speech and other types of offensive speech. For many years, NSFnet, long the major backbone network of the Internet, had rules forbidding commercial use of its networks. While some people see those rules as infringing on First Amendment rights, it is not clear at all that they do.

After all, the FCC is allowed to ban indecent speech from radio and television airways at certain periods of the day even though indecent speech merits First Amendment protection. It is hard to imagine the Supreme Court compelling a company to allow its computers to be used for obscenity or other forms of speech that warrant even less First Amendment protection.

And while people who use the Internet like to believe that they also own it and should be able to establish the rules which cover its use, they don't and can't. The computers that are linked through the network are each owned by an organization or person. Those owners have the right to establish rules that govern their use. Journalists should take care not to violate those rules.

And, in fact, owners of computer-based communications networks have to be sensitive to more than just free speech concerns in controlling what is posted on their computers. In the fall of 1994, Santa Rosa Junior College reached a settlement with the U.S. Department of Education in which the college agreed to pay three students $15,000 to settle sex-discrimation charges related to men-only and women-only online computer conferences conducted by the school.

The students charged that the single-sex conferences violated a federal law that prohibits sex discrimination in schools that receive federal funds. The computer bulletin board, which was launched by a professor of journalism and hosted more than 100 online conferences, was seen as an educational activity of the school and, therefore, subject to what are known as Title IX regulations.

Federal investigators found that derogatory remarks about two women posted on the men-only conference were a form of sexual harassment creating a hostile educational environment. The Department of Education's Office of Civil Rights argued that computer bulletin boards do not enjoy the same level First Amendment protection as the campus newspaper. The office has proposed banning comments that harass or denigrate people on the basis of sex or race.

The school's lawyer argued that the online conference should have been protected by the First Amendment. Nevertheless, the college felt compelled to settle the case.

Open meetings and freedom of information

Journalists are not the only community taking advantage of computer-based communications networks. Public officials and government agencies are also incorporating new technology into their work. Their activities raise two vital concerns for journalists. First, are open meeting laws being circumvented through the use of computer networks? Second, how much of the information collected by governments should be available to journalists in an electronic format and how much should that information cost?

Since the mid-1970s, many states have passed what are called Sunshine or Open Meeting laws.The purpose of these laws is to ensure that public business is conducted in the open where the public can see what happens. Except under specified conditions, members of many school boards, local government commissions and other agencies cannot conduct official business without first notifying and inviting the public to observe or participate.

As new forms of communication become available, the definitions both of "meeting" and public access to meetings have come under pressure. Can officials "meet" online or via a video conference to conduct business? Does inviting the public to a video or online conference fulfill the spirit and letter of the open meeting laws?

Sunshine laws vary from jurisdiction to jurisdiction. Journalists must be on guard to ensure that agencies do not try to use new communication technology to conduct the public business in a covert or hidden fashion.

Along the same lines, public access to government computer files has been a significant issue for several years. The question has three important aspects. First, are electronic records considered records under Freedom of Information laws and therefore must be made available on request? Second, must government agencies provide information to journalists and the public in an electronic format? Third, how much can government agencies charge for access to electronic information? Can agencies give exclusive rights to information to private data providers who in turn can charge whatever the market will bear for the data, even if the pricing makes it prohibitive for smaller publications and individuals to purchase?

Once again, these questions are being decided at all levels of government. Journalists must stay aware of the deliberations that will resolve them as they will have a profound influence on the practice of journalism.

Obscenity and other free speech issues

As participants in the robust debate protected by the First Amendment, journalists should also be aware of free speech issues that may not have a direct impact on the way they do their jobs. They include the ability of one jurisdiction to impose its standards for speech in another jurisdiction and the ability networks give journalists to circumvent international press law.

As in other media, obscenity serves as the flash point of one locality imposing its standards on another. In its pivotal ruling in *Miller v. California* (1974), the Supreme Court decided that community standards should be used to evaluate if material was obscene. In the summer of 1994, the city of Memphis won a decision against a computer bulletin board operator in the San Francisco Bay area for distributing obscene pictures. Law enforcement officials had actively requested that the material on the bulletin board be sent to them.

This was not the first time that Memphis had used this tactic to shut down what its local officials believed were companies distributing pornography using new technology. In the late 1980s, a similar suit helped close the XXXCTASY channel, a California-based company that was broadcasting hardcore pornographic films via satellite. By the standards of Memphis officials the films may have been obscene, but officials in other cities had felt differently. The movies were available in video stores and in movie theaters. The growth of computer-based networks could ultimately bring pressure to change the community-standards aspect of the obscenity debate.

Computer-based pornography suggests another perplexing problem. The Supreme Court has regularly acknowledged that one of the roles of government is to protect children, and First Amendment rights had to be weighed against that obligation. (For example, see *FCC v. Pacifica Foundation* 1978). As the mainstream media delight in reporting, pornographic material is available via computer bulletin boards and networks, and children who are savvy enough with their computers can figure out how to access it. It is not clear what kind of laws, if any, will be drafted in order to curtail the access of underage people to computer-generated pornography

In the same way that computer networks are avenues for circumventing restrictions on the distribution of pornography, they are also a way to circumvent national press laws in other countries. As we reported in the Karla Homulka case, Canadians used network news groups to spread information about a grizzly murder case even though the judge in the case had imposed a news blackout.

In many cases, people will be applauded for circumventing press laws. They will be seen as defying the heavy hand of censorship. But people who do violate those press laws could have to pay a heavy price. The judge in the Karla Homulka case threatened to shut down specific computers suspected as the vehicle for violating his gag order. Journalists who receive information that has been distributed in violation of national press laws must keep in mind that somebody may have to pay a price for making that information available. It should not be published frivolously.

Online ethics

Consider this scenario: You are walking along a road and you come across a knapsack. You stop, pick up a book that has partially fallen out and open it. The first page reads that the information is to be read and used only by people who have purchased the book.

At that point, is it unethical to read on, if only to see if you can find the name and address of the person who owns the knapsack? If, in looking for the person's name, you read something which could be of value to you, is it wrong to use that information? If you read the entire book and then return it to the knapsack and leave, have you stolen anything?

As you use online information, you will frequently come across information that was not intended for your eyes. As a reporter, you may join a list without the others knowing your interest. They think the discussion is just among specialists in a specific area. A private e-mail message might be posted or forwarded to a discussion list mistakenly or maliciously. Navigating through the maze of computers on the network, you may find a back door to a commercial data base open only to those with paid subscriptions.

In other words, from time to time you will find a knapsack with a open book on the road. Online journalism promises to open a whole new arena for discussions of media ethics. And the ethical boundaries, what journalists morally should or should not do online will only be worked out over time as more journalists use electronic services and more journalists debate their use.

Nevertheless, all journalists should adhere to certain ethical guidelines. First, journalists should almost always identify themselves as such if they plan to use information from discussion lists or network news groups. In most cases, journalists have the ethical obligation to allow people to choose to go on the record or not.

Using hidden cameras is very controversial in standard journalism. To lurk on a discussion list and then quote people who did not know that what they wrote would be used in a different context is as deceptive as posing or going undercover to report a story. While from time to time in traditional journalism the benefit of posing to reveal a significant social wrong may outweigh the deception involved, that probably will not be the case in most instances in online journalism. In almost all cases, journalists have an obligation to let the people with whom they interact know that they are talking to a reporter.

Second, journalists must identify the source of their information in their reporting. Attribution is an essential element of journalism. If you don't know definitively who the source of information is, you must be very careful if you choose to use it. Widely published journalism codes of ethics frequently warn that journalists should verify all information. At the same time, you should not claim credit for information that somebody has published on a network without crediting that source.

Third, journalists have to respect the limitations of the information they gather online. Online information should be treated in the same way as information gathered through any other technique.

While the three operational rules outlined above can help steer journalists in the right decision, they will not, and cannot, cover every situation. For example, was Daniel Ellsberg justified in stealing the Pentagon Papers in the early 1970s? Those papers laid out in vivid detail the way the U.S. government had misled and lied to the American people about its policies in Vietnam. Were *The New York Times* and the *Washington Post* justified in publishing that information even though the information was both classified and stolen? Whatever you feel, Ellsberg could not have passed the Pentagon Papers along to *The New York Times* and *Washington Post* as easily if photo-copying – a new communications technology – had not been invented.

Like photocopying, and radio and television before it, computer-based networks are a new communciation technology. Legal and ethical controversaries will only be decided in action, as people like yourselves try to decide the correct course of action in the complex situations that will arise in the future.

Further reading

Widespread public use of computer communications is a relatively new area, as this chapter has explained. A few resources may prove helpful.

1. Kenneth C. Creech. *Electronic Media Law and Regulation*, Boston: Focal Press, 1993. While the book deals primarily with "traditional" electronic media, Chapter 13 touches upon issues of the "evolving electronic landscape," and the FCC does have authority over computer communications.
2. Jane Kirtley, ed. *Access to Electronic Records*, Reporters Committee for Freedom of the Press: Washington, D.C., 1990.
3. Electronic Frontier Foundation maintains at eff.org online Gopher and World Wide Web servers that carry current information on legal and ethical issues of online access. To reach them, for example, aim your Gopher (or WWW) client at eff.org.

How to access the Internet

Access to the Internet has become increasingly open over the past few years. Once restricted to the educational and research communities, many companies now are online. So, if you are working for a company, you should first check to see if it is already connected.

If not, several concerns provide public access to the Internet; user groups and community Free-nets that provide online services to specific communities are linking to the Internet; and commercial information services are increasing the Internet services they offer as well.

The cost of access to the Internet, a major concern for reporters in smaller operations and for freelancers, varies dramatically among service providers. The most efficient and cost effective way to be able to use the Internet is to establish an account at a local college or university, business, or library that is already on the Internet. In many cases, the institution itself pays a flat fee for Internet access and does not charge users.

Some journalists either enroll for course at a local community college or take jobs as adjunct instructors primarily to establish a computer account through which they can access the Internet. Some universities offer Internet accounts to people in the community. Some public libraries are also on the Internet, and you may be able to arrange an account through them.

If that approach is not feasible, you have three options: commercial information services, community Free-nets, or public access Internet providers. An explanation of each type of provider and selected contacts are listed below.

Commercial information services

Commercial information services offer much more than just Internet access. They support a wide range of services including news, discussion groups, directories, and gateways to other interesting information. Most commercial information services provide e-mail access to the Internet. Over the past year, they have begun to offer access to other Internet functions as well including Usenet news groups and Gopher.

On the down side, commercial information services generally charge hourly fees and surcharges for extended services. They also limit the number of mail messages you may send and receive, and some charge if you send and receive large messages. Finally, most restrict the amount of online disk storage space any user can have.

Despite the cost, however, millions of people have found commercial information services extremely valuable. As their Internet capabilities increase, they promise to be even more useful.

Major commercial information services include:

America Online (Tel: 800-227-6364)

CompuServe (Tel: 800-848-8199)

Delphi (Tel: 800-544-4005)

GEnie (Tel: 800-638-9636)

Prodigy (Tel: 800-822-6922)

Several other companies, including Apple Computer Corp., Microsoft, and Ziff-Davis Interactive, have new commercial information services in various stages of development. Commercial information services should become even more viable as a tool for journalists in the years to come.

Community Free-nets

As the potential benefits of computer-based communications networks became apparent in the late 1980s, a movement developed to form community-wide computer networks. This effort was organized under the umbrella of what is called the National Public Telecomputing Network (NPTN). You can receive more information about the NPTN from T.M. Grundner, President, NPTN, Box 1987, Cleveland, OH. (Tel: 216-247-5800, Fax: 216-247-3328, E-mail: tmg@nptn.org, ftp nptn.org cd /pub/info.nptn).

Many community Free-nets now provide Internet access as well, although the Internet access may not be free. Below is a selected list of Free-nets connected to the Internet, their dial-in access numbers, and log-in information.

Big Sky Telegraph	Dillon, Mont.	(Modem: 406-683-7680)	Visitor login: bbs
Buffalo Free-net	Buffalo	(Modem: 716-645-6128)	Visitor login: freeport
Cleveland Free-net	Cleveland	(Modem: 216-368-3888)	Visitor: Select 2 at menu
Columbia Online Information Network			
(COIN,)	Columbia, Mo.	Modem: 314-884-7000)	Visitor login: guest
Dayton Free-net	Dayton	(Modem: 513-229-4373)	Visitor login: guest
Denver Free-net	Denver	(Modem: 303-270-4865)	Visitor login: guest
Great Lakes Free-net	Battle Creek, Mich.	(Modem: 616-969-4536)	Visitor login: visitor
Heartland Free-net	Peoria	(Modem: 309-674-1100)	Visitor login: bbguest
Lorain Co. Free-net	Elyria, Ohio	(Modem: 216-366-9721)	Visitor login: guest
Nat'l Capital Free-net	Ottawa, Canada	(Modem: 613-780-3733)	Visitor login: guest
Prairienet	Champaign-Urbana	(Modem: 217-255-9000)	Visitor login: visitor
Tallahassee Free-net	Tallahassee	(Modem: 904-488-5056	Visitor login: visitor

Additionally, several cities and states are opening publicly funded computer networks for their residents. The best known is Santa Monica's Public Electronic Network for residents of Santa Monica, Calif. (Tel: 310-458-8383). Maryland has implemented a network called Sailor through its public library system with Internet access. Users who access the system through

Baltimore City's Enoch Pratt central library can also receive e-mail accounts as well (410-396-4636 for information, 410-605-0500 to access Sailor through Pratt Library).

Public access internet providers

As the Internet has grown in popularity, several companies have begun to offer access. The fees charged by these service providers vary greatly. Moreover, many offer more than just Internet access. The WELL in San Francisco, for example, has many discussion groups of its own.

Service providers also offer different types of connections to the Internet. To be able to use graphic browsers like Mosaic, you need a SLIP or PPP connection (Chapter 4, 7).

Finally, in most cases users dial in to these service providers. Some providers offer 800 numbers but charge users for these services. Others offer access through what is called the Public Data Network or PDN. Public Data Network access allows you to make a local call to the network and then connect to the service provider of your choice. Most of the commercial information services route their users through the PDN. There often is a additional charge for using the PDN as well.

It may be difficult to immediately determine which service provider best meets your needs. Once you have e-mail access to the Internet, you can receive a lengthy list of Internet access providers by sending the message "Send PDIAL" to "info-deli-server@netcom.com"

The following is a partial list of Internet access providers.

Anomaly - Rhode Island's Gateway To The Internet
local access: Providence/Seekonk
long distance: provided by user
services: shell, ftp, telnet, SLIP
email: info@anomaly.sbs.risc.net
voice: 401-273-4669

Clark Internet Services, Inc. (ClarkNet)
local access: MD: Baltimore; DC: Washington; VA: Northern VA
long distance: provided by user
services: shell, menu, ftp, telnet, irc, gopher, hytelnet, www, WAIS,
    SLIP/PPP, ftp space, feeds (UUCP & uMDSS), dns, Clarinet
email: info@clark.net
voice: Call 800-735-2258 then give 410-730-9764 (MD Relay Svc)
fax: 410-730-9765

Community News Service
local access: Colorado Springs, Denver, Colo.
long distance: 800 or provided by user
services:UNIX shell, email, ftp, telnet, irc, USENET, Clarinet, gopher,
    Commerce Business Daily
email: service@cscns.com
voice:719-592-1240

CR Laboratories Dialup Internet Access
local access: In California: San Francisco Bay area + San Rafael,
    Santa Rosa, Los Angeles, Orange County; In Arizona: Phoenix,
    Scottsdale, Tempe, and Glendale; In Georgia: Atlanta metro area
long distance: 800 or provided by user
services: shell, ftp, telnet, feeds, SLIP, WAIS
email: info@crl.com
voice: 415-381-2800

Dial n' Cerf USA
local access: anywhere (800) service is available
long distance: 800
services: shell, menu, irc, ftp, hytelnet, gopher, WAIS, WWW, terminal
    service, SLIP
email: help@cerf.net
voice: 800-876-2373 or 619-455-3900

HoloNet
local access: Berkeley, Calif.
long distance: PDN
services: ftp, telnet, irc, games
email: info@holonet.net
voice: 510-704-0160

Institute for Global Communications/IGC Networks
   (PeaceNet,EcoNet, ConflictNet, LaborNet, HomeoNet)
local access: Palo Alto, San Francisco
long distance: PDN
services: telnet, local newsgroups for environmental, peace/social
    justice issues; NO ftp
email: support@igc.apc.org
voice: 415-442-0220

MCSNet
local access: Chicago
long distance: provided by user
services: shell, ftp, telnet, feeds, email, irc, gopher, hytelnet, etc.

email: info@genesis.mcs.com
voice: (312) 248-UNIX

MSen
local access: All of SE Michigan (313, 810)
long distance: provided by user
services: shell, WAIS, gopher, telnet, ftp, SLIP, PPP, IRC, WWW,
    Picospan BBS, ftp space
email: info@msen.com
voice: 313-998-4562
fax: 313-998-4563

Netcom Online Communication Services
local access: In California: Alameda, Irvine, Los Angeles, Palo Alto,
    Pasadena, Sacramento, San Diego, San Francisco, San Jose, Santa
    Cruz, Walnut Creek; Denver Colo.; Washington D.C.; Atlanta,
    Ga.; Chicago, Ill.; Boston, Mass.; Portland, Ore.; Dallas, Texas;
    Seattle, Wash.
long distance: provided by user
services:shell, ftp, telnet, irc, WAIS, gopher, SLIP/PPP, ftp space,
    feeds, dns
email: info@netcom.com
voice: 408-554-8649, 800-501-8649
fax: 408-241-9145

PANIX Public Access Unix
local access: New York City
long distance: provided by user
services: shell, ftp, telnet, gopher, wais, irc, feeds
email: alexis@panix.com, jsb@panix.com
voice: 212-877-4854 [Alexis Rosen], 212-691-1526 [Jim Baumbach]

PSILink - Personal Internet Access
local access: PDN
long distance: PDN
services: email and newsfeed, ftp
email: all-info@psi.com, psilink-info@psi.com
voice: 703-620-6651
fax: 703-620-4586

NeoSoft's Sugar Land Unix
local access: Houston, New Orleans
long distance: provided by user
services: bbs, shell, ftp, telnet, irc, feeds, UUCP
email: info@NeoSoft.com

voice: 713-438-4964

The Whole Earth 'Lectronic Link (The WELL)
local access: Sausalito, Calif.
long distance: PDN
services: shell, ftp, telnet, bbs
email: info@well.sf.ca.us
voice: 415-332-4335

The World
local access: Boston, Mass.
long distance: PDN
services: shell, ftp, telnet, irc
email: office@world.std.com
voice: 617-739-0202

GLOSSARY

Archie—a software program that locates files that can be received via FTP on the Internet.

ASCII—the ANSI Standard Code for Information Exchange format to store information. When information is stored in an ASCII format, it generally can be used by many different programs. ASCII is generally used for text information.

binary—another format in which information can be stored in computers. Binary information is often used for non-text data such as instructions for applications programs.

BPS or Bits Per Second—the measure used to gauge the speed of a modem. The more bits per second a modem can transmit, the faster it is. Although slightly different, baud rate is another term that refers to the speed of a modem.

Boolean — the logic used in searching for information. Boolean logic uses terms such as "AND" "OR" and "NOT" to limit the results of information searches. A search for "defense AND policy NOT nuclear" would produce a list of files and directories containing both defense and policy in them but would eliminate from the list any such files or directories that contain the word nuclear in the title.

client —a software application program that extracts a service from a server somewhere else on a network. Clients organize information gathered from elsewhere on the network and are the interface for the user.

Commercial Information Services—commercial enterprises that provide information online for a fee. The largest consumer oriented commercial information services are Compuserve and America Online. Many more services are in the planning stages. Most commercial information services provide at least e-mail access to the Internet as well and many are offering additional Internet services.

cyber—a general term that refers to the online world.

data base—a systematic organization of information that can be added to, modified, or retrieved online.

discussion list—a method of using e-mail in which individuals can communicate easily with many people. People subscribe to discussion lists and then automatically receive any messages other subscribers send to the list.

E-mail—a method to send messages back and forth via computers. E-mail can be sent among many different computer networks.

Ethernet—a kind of local area network

FAQ—Frequently Asked Questions is the name for files that store the answers most beginners ask about a Usenet News Group or discussion group. Many FAQs also often include other useful information about a specific area.

file—a self-contained unit of information online.

FTP—an acronym for File Transfer Protocol, FTP is a program used to move files across the network from one computer to another. Sometimes employed as if it were a verb.

Gopher—a program used to locate and transfer information on the Internet.

Gopherspace—a term to describe the network of gopher servers.

host —a computer that provides to other "client" computers access to files or to the network itself.

Gateway—a method that allows computer system to transfer data between normally incompatible applications or networks.

Internet—the network of computers that use the TCP/IP communication protocol and can communicate with each other. Some people see the Internet as the prototype of the Information Superhighway.

Internet Relay Chat—Internet software that allows for real-time interactive multiparticipant exchanges.

listserv—software used to organize on type of online discussion.

local area networks—networks that run over short distances, generally at high speed.

network—linking computers in order to transfer information and share other resources.

news group—a method in which many people can communicate online. Through the Usenet network, in newsgroups individuals post messages to a central site, which are then passed to different computers that receive a "news feed." Subscribers can then read those messages and post replies. Unlike discussion lists, with news groups messages are not sent to people's individual accounts.

Post—sending a message to a discussion list or a news group.

PPP—Point to Point Protocol is a protocol that defines the connection of a personal computer to the Internet.

packet—a unit of information transmitted over network connections

protocol—a commonly agreed upon method or set of instructions. Computers need to use the same communications protocols if they are to send information back and forth. TCP/IP is the primary protocol for the Internet.

server—software designed to perform specific tasks at the request of its clients.

SLIP—Serial Line Internet Protocol is another protocol that defines the connection of a personal computer to the Internet

system prompt—a character or string of characters that tell the computer user in a command line environment that the machine is waiting for a new command and that all non-system programs have terminated. In DOS, the system prompt is typically a "C:>"; in UNIX it is "%"; in VMS it is "$".

TCP/IP—the communications protocol used by computers linked to the Internet.

Telnet—an Internet application program that allows you to log onto another computer.

terminal —computer workstation composed of a monitor (VDT) for viewing computer output and a keyboard for talking to the computer or network. Once online, personal computers often serve primarily as terminals.

UNIX—a popular operating system used by computers more powerful than PCs. Server software is often based on computers running UNIX and many times people will log onto UNIX-based machines to access the Internet.

WAIS—Wide Area Information Servers allow for the indexing, identification, and retrieval of information located on specific Internet computers. WAIS servers are accessed by WAIS client programs.

World Wide Web—allows for information located on many different computers to be linked through key terms. This approach is called Hypertext or Hypermedia. The Web is accessed through client programs such as Mosaic and Lynx.

Net Slang and Short Hand

Bandwidth—a term used to imply that the online communication is a limited resource that should not be wasted frivolously.

BTW — By The Way.

Emoticon—symbols to express emotions in computer communications. The most well-known is called a smiley and looks like :-).

Flame— A heated response/insult directed at an individual who has said something on the net to which the responder is reacting.

FWIW —For What It's Worth.

FYI—For your information.

IMHO — In My Humble Opinion.

IMNSHO —In My Not-So- Humble Opinion.

lurk —to "hang around" in or read a mail discussion list or news group postings without adding your own comments. A person who lurks is known as a lurker.

newbie — (n.) a person new to the network or any "place" (such as a discussion list) on it.

RTFM—Read the Manual. A nasty response when somebody asks a question for which the answer is readily available elsewhere.

Electronic information sources

Beat organized online catalog

All the places listed in this catalog were active in 1994. Because the online world is rapidly changing, it is expected that several places listed here will be obsolete addresses, "wrong numbers," so to speak, in 1995. Addresses ending with "->" are continued in the next field.

Beats are abbreviated according to the following scheme: Agri = agriculture; Arts = arts and entertainment; BizEc = business, banking, and economics; Court = courts, crime, and law enforcement; Educ = education; Envir = environment; Feds = federal government; Genl = a broad, multipurpose general information resource often crossing many beat lines; Intl = international; Life = lifestyles, hobbies, travel; Media = news media specific resources; Medic = medicine and health; Nets = information helpful for navigating networks; Scitk = science and technology; Sport = sports; State = state and local government.

Many online sites could logically be listed in two different places. For example, a Department of Commerce information service could be logically listed under "federal government" or under "business, banking, and economics." When you are looking for a resource, consider multiple beat approaches. After the beat listing is the access tool from the book (gopher, telnet), the address (or telephone number) appears above the log-in instructions, and pertinent notes follow.

Beat	Access	Address/ Login	Notes & Special Instructions
Agri	gopher	esusda.gov N/A	Also has White House policy statements, Cong. action on such as NII, NAFTA, Health Care, NPR
Agri	mail	almanac@wisplan.uwex.edu send haylist <a.c.> <hay type>	Hay type may be alfalfa, mixed, or left blank. Updated daily. "send haylist price" returns only the average price of hay listings and the GovtBBS list
Agri	modem	301-504-5496 Register at first login	
Agri	telnet	psupen.psu.edu 2 char state postal code (TX)	Login with your state's postal code
Arts	ftp	ra.msstate.edu anonymous	pub/archives/fineart_online/Online_ Directory CARR0708.93 internet
Arts	mail	mailserv@acfcluster.nyu.edu sub perform-l <yourname>	resources related to the arts TDR addresses performance issues of every kind:
Arts	telnet	ursus.main.edu ursus	theatre, music dance, entertainment, media, sports, politics, aesthetics of everyday life,
Arts	www	http://rg.media.mit.edu/RG/-> /RG.html	@Main menu B, then 2; takes you to National Gallery of Art. Login may not be required Rare Grooves, a tipsheet for some kinds of music; charts, playlists, short sound clips
BizEc	ftp	town.hall.org anonymous	EDGAR filings. First get file "index"

BizEc	gopher	cscns.com N/A	Commerce Business Daily
BizEc	gopher	fdic.sura.net 71 N/A	
BizEc	gopher	gopher.fonorola.net N/A	Internet Business Journal from root directory
BizEc	gopher	gopher.nijenrode.nl N/A	Choose "Business Resources" from the root directory
BizEc	gopher	town.hall.org N/A	SEC's Edgar filings beginning 1994. Get index first.
BizEc	mail	listserv@indycms.iupui.edu subscribe prforum	List for gathering of Public Relations folks
BizEc	modem	202-566-4699	Program into, seminar skeds, press releases, bulletins of special interest (city-state programs).
BizEc	modem	303-208-7679	Voice 202-566-8818 Press releases, pamphlets on products and classes of products; how to buy
BizEc	modem	314-621-1824	Info on banking, interest rates, & economy. Operated by Fed. Res. Bank of St. Louis. Voice 314-444-8562
BizEc	modem	414-789-4210 Register, costs $$ to stay	
BizEc	modem	602-881-8144	Real Estate information
BizEc	modem	614-538-9250 Register	Focus on helping small businesses. Must subscribe to have full access.
BizEc	modem	617-662-2600	Aviation BBS, source of FAA records.
BizEc	modem	702-566-6840	Pictures of real estate offerings
BizEc	modem	800-859-4636	
BizEc	telnet	iron.nttc.edu visitor	databases on federal funding
Court	ftp	128.204.33.18 anonymous	Data sets of U.N. Surveys of Crime Trends and Criminal Justice Systems back to 1970.
Court	ftp	eff.org anonymous	pub/academic/law[filename] directory Legal cases involving electronic information, alt address 192.88.144.4 CAF Archive
Court	ftp	ftp.cwru.edu anonymous	Supreme Ct. decision archive. From the hermes directory get the decision index as a guide.
Court	ftp	ftp.midnight.com anonymous	pub/legalList/legallist.txt
Court	ftp	una.hh.lib.umich.edu anonymous	
Court	gopher	fatty.law.cornell.edu N/A	many govt. resources
Court	gopher	gopher.cni.org N/A	In the Workgroups/forums path are the arcives of copyright mailing list
Court	gopher	gopher.law.cornell.edu N/A	LII gopher with Supr. Ct. decisions
Court	gopher	gopher.nwu.edu N/A	In /Library Services/Law & Courts Preprint path is legal preprints archive.
Court	gopher	niord.shsu.edu N/A	Choice 4 at root opens extensive data resource gateway for economics
Court	gopher	trout.ab.umd.edu N/A	/Legal Information Resources
Court	mail	lii@fatty.law.cornell.edu subscribe liibulletin	Listserv@fatty.law.cornell.edu subscribe liibulletin Name, address, telephone Num. all on one line
Court	modem	202-482-3870 Register at first login	Economic Bulletin Board also available on Internet

Court	modem	301-738-8895 Register at first login	Nat'l Criminal Just. Reference Service
Court	modem	301-763-7554 register	
Court	modem	317-780-5285 Register	Civil liberties watchdogs. Have complete files on ATF vs. Branch Davidians at Waco
Court	modem	405-536-5032 Register	
Court	modem	612-340-2489 Register	
Court	modem	619-299-0351 Register	
Court	modem	908-254-8117 Register	
Court	telnet	acc.wuacc.edu washlaw	Washburn University Gopher pointed at law related resources
Court	telnet	ebb.stat-usa.gov TRIAL	Has some notes, trouble? e-mail to awilliams@esa.doc.gov
Court	telnet	fatty.law.cornell www	www server; choose NFEJ for Nasdaq Financial Exec. Journal
Court	telnet	fatty.law.cornell.edu www	www server, move on hilited terms
Court	telnet	hermes.merit.edu @ Which Host um-gomlink	Gopher for Census, business, economics data and statistics. Gopher root server
Court	telnet	teetot.acusd.edu	
Court	telnet	privacy vienna.hh.lib.umich.edu mlink (all l.c.)	Economic and business area
Court	www	http://www.law.cornell.edu none	Supreme Court decisions on line, searchable
Educ	ftp	ftp.ed. gov anonymous	Education Dept. online library
Educ	gopher	ericir.syr.edu N/A	
Educ	gopher	gopher.cua.edu N/A	11. Special Resources has ERIC Clearinghouse on Tests & Measurement data and others focusing on
Educ	gopher	gopher.ed.gov N/A	testing and alternative assessment. Also GIF graphics, stats
Educ	modem	407-687-8712	Focus on Homeschool Families
Educ	modem	701-237-3383	
Educ	modem	916-657-4881	
Educ	telnet	fedix.fie.com new	Includes HERO (Higher Education Opportunities for Minorities & Women) Grants, jobs, etc.
Educ	www	http://www.clas.ufl.edu/CLAS/ american-universities.html	Home page of home pages for 145 American Universities
Educ	www	http://www.ed.gov	Education Dept. online library
Envir	ftp	una.hh.lib.umich.edu anonymous	Guide to environmental resources on the internet in /inetdirsstacks file is environment:murphybriggs
Envir	gopher	csf.colorado.edu N/A	Environment from root menu.
Envir	gopher	gopher.ns.doe.gov 70 N/A	
Envir	gopher	una.hh.lib.umich.edu N/A	North America/ USA / Michigan / Clearinghouse of Subject-Oriented Internet Res. Guides / All Guides/ Environment

Envir	modem	202-234-8570	Right to Know network: Must register to have
		@ USERID "public"	access to databases
Envir	modem	301-585-6697	
Envir	modem	301-589-8366	
		Register at first login	
Envir	modem	415-512-9108	
Envir	modem	805-833-1437	
Envir	telnet	happenings.ncsu.edu	Get down about three levels into government files,
		info	and you have some interesting stuff. Esp,
			SuperFund, and water purity.
Envir	telnet	ttnbbs.rtpnc.epa.gov	
Feds	ftp	ftp.cni.org	Govt. Info. Locator Service text file in pub/docs/gils
		anonymous	= gils1111.txt (date will change with update). Also
			gopher
Feds	ftp	ftp.cpsr.org	
		anonymous	
Feds	ftp	ftp.cu.nih.gov	Electronic Records in NARA_ELECTRONIC
		anonymous/guest	directory. Some contain raw data.
Feds	ftp	ftp.fcc.gov	
		anonymous	
Feds	ftp	ftp.loc.gov	Wide range of documents available.
		anonymous	
Feds	ftp	maristb.marist.edu	clinton directory has clinton logyymm where yymm
		anonymous	is date into.
Feds	ftp	nctamslant.navy.mil	Navy policy, strategy; docs from Joint Forces
		anonymous	Quarterly; announcements and speeches
Feds	ftp	sunsite.unc.edu	pub/academic/political-science has govt docs
		anonymous	
Feds	gopher	ace.esusda.gov	Clinton Adm. dev. of communications network
		N/A	program between the federal govt and American
			public. Incl. Nat'l Performance Review
Feds	gopher	cpsr.org	Taxpayer Assetts Project TAP-INFO archives
		N/A	available here.
Feds	gopher	disaster.cprost.sfu.ca 5555	
		N/A	
Feds	gopher	ftp.cc.utexas.edu 3003	/pub/lbj-library
Feds	gopher	gopher.counterpoint.com 2002	Federal Register, posted daily in file named, e.g.
		N/A	030794—searchable Counterpoint will charge for
			access.
Feds	gopher	gopher.cqalert.com	Congressional Quarterly documents
		N/A	
Feds	gopher	gopher.house.gov	
		N/A	
Feds	gopher	gopher.hud.gov	HUD information, incl. mortgage assn., research,
		N/A	inspections
Feds	gopher	gopher.senate.gov	
		N/A	
Feds	gopher	marvel.loc.gov	Far-reaching gopher
Feds	gopher	mudhoney.micro.umn.edu 7000	Legis-Late experiment, Federal Register
		N/A	
Feds	gopher	peg.cwis.uci.edu 7000	Government gophers. Also accessible through
		N/A	Library of Congress gopher
Feds	gopher	toby.scott.nwu.edu	American politics Gopher.
		N/A	

Feds	gopher	wiretap.spies.com	
		N/A	
Feds	mail	listserv@gibbs.oit.edu	
		subscribe gov_on_inet	
Feds	modem	202-225-5527	
Feds	modem	202-501-2014	GRA sked and products authorized for purchase by fed govt. voide 202-501-1404
Feds	modem	202-523-1186	
Feds	modem	202-708-3653 or 708-3460	HUD news releases, speeches by HUD officials, fact sheets about major programs, biographies of senior
Feds	modem	301-753-7554	Messaging to census analysis experts from media and government; press releases
Feds	modem	703-321-8020	FedWorld BBS
Feds	phone	301-258-4097	leave your fax #; they send
		none: pure telephone	
Feds	telnet	fedworld.gov	Requires a user to register on FedWorld, then
		must register 1st time	access the Gateway system via the "D" command from main conference.
Feds	telnet	info.umb.edu	Go to government area for govt. facts
		info	
Feds	telnet	locis.loc.gov	Federal legislation abstracts since 1973
		none necessary	
Feds	telnet	marvel.loc.gov	Super gopher with access to much govt. info as well
		marvel	as Internet wide tools.
Feds	telnet	sunsite.unc.edu	
		politics	
Feds	www	http://www.npr.gov	Interactive online window for people to participate
		N/A	in national govt.
Genl	ftp	ftp.clark.net	Journalism list by John Makulowich
		anonymous	
Genl	gopher	cix.org	Commercial Internet Exchange
		N/A	
Genl	gopher	cwis.usc.edu	/Other Gophers/Gophers by Subject/Gopher Jewels
		N/A	This is the "live" gopher jewels server
Genl	gopher	enews.com	Electronic Newsstand
		N/A	
Genl	gopher	gopher.chico.rice.edu 1170	General gopher server
		N/A	
Genl	gopher	gopher.netsys.com 2100	Electronic Newsstand: access to mags
		N/A	
Genl	gopher	gopher.utdallas.edu	Choose "Subjects" from menu
		N/A	
Genl	gopher	gopher.well.sf.ca.us	Electronic magazines (e-zines) and much more.
		N/A	
Genl	gopher	igc.apc.org	Includes environmental, labor, peace interest
		N/A	groups
Genl	mail	mail-server@rtfm.mit.edu	subject blank: in message body type: send usenet-
		N/A	addresses/lastname where lastname=that you are looking
Genl	mail	netnews@db.stanford.edu	Ex: "subscribe Clinton Health Plan" "Period 2" will
		subscribe <keywords>	return every 2 days a listing of Newsgroup hits on keywords
Genl	modem	410-363-0834	Press releases on various topics
Genl	telnet	consultant.micro.umn.edu	The Mother of all Gophers
		gopher	
Genl	telnet	cs.indiana.edu 2627	Basic command DEFINE <word>
		@ cnxn type HELP (u.c.)	

Genl	telnet	database.carl.org follow instructions	Journal articles may be faxed
Genl	telnet	gopher.netsys.com enews	
Genl	telnet	igc.org none	Sections of environmental, peace, and labor interest
Genl	telnet	pac.carl.org follow instructions	Journal articles may be faxed
Genl	telnet	sunsite.unc.edu gopher	Access -IT gopher
Genl	www	http://www.delorme.com N/A	Catalog includes mapping software.
Intl	ftp	ftp.netcom.com anonymous	pub/amcgee lists of where (on Internet) to find info on African ancestry/ethnic development, pursuits, etc. Art McGee
Intl	ftp	ftp.voa.gov anonymous	VOA (US Inf Agency) Int'l news and English broadcasts radio newswire and other USIA stuff.
Intl	ftp	if css.org anonymous	Immigration information
Intl	gopher	gopher.austin.unimelb.edu.au N/A	World Country & Area Telephone Codes Index (not USA or CANADA)path=waissrc:/general/ country=codes
Intl	gopher	gopher.eunet.sk N/A	Slovakia information
Intl	gopher	gopher.psg.com N/A	Information about countries without Internet access
Intl	gopher	gopher.rcp.net.pe N/A	Access to gophers at ministries & universities in Mexico, Costa Rica, South America
Intl	gopher	gopher.ru.ac.za N/A	Zaire, South African politics
Intl	gopher	gopher.vanderbuilt.edu N/A	Voice of America, Radio Free Europe, Radio Liberty, State Dept. travel notes
Intl	gopher	gopher.voa.gov N/A	VOA (US Inf Agency) Int'l news and English Broadcast radio newswire & other USIA stuff.
Intl	gopher	gopher.who.ch N/A	World Health Organization
Intl	gopher	gopher.worldbank.org N/A	World Bank
Intl	gopher	israel-info.gov.il N/A	Policies, facts, graphics, statistics, issues from Israeli POV
Intl	gopher	jerusalem1.datasrv.co.il N/A	Resources focused on maintaining Jewish identity vs. assimilation
Intl	gopher	nywork1.undp.org N/A	U.N. Information
Intl	gopher	telecom.mty.itesm.mx N/A	Main material in Spanish. Choice 3, "Otros Gophers" is English directory.
Intl	gopher	uacsc2.albany.edu N/A	Path=1/7 U.N. Criminal Justice Network
Intl	gopher	umslvma.umsl.edu N/A	In The Library section are U.S. Army Area Handbooks on many nations
Intl	gopher	vita.org N/A	Disaster (emergency) situation info from around the world.
Intl	mail	listserv@cc1.kuleuven.ac.be subscribe NATODATA	NATO information mailing list
Intl	telnet	freenet.carleton.ca guest, select 10	www server; choose NFEJ for Nasdaq Financial Exec. Journal
Intl	telnet	gopher.who.ch gopher	
Intl	telnet	lanic.utexas.edu lanic	Latin American network info center

Intl	telnet	wchr.apc.org login: guestpwd: guest	Register as new user. Group is synthesis for Human rights groups incl. U.N. Centre for Human Rights
Intl	www	http://debra.dgbt.doc.ca/ opengov N/A	Open governments server.
Intl	www	http://www.eunet.sk N/A	Slovakia information
Intl	www	http://www.worldbank.org N/A	World Bank files
Life	gopher	gopher.moon.com:7000 N/A	Travel information.
Life	gopher	mojones.com	Mother Jones
Life	gopher	path.net N/A	Self Awareness, Women's Wire
Life	mail	listserv@vm3090.ege.edu.tr subscribe homefix <your name>	HOMEFIX is a non-edited list on home improve- ment, repairs, electricity, plumbing, etc.
Life	modem	212-274-8110	Weird and wacky stuff
Life	www	http://www.mojones.com N/A	Mother Jones
Media	mail	71344.2761@compuserve.com N/A	Ask for User's Guide. Run by journalists, MediaNet is a free research service connecting journalists
Media	mail	Listserv@cmuvm.edu subscribe NPPA-L <your name>	with corporations, non-profit groups, National Press Photographers Assn. List started June of 94
Media	mail	cma-l-request@vm.cc.latech. edu subscribe CMA-L <your name>	List for college media advisers
Media	mail	listserv@netcom.com subscribe SPJ-online <your name>	Society of Professional Journalists list.
Media	mail	listserv@vm.cc.latech.edu subscribe HSJOURN <your name>	List for high school journalism teachers and advisers
Media	mail	nit-request@chron.com subscribe list	nit-chron is moderated and membership is granted to working journalists by request
Media	mail	profnet@sunysb.edu N/A	Profnet forwards requests for information to university PIOs across nation. Quick way to get expert sources for interview.
Media	modem	202-371-9053	Media watchdog monitors criticisms of media accuracy. Researches reports of errors, has library files
Media	modem	301-725-1072	Info on FCC rulemaking, specific refs to investiga- tive dockets, telecom. topics of special interest
Media	modem	504-769-3896	
Media	news	alt.journalism	
Media	news	alt.journalism.criticism	
Media	news	alt.news-media	
Media	news	alt.politics.media	
Media	news	uk.media	
Medic	ftp	cu.nih.gov anonymous	

Medic	ftp	ftp.gac.edu anonymous	Binary get /submissions/a:matrix for Win3 hypertext presentation of health matrix, Internet health resources
Medic	ftp	ftp.hivnet.org anonymous	Global Electronic Network for AIDS data base
Medic	ftp	ftp.temple.edu anonymous	Nat'l Institutes of Health Guide in /pub/info/listserv/research/NIH_Guide
Medic	ftp	helix.nih.gov anonymous	
Medic	ftp	nlmpubs.nlm.nih.gov anonymous	AIDS articles, others
Medic	ftp	oak.oakland.edu anonymous	Binary get /simtel/pub/msdos/windows3 / hmatrix.zip for Win3 hypertext vers. of health matrix, Internet health resources
Medic	gopher	gopher.brown.edu N/A	/11/brown/departs/worldhun/hungerne Detailed hunger information, interactive
Medic	gopher	gopher.hivnet.org N/A	Global Electronic Network for AIDS database
Medic	gopher	gopher.nih.gov	National Institutes of Health
Medic	gopher	gopher.nlm.nih.gov N/A	National Library of Medicine
Medic	gopher	welchlink.welch.jhu.edu N/A	Access to other Johns Hopkins resources.
Medic	mail	listserv@calvin.dgbt.doc.ca subscribe healthnet <your name>	
Medic	modem	301-443-7496	Info re: FDA's procedures for evaluating and approving medical devices
Medic	modem	800-222-0185 name, password	On first signin, you work out your password, login by name. Hope.
Medic	telnet	debra.dgbt.doc.ca chat	Files on AIDS and Epilepsy
Medic	telnet	fdabbs.fda.gov bbs/ then name, password	On first signin, you work out your password, login by name. Hope.
Medic	www	http://utsph.sph.uth.tmc.edu N/A	Access to topics on Public Health
Medic	www	http://www.hunger.brown.edu/-> N/A	/oxfam Hunger information interactive
Nets	ftp	csd4.csd.uwm.edu anonymous	pub/inet. services.txt is Scott Yanoff's "Special Internet Connections":
Nets	ftp	ftp.clark.net anonymous	pub/journalism Journalism List and exercises
Nets	ftp	ftp.rpi.edu anonymous	pub/communications/internet-cmc
Nets	ftp	nic.ddn.mil anonymous	rfc dir has net helps
Nets	ftp	rtfm.mit.edu anonymous	pub/usenet/news.answers get internet-services/faq
Nets	gopher	csd4.csd.uwm.edu N/A	Remote Inf. Servers/Special Internet Connections has Yanoff List
Nets	gopher	ds.internic.net N/A	
Nets	gopher	gopher.cic.net	
Nets	gopher	gopher.internet.com	Electronic Newsstand includes New Yorker, Economist, New Republic
Nets	gopher	sluava.slu.edu N/A	Internet access files in "Library Services/SLU Law Library Services/ Internet Training and Access

Nets	gopher	snymorva.cs.snymor.edu	library services/electronic journals
Nets	gopher	tic.com N/A	Information on the network(s) and their resources. Quarterman and MIDS group (Matrix)
Nets	mail	whois@nist.gov N/A	Send mail message. On the Subject line, enter "whois smith"
Nets	telnet	access.usask.ca hytelnet	Public Hytelnet client
Nets	telnet	ds.internic.net netfind	Netfind server for searching and for "seed database lookup"
Nets	telnet	infotrax.rpi.edu LIST at : prompt	Searchable list of listservs
Nets	telnet	sunsite.unc.edu 23 swais	WAIS searches. Port 70 is gopher
Nets	telnet	wugate.wustl.edu servicespwd: <CR>	
Nets	telnet	www.law.cornell.edu www	WWW public client
Nets	www	http://ds.internic.net N/A	Network services directory from NSF, AT&T, General Atomics
Nets	www	http:// www.biotech.washington.ed N/A	
Nets	www	http://www.cs.colorado.edu N/A	WWW Worm searching device at http://www.cs.colorado.edu/home/mcbryan/ WWW.html
Scitk	ftp	csd4.csd.uwm.edu anonymous	cd/pub get to internetwork mail guide
Scitk	ftp	enh.nist.gov anonymous	Dir. /WERB for Washington Editorial Research Board has files of titles and authors of papers
Scitk	ftp	ftp.temple.edu anonymous	approved for pub. ed pub/info/help=net information on the network
Scitk	ftp	media-lab.media.mit.edu anonymous	cd /access provides access to MIT's current Project, Publication, Sponsor, and Thesis list.
Scitk	ftp	naic.nasa.gov anonymous	
Scitk	ftp	oak.oakland.edu anonymous	Software repository
Scitk	ftp	pubinfo.jpl.nasa.gov anonymous; city/ST	Information on and GIF images from NASA space missions. MAIL0201 (93)
Scitk	gopher	farnsworth.mit.edu N/A	Digital Information Infrastructure Guide; other things on information policy
Scitk	gopher	gopher.econ.lsa.umich.edu	Hal Varian economics of the Internet
Scitk	gopher	gopher.eff.org N/A	Monitors cases, lobbies for access for all to telecommunications services and information. CAF Archive
Scitk	gopher	gopher.gdb.org N/A	
Scitk	gopher	gopher.gsfc.nasa.gov 4320 N/A	port may not be necessary. Has telephone directory
Scitk	gopher	gopher.nodc.noaa.gov N/A	Global holdings of oceanographic data physical, chemical & biological
Scitk	gopher	gopher.ns.doe.gov 70 N/A	Access government info. Gopher under construction.
Scitk	gopher	huh.harvard.edu N/A	Biological information systems access, includes images
Scitk	gopher	iitf.doc.gov N/A	

Scitk	gopher	kilburn.keene.edu N/A	Earth Science & Environment gopher
Scitk	gopher	stis.nsf.gov N/A	Government Gopher Servers going beyond Science & Technology
Scitk	gopher	wealaka.okgeosurvey1.gov N/A	Seismic Gopher + server. Data open. Nuclear testing and treaty info. Connect to non Okla. seismic sites.
Scitk	gopher	zserve.nist.gov /NIST General Information	Includes "Science Beat" tip sheet for science journalists; biweekly NIST Update
Scitk	modem	202-501-1920	
Scitk	modem	303-273-8508 GUEST (or NEW and register)	Provides both scientific and general information on Seismology and Geomagnetism. 8-N-1 only 1200 baud?
Scitk	modem	703-648-4168	Public domain files dealing with mapping and earth science info. 9600 baud
Scitk	modem	818-354-1333 anonymous; city/ST	Information on and GIF images from NASA space missions.
Scitk	telnet	archie.sura.net 23 qarchie	Basic Archie commands given at login. Some help available.
Scitk	telnet	downwind.sprl.umich.edu 3000 none	In some cases may use switch in address
Scitk	telnet	ds.internic.net guest	Tools for searching the Internet. Interface has AT&T name. Leave comments to admin@ds.internic.net
Scitk	telnet	gopher.nist.gov gopher	News releases, announcements, and newsletters from the National Institute of Standards and Technology such as the biweekly NIST
Scitk	telnet	iitf.doc.gov gopher	
Scitk	telnet	neis.cr.usgs.gov Usrname: QED	Earthquake info, geomagnetism
Scitk	telnet	stis.nsf.gov 23 public	On first login, you are asked to register a user id. Can do Boolean searches.
Scitk	telnet	walrus.wr.usgs.gov anonymous	maps of earth
Scitk	www	http://farnsworth.mit.edu N/A	Digital Information Infrastructure Guide; other things on information policy
Scitk	www	http://www.esd.ornl.gov/ BFDP/-> N/A	BFDPMOSAIC/binmenu.html This is U.S. Dept. of Energy Biofuels Information Network
Scitk	www	http://www.nodc.noaa.gov N/A	Global holdings of oceanographic data physical, chemical & biological
Sport	www	http://www.mit.edu: 8001/-> /services/sis/sports.html	NFL draft results listed by team and by rankings. Other sports info
State	ftp	ftp.utexas.edu anonymous / guest	WordPerfect and Text files
State	ftp	leginfo.leg.wa.gov anonymous	Legislative documents for Washington in the /pub/ directory
State	ftp	zoo.dir.gov anonymous	VMS system; CD, CDUP
State	gopher	badger.state.wi.us N/A	Wisconsin government info.
State	gopher	ocs.dir.texas.gov N/A	
State	gopher	unix2.nysed.gov N/A	Government Info Locator System for New York State; variety of State docs and pubs; access to fed systems
State	gopher	vixen.cso.uiuc.edu N/A	/cu houses Urbana-Champaign and Regional Information

State	gopher	window.texas.gov N/A	
State	mail	listserv@rutvm1.rutgers.edu N/A	Subscribe DOXNJ firstname_lastname gets you onto New Jersey government documents forum
State	modem	800-227-8392 Register at first login	
State	telnet	access.uhcc.hawaii.edu none	
State	telnet	cap.gwu.edu Lgn: guest / Pwd: visitor	To gain full access, (to post messages, enter chat areas) you have to register. As name implies, it's free.
State	telnet	oes1.oes.ca.gov 5501 none	Flat info server run by EDIS
State	telnet	window.texas.gov register at first connect	Need Kermit to download

Index